After Trump

After Trump

Achieving a New Social Gospel

DONALD HEINZ

CASCADE *Books* · Eugene, Oregon

AFTER TRUMP
Achieving a New Social Gospel

Cascade Books
An Imprint of Wipf and Stock Publishers
199 W. 8th Ave., Suite 3
Eugene, OR 97401

www.wipfandstock.com

PAPERBACK ISBN: 978-1-5326-9531-5
HARDCOVER ISBN: 978-1-5326-9532-2
EBOOK ISBN: 978-1-5326-9533-9

Cataloguing-in-Publication data:

Names: Heinz, Donald, author.

Title: After Trump : Achieving a New Social Gospel / Donald Heinz.

Description: Eugene, OR: Cascade Books, 2020 | Includes bibliographical references and index.

Identifiers: ISBN 978-1-5326-9531-5 (paperback) | ISBN 978-1-5326-9532-2 (hardcover) | ISBN 978-1-5326-9533-9 (ebook)

Subjects: LCSH: Christianity and politics—United States. | Church and state. | Church and the world.

Classification: BR526.H36 2020 (paperback) | BR526 (ebook)

Manufactured in the U.S.A.   03/18/20

Contents

Preface

After the Civil War, the reconstruction of the South ended in failed promises and the reestablishment of white supremacy. But an emancipatory vision emerged as the black social gospel movement. At the beginning of the twentieth century a new social gospel arose as a liberal Protestant response to the Gilded Age, and lingered in the New Deal and the Great Society. In the 1960s, amidst much dissatisfaction with American society and culture, another black social gospel movement arose, led by Martin Luther King Jr., who died for it and made it an exemplary instance of new liberation movements. But social justice was overwhelmed in the times after Reagan when late capitalism triumphed. The purpose of this book is to imagine and proclaim another new social gospel, one that would redeem American Christianity in the time after Trump. It is an invitation and a manifesto.

Introduction

The Looming Tower

> The LORD enters into judgment with the elders and princes of his people:
> It is you who have devoured the vineyard, the spoil of the poor is in
> your houses. What do you mean by crushing my people, by grinding
> the face of the poor?
> Isaiah 3:14–15

> But if any one has the world's goods and sees his brother in need,
> yet closes his heart against him, how does God's love abide in him?
> 1 John 3:17

SECULARISM AND MATERIALISM

In contemporary America, secularism is the native language in the "naked
public square," a space cleared of religion and the historic virtues that once
constituted a prevailing Christian humanism. Social, cultural, and economic forces have subtracted religion from the commons. Sociology names
this process "secularization theory" and Max Weber, a founder of the discipline, foretold the *disenchantment* of the world that would follow. American
courts tend to declare religion off limits on the public grounds patrolled
by the First Amendment's "establishment clause" that shields us from theocracy. Public intellectuals and scientists and economic forces lean toward
a materialist philosophy of human life and the universe. Matter and spirit
are no longer in balance. They used to be like a teeter-totter in the game
of life. Long ago some villages would connect their playground see-saws
to a mechanism that pumped water to the community well. Community

1

play supported the common good. But now just one end stubbornly anchors reality, while the opposite floats inaccessibly in the air. No balance. No water for the village gets pumped.

no balance

Lenski

We no longer strive for ways of being human that balance spirit and matter, sacred and profane, or individualism and community. No civic virtue accumulates social capital in the commons. Social imagination dwindles to disencumbered individuals "bowling alone," to rapacious capitalism ruling society, to government deliberately made small and with little ambition or means to bring justice to all. Around despoiled parks vast and heartbreaking inequalities dominate. Wealthy oligarchs rule. Diversionary entertainment consists of apocalyptic movies persistently picturing where we are heading and offering desperate plots in which solitary individuals rise up just in time to save the human project. The entertainment ends as we leave the theater.

A new book, *Seven Types of Atheism,* contends that twenty-first-century dismissal of god talk is nearly always a *form of materialism* and that the secular humanism that prevails today offers at best a hollowed-out world. A *New York Review of Books* review suggested that our post-Enlightenment age pits the full implications of a materialistic worldview against the ghosts of Western Christianity once seen in moral progress, universal values, and human exceptionalism. In his game-changing book *After Virtue,* Alasdair MacIntyre deplored the collapse of moral reasoning in the modern age and its inability to foster the virtue-laden (religious) humanism civilization requires. Especially in the United States *late capitalism* spans politics, society, and culture while steadily withdrawing social capital from the commons and transferring the economy from the control of government, social institutions, and the demands of the common good—into the hands of unconstrained and unencumbered corporate capitalism and the all-consuming ends of the free market. In *People, Power, and Profits,* Joseph Stiglitz diagnoses "market fundamentalism" and argues that capitalism has fallen down and needs government help to get back up. But both politics and economics have failed us and seem to be entrenched beyond Stiglitz's exhortations. Hope for a just society and care for the earth does not grow inside the beltway. Where to look for remedies? This book will argue that religion, and specifically a Christian social gospel, can become a counterbalance to prevailing forces and a stimulus to new social and political action. Meanwhile, we are in deep trouble. The Bible verses at the beginning of this Introduction tell the truth, but people, including Bible believers, are determined not to hear it.

From a materialist secular discourse, the eclipse of historic moral reasoning, and the triumphalism of the free market flow all manner of human deficits—the ravages of deregulated capitalism, the dehumanization of the commons, a profound and thoroughly entrenched inequality between the 1 percent and the 99 percent, the destruction of ideas of interdependency among peoples and with the environment. Once "the commons" referred to the social, cultural, and natural resources accessible to all members of society. The Eisenhower Republican platform of 1952, still influenced by FDR's New Deal, suggested such a vision. This was before the "rise of a new king who did not know Joseph" (Exodus 1:8) and who brought oppression to the people and made necessary the exodus from oppression we still seek. Our story with a biblical ring would be the legacy of Ronald Reagan, who forgot the old covenant, while the oligarchs who now mostly reign grind the masses into the ground.

We now lack, by choice or by default, the "ability to think the commons" or to imagine government as a prospective social good or to see spirit and matter in mutual embrace. On one end of the social spectrum we have lost the voice to name these deficits, and so we wander in anger and resentment without help or diagnosis. On the other end we have militantly installed late capitalist moral and economic failures as the way things are and must be. One side has lost the ability to imagine that we need field hospitals in the public spheres of modern life. The other side has seen to the dismantling of religion as the healer and visionary for regrouping and reimagining. This is because religion might call for fundamental change in *dominance* direction or constitute a moral hazard to the current assumptions of the American way of life or call into question the hegemony of secular ideology and its occupation of the public square. Social gospels, though they periodically reappear, are now out of style or even unimaginable.

An overconfident metaphysical abstention, sometimes in the guise of *wow* "ironic detachment," assures there are no grand narratives worth believing, no moral questioning of markets. The newly installed stories leave us alone in the universe and unable to move beyond the field where the strong plunder the weak. Those who cannot diagnose what has happened to them are "left behind" (Robert Wuthnow's lament for small-town America) or find themselves "strangers in their own land" (Arlie Hochschild's study of anger and mourning on the American Right). People find themselves in a Tea Party rage of racism and sexism, and a civil religion that has lost its integrating power and substituted a popular idolatry with Christ reduced to a national icon and a God who cannot hear the cries of the people. Cartoonists depict Trump as the golden calf to whom the people bowed and prayed.

A questioning common faith or a tradition of vigorous moral discourse might have explored the limitations of competing answers to the problems that beset us, perhaps even envisioning a new social gospel. But such a search cannot succeed while hands are tied behind one's back by a materialist philosophy, aggressively asserted or assumed by default. Or while blind to a Christianity that witnesses to a reconciling God who saves us in community and calls us to earthcare. For some, a hard-fought-for meaning of life ended in civilizational despair sitting astride the death of God as the "assured result" of modern thought. A go-it-alone materialism produces lives disencumbered of spirit, its lost binary in the universe, and leaves us in a locked-in syndrome. Unable to take the steps beyond our confinement, we look through dimmed eyes at devastated landscapes that mirror our own psyches and social conditions. We lack the ability to imagine our interdependent humanity, to call earth mother and each other brother and sister, to commit to effective government and healthy institutions dedicated to the common good, to find images of God or justice arcing down on the road ahead. "Without vision the people perish" is a biblical proverb.

Whom can we blame? Where are solace and solution to be found? It is argued by conservative nationalists that Islamic emigration and especially Islamic jihad are the real problems in the world, the real threat to American well-being. Ironically, it is Islamic radicals themselves who believed they had diagnosed *Western materialism* as the crisis of the modern age. Osama bin Laden's plan for 9/11 was inspired by a verse from the Quran, "Wherever you are, death will find you, even if you are in lofty towers." In other words, jihad would come to New York to bring down the edifice of secular materialism. And so Lawrence Wright called his book about Osama's plot for the death of Western Civilization *The Looming Tower.*

But we seriously (and conveniently) misdiagnose the American dilemma if we think it is the onslaught of people of color that adequately names our fears and gives meaning to the agendas that will save us. Under closer inspection and critical reflection, the looming tower turns out to be a much closer contemporary meme in American discourse—*Trump Tower*, the icon of materialism and greed and self-dealing and white racism and nearly every corruption gone wrong with the country. A paradise for grifters. But Trump is only the ephemeral icon on the building that has come to stand for us, with many others in line to name our false hopes and values. Altogether this looming tower amounts to a self-congratulatory materialism that denies or discards its birthright twin—spirit in the world, human interdependence on a good earth with God-given treasures available to all, as countless verses in the Hebrew Bible had imagined and for which Jesus' vision of the reign of God opened new space on earth.

THE RISE OF THE CHRISTIAN RIGHT

As icon of our age we might consider Albrecht Durer's famous woodcut of the "four horsemen of the apocalypse," with secularism, materialism, libertarian individualism, and pillaging capitalism riding hard over the earth. Once it was assumed that religion, perhaps especially American civil religion, was the answer to refreshing the commonwealth. How's that going? John Winthrop, who became the first governor of the Massachusetts Bay Colony, preached a sermon on board the ship Arbella before disembarking, that looked back to the exodus story in the Old Testament and extolled a Puritan vision of a new community in a new land, responsible to God for constructing a "city on a hill" that would be God's beacon for all who hoped for a new world.

So the answer to looming American greed and materialism and self-dealing and contempt for the downtrodden must surely be religious revival, the resurgence of the American civil religion that once projected the American experiment to a city on a hill and united us in a national narrative knit together with religious symbols, right? Surely the religious answer to our malaise would be an American evangelicalism, heir to the vigorous founding Puritans, continuous with earlier religious awakenings? The hope at hand would lie within the resurgence of the religion already deeply engaged and well practiced in the culture wars against secularism.

But in the late twentieth century, beginning with the Moral Majority and nationalist sentiment and captive to the "original sin" of racism, then built up or coopted by corporate capitalism, the New Christian Right has emerged to define the shape and piety of the American evangelical tradition. Some argue that it was not political operatives who turned the South into conservative godly Republicans, but Southern Baptist pastors. Now this legacy is a political-religious cult surrounding Donald Trump as God's anointed. In spring 2019, a group of evangelical Christians sponsored a large billboard along a Texas freeway. It featured a looming picture of Trump, the slogan "Make America Great Again," and a quotation from John 1:14: "The Word became flesh and dwelt among us." Is this fearless leader to be the American contribution to a postmodern, post-Christendom grand narrative that will shape the dawn of the third millennium and return religion as a public good in a secular age? What is the carrying capacity of this vision? In whose interest?

But when the God who will save the nation no longer sounds like the one we can recall through the prophets and Jesus Christ, and when God's up-to-date voice sounds suspiciously channeled through anti-government, anti-commons, Wall Street self-regarding corporate interests, we suspect that a popular religion of self-congratulation, or resentment, or social Darwinist delusion has distanced itself from a biblical theology of the cross. Robert Bellah observed that America once kept in tension civic virtue and utilitarian individualism, but that now the latter has far outdistanced the former and the "habits of the heart" that make for a good society are unpracticed. Many leaders seem to be virtue-free.

It turns out that the loudest form of religion proposing to re-occupy the public square and save our country is the New Christian Right (with assistance from Catholic billionaire-supplied economic conservatives), a uniquely American evangelicalism that proposes to make America great again by advancing a *Southern Orthodoxy* of American exceptionalism, white nationalism, anti-immigration, anti-feminism, anti-LGBTism, anti-environmentalism, the hard ethic of free markets, and a peculiar revulsion to kneeling black football players. In this prosperity-promising theology of glory, as Luther would have derided it, God's foolish wisdom of grace on the way to the cross and ultimate redemption tarries, and the arrival of the reign of God and the new creation the New Testament proclaimed is usefully postponed for an end-time dispensation that does not trouble contemporary pursuits. The Jesus who delivered the Sermon on the Mount is not only not on offer, but would be a moral hazard to the American way of life if he were to come riding into the capital city. New Testament Christianity produces an excess of grace and gratitude and empathy, but religious nationalists do not demand radical change of the American way—except for cleansing society of gays and dangerous women and reducing and confining pro-life ethics to fetuses stored in female bodies under guard. The sign outside the church door would have to say to any who show up by mistake or with false hopes: *Nothing to see here*—for the poor, the downtrodden, immigrants looking for a place, peace-making, transforming life in a covenanted community, earth's bounties for all. Jerry Falwell's Liberty University means to graduate citizens certain of the smooth continuity between the way ambitious Americans are and God's own way, the divine hand stimulating the free market.

Trump Tower has become a fortified citadel, a pseudo-Christian cathedral where Trump is periodically reanointed as God's just-in-time good news. One in four Americans believes that God elected Trump to be our contemporary savior. Eighty-two percent of evangelicals voted for him and still sing in his choir. Celebrities like the national chaplain, Paula White, Billy Graham's heir Franklin, the Moral Majority heir Jerry Falwell, Jr., and many megachurch pastors have assembled as Trump's "evangelical cabinet," the king's court, domesticated prophets on retainer, arisen to proclaim Trump as God's last, best hope.

Consider a 2019 Facebook outing of those who gather for worship at Trump rallies: "If you want to better understand Trump supporters, we should think of them as his congregation. He is their savior. He preaches to their fears and sense of victimhood. He empowers them. He rallies them. He emboldens them. He tells them whom to blame. He becomes their truth. He is the answer. Any assault on him is an assault on them. Do not deceive yourself into thinking your facts and logic can penetrate that emotional armor." After the massacre on Muslims in New Zealand for which the white terrorist saw Trump as his inspiration (as did the synagogue shooter, the mail bomber, and the Coast Guard white supremacist), a columnist for the *New Zealand Herald* wrote: "Trump personifies everything the rest of the world despises about America: casual racism, crass materialism, relentless self-aggrandizement, vulgarity on an epic scale." Is this then the tower that looms?

No doubt many who look to Trump Tower, evangelical and even Catholic Christians as well as "nones," fear being left behind or disinherited in their hopes for well-being and (white nationalist) identity. They do not notice, or cannot name, the self-perpetuating extreme wealth and corporate greed that keep the 99 percent down and gradually lay waste to the earth. Socialism for hedge funds and scarcity for the middle class and the poor is the economic program. The 1 percent are pleased to help fund and cheer on the new religion because it serves their purposes. Wall Street is doing God's work on weekdays, its CEOs like to say. Climate science denial, for example, is not a matter of ignorant yokels, but a well-financed and deliberately conceived corporate plan to protect vested interests. In the Gospels, Jesus regularly condemned the managers of God's vineyards. Countless Americans are losing in a desperately unequal society, but the God-as-liberator and the love-as-justice traditions of the Bible do not loom. That would be socialism.

We are at a religious impasse. The very social gospel, once regarded as America's distinctive contribution to world Christianity, was derided by American fundamentalists in the early twentieth century as a false delusion that would lead Christians away from the salvation in the hereafter that was their destiny and calling. And relieve the expected behaviors of sanctified selves by displacing them onto government. Christianity is about individual freedom and individual redemption, not to mention holding the line on women and gays.

CRITIQUES OF THE CHRISTIAN RIGHT

Today one hears post-evangelicals and neo-Anabaptists, not to mention mainstream Protestants and Catholics, assert that *the death of Christian*

Right evangelicalism may have to occur if the Christian tradition, and American Christianity, is to survive in its historic mission and calling.

The wasting of American evangelicalism, together with the denigration of Catholic social thought in a corporate-funded Catholic neoconservatism, began to come in recent years under scrutiny—especially among evangelicals themselves and eventually in the religious press. The apotheosis of an evangelicalism gone dangerously wrong under Trump came to be seen and lamented, or denounced, as a great tragedy in American Christianity. It is not too much, in this time of Trump talk, to speak of a *great collusion* between Catholic and evangelical conservatism on the one hand and capitalist dark money on the other. The 1986 Catholic Bishops' pastoral letter, "Economic Justice for All," had been meant to revive historic Catholic social teaching and severely critique Reaganesque economics. Instead, it made Catholic conservatives crazy. So a Catholic Right arose to oppose this new social gospel, seemingly bent on creating their own counter-magisterium, for example in organizations like the Knights of Columbus. Catholic economic conservatives and libertarians, with funding from right-wing billionaires, seemed bent on a hostile takeover of American Catholicism. Their platform was unrestricted capitalism and small government, often meaning the diminishment of government services on behalf of the poor.

Toward the end of the twentieth century, "post-evangelical" became a meme. In 2010, Brian McLaren called for "a new kind of Christianity that would move beyond theological rigidity, biblical literalism, and overly confident answers to everything instead of a new more open-ended approach—"living the questions." McLaren also denounced the increasing alignment with rightist politics, as did Fuller Seminary President Mark Labberton in a speech at Wheaton College that castigated evangelicals for political dealing, grasping at political power, racism, nationalism, and lack of concern for the poor. The evangelical stalwart InterVarsity Christian Press commissioned a book devoted to the meaning and future of the movement and titled it: *Still Evangelicals? Insiders Reconsider Political, Social, and Theological Meaning.* An anthology by several evangelical heavyweights called itself "The Compromised Church: The Present Evangelical Crisis." The blogger Michael Spencer aroused many with his essay, "The Coming Evangelical Collapse, and Why It is Going to Happen." Would an American evangelicalism seriously off course bring down much of Christianity with it? Would many Americans say, good riddance?!

In a March 2018 *Atlantic* article, the former Republican speech writer and political operative Michael Gerson, a devout evangelical, denounced the political pandering of contemporary evangelicals willing to abandon everything for unprecedented access to a White House with a "dream president."

Jared and Ivanka made some evangelicals think of Joseph and Mary. Tony Perkins of the evangelical Family Research Council thought Trump should be given a mulligan for past infidelity. The influential post-evangelical Tim Keller thought *evangelical* was now synonymous with *hypocrite*. A few decades earlier the dominating Carl Henry was writing about the "uneasy conscience of modern fundamentalism" and urging greater cultural and intellectual engagement with the modern world. The downward evolution was marked in 1980 when President Reagan went public with "You cannot endorse me, but I endorse you." Billy Graham, a man of considerable distinction and honor, would become the chaplain to the powerful. Since Trump's election, the sons of Billy Graham and Jerry Falwell of the Moral Majority, namely Franklin Graham and Jerry Falwell Jr., would be the first in line to become political kingmakers. Fox News, the new voice of the Christian Right, would become far more influential than the National Association of Evangelicals ever was.

Gerson and especially John Fea's book, *Believe Me: The Evangelical Road to Donald Trump*, see that it is no surprise that Trump depicts evangelicals as they do themselves—a mistreated minority, in need of a defender who plays by worldly rules, a bully and a strongman who comes through with a protection racket and a religious cover for moral squalor. Intentionally, or in a great tragedy of misperception, the evangelical faith has become twinned with racism, nativism, misogyny, lawlessness, corruption, and deception. Christians look like another interest group scrambling for benefits at the expense of others rather than seeking the welfare of the commons. Gerson's summary: "We sell our souls to buy our wins."

EARLY SOCIAL GOSPEL MOVEMENTS

At the turn of the twentieth century a new social gospel had become a notable American Protestant contribution to world Christianity. It was a social reform movement that flourished from 1870 to 1920, left a significant legacy in the New Deal and the Great Society, and was clearly over by the Reagan years beginning in 1980s. Key to its self-understanding was the "social salvation" interpretation of the New Testament concept of the reign of God, as a correction to the "individual salvation" understanding of the church's common ambition and purview. Christians were reminded that the "Thy kingdom come" petition in the Lord's Prayer was meant to take up social space.

The setting for the first American social gospel movement was the Gilded Age, when unimaginable wealth was accumulated and gilded a social scene from which city workers and farmers had been excluded. Social justice was not in the news. It seemed clear to Protestant thinkers like Washington Gladden and Walter Rauschenbusch that labor reforms—including abolition of child labor, a shorter workweek, a living wage, and factory regulation—were the purview of Christianity and the mission of the church. By the 1930s, and after a Great Depression, many of these ideals would come to be realized through the rise of organized labor and the ambitions of President Roosevelt's New Deal. A movement that applied Christian ethics to social problems would also address economic inequality, poverty, alcoholism, crime, racial tensions, slums, and an unclean environment. Lyndon Johnson had grown up with the piety of the social gospel.

In terms of Christian eschatology, a subject to which this book returns in the Epilogue, the social gospelers were postmillennialist, which is to say they were optimistic about how much social salvation could be achieved on earth and that Christ's return would come as the culmination of the earthly achievements of his kingdom—when social evils were mostly abated. The social gospel was preached and put into practice by Protestant progressives who were mostly theologically liberal. Their reach was ambitious. Gladden assumed that Christian public theology should reach, for example, to the relationship between employers and employees. Rauschenbusch, the most prominent social gospel thinker, railed against the selfishness of capitalism and promoted a form of Christian socialism that supported labor unions and cooperative economics. The American Federation of Labor was deeply influenced by social gospel activists. Rauschenbusch provided a theology to make the social gospel effective and insisted that *theology needed the social gospel to be vital*—and vice versa. The Christian diagnosis of sin must reach from individuals to social institutions and would require structural responses from the government, spurred on by the churches. Sometimes the church took the initiative itself, as in the "settlement houses" that offered daycare, education, and health care to needy people in slum neighborhoods. That example may be crucial as I come to appeal not only to mainstream Protestants comfortable with structural approaches but also to evangelicals more likely to insist on Christian charity or what can be accomplished by individual, born-again Christians.

Meanwhile, the famous evangelist Dwight Moody was claiming that concentrating on social aid distracted people from the life-saving message of the gospel. But social gospel Presbyterians countered: "The great ends of the church are the proclamation of the gospel for the salvation of humankind; the shelter, nurture, and spiritual fellowship of the children of God; the maintenance of divine worship; the preservation of truth; the promotion of social righteousness; and the exhibition of the Kingdom of Heaven to the world."

Often forgotten is the *black social gospel movement* led by Martin Luther King Jr. and by predecessors who greatly influenced him like W. E. B. DuBois. In *Breaking White Supremacy: MLK and the Black Social Gospel* and *The New Abolition: W. E. B. DuBois and the Black Social Gospel,* Gary Dorrien tells the well-known history of Martin Luther King Jr.'s social gospel activism and the mostly forgotten history of the movement that preceded him in the nineteenth century. The full-fledged black social gospel combined an emphasis on black dignity and personhood with activism for racial justice, an insistence that authentic Christian faith is incompatible with racial prejudice, an emphasis on the social teaching of Jesus, and an acceptance of modern scholarship and social consciousness.

The earlier black social gospel had emerged from the trauma of Reconstruction at the end of the Civil War, to ask what a "new abolition" would require in American society. After a brief attempt at reparations, in which newly freed black slaves would be allocated "forty acres and a mule," the forces of Southern revisionism reasserted themselves, the Civil War was declared a war about states' rights, the White plantation class got the reparations, and blacks got nothing but Jim Crow and the Klan. So the black attempt at a new abolition became an important precursor of religious thought and resistance. It is evidence that the myth of blacks always waiting for initiative and deliverance from whites is false. And of course the black exclusion from the public square came by force, and sometimes lynching. The recovery of this history in our time is evidence and exhortation that a new social gospel movement is worthy and possible.

When Martin Luther King Jr. preached in Washington DC, he was dreaming God into the end of the second millennium. He pictured a social order coming into being not miraculously, but by human effort and will. If so many are held in the bands of poverty, violence, loss of place, the destruction of nature, and meaninglessness, his dream was to set them free to live in a community of justice, democracy, cultural identity, peace with nature, and ultimate meaning. If ascetics found the world wanting and fled it, King and those like him found the world wanting and determined to change it. This is the agenda of progressive religion, the enactment of a succeeding social gospel, and King is one of the patron saints.

Then what happened? America shifted. The Reagan years arrived. Reagan took it all from the middle class and the poor and gave it to the wealthy in a massive redistribution scheme. Mainstream Protestants lost their voice in the public square or spoke softly. American Catholics forgot their rich heritage of social thought in Europe at the same time as the American

Protestant social gospel. Evangelicals, always suspicious of the theological modernism that seemed to accompany the social gospel, came to emphasize individual salvation much more powerfully and persuasively—sometimes abetted by corporate interests that made common cause with them and were certainly motivated by white racism.

THE SETTING FOR A NEW SOCIAL GOSPEL IN AMERICA

Beginning well before the Reagan years, and epitomized by the anti-Vietnam movement, the civil rights movement, the women's movements, and the gay liberation movement, a *new religious left, or progressive Christianity,* began to emerge. It had begun already in neo-evangelical and then post-evangelical and neo-Anabaptist social statements and activist movements in the 1970s, a renewing, then repressed, then recovered Catholic liberation theology that built on historic Catholic social teachings, and a liberalism within mainline Protestantism that found a more vigorous theological underpinning of the social gospel and then, slowly, recovered its own voice. It occurred to the thoughtful that European democratic socialism had often been grounded in Christian values and was not merely an echo of Marxism. There were faint projections on the social imaginary of a new social gospel, much more theologically grounded and without so many compromises with modernism. But these did not effect a reversal of the "government is the problem" period that was Reagan's legacy. By the time of the apotheosis of greed and neglect and the degradation of social justice under Trump, it seemed that the *loss of a prevailing social gospel had in fact enabled the triumph of Trump.* The loudest Christian voice was the Christian Right, which had already emerged under Reagan and decisively voted for Trump.

This book calls for redeeming American Christianity after Trump. Trump by himself is a towering icon of this age, and he has come to sum all the American voters and the economic system that brought him forward—from the Christian Right to angry and disaffected voters feeling left behind and disinherited to libertarianism to corporate capitalism to a secular society from which genuine religious discourse and a vigorous Christian humanism have departed. In this wake we see the dominance of a ruthless, deregulated capitalism which pillages the earth and opens an ever widening gap between the 1 percent and the 99 percent and from which structural responses to tending the common good are steadily eroded and all social capital withdrawn from political action.

Trump and Trumpism became possible because of an ever widening gap between conservative political action and public support for the common good and the regulation of capitalism. Because American Christianity mostly was failing, in the right places, to proclaim and embody a social gospel in our time and to be a vital presence in the public square and in all discourse about social justice in the commons, and because across Christianity itself there was little engaged debate about what the gospel enables and requires and how that might differ drastically from American economic assumptions, there was open space for Trump and his evangelical court to emerge and triumph.

A new social gospel would recall the God of the Exodus and the Hebrew prophets and invoke the God whose reign Jesus proclaimed and enacted. A proclaimed gospel and an enacted social gospel must be the test of each other. The kingdom of God central to the eschatology of the New Testament should be experienced today reaching back to us from the future, evoking projects of social praxis on the road ahead.

A new social gospel requires the evocation of a pilgrimage towards God that brings all the neighbors along. This requires first of all the church *being the church*, the worshiping community that holds aloft in the human parade the God who in Christ reconciled with humanity, a religious community called out to become a colony of heaven.

This then means the return of Christianity to public discourse. A new social gospel requires a recontested public square in which Christianity, and all contenders for the good of the commons and justice for all, take their rightful place as vigorous discourse communities among the grand narratives that rightfully compete for public space, mount a new Christian humanism, enter the world of economics and contend for the vision of a godly economy, and strive for a collaborative eschatology in which anticipation of God's presence stirs earthly achievement.

BUILDING ON AMERICAN ROOTS AND HISTORIC CHRISTIAN TRADITIONS

Is there sufficient oomph for such a (probably unwelcomed) venture? A new social gospel does not have to be created out of nothing—though that too is possible for God. America has a history of Great Awakenings, so why should they not come to mind as we ponder redeeming American Christianity after Trump? The first Great Awakening of the 1740s was replete with a pietism that left no realm of a rigid doctrinal Protestantism untouched. The second Great Awakening of the 1820s evoked a romanticism that would counter Enlightenment rationalism. The third Great Awakening of the early twentieth century was many things, from a fundamentalist protest against liberalism to the emergence of the social gospel. There were also Holiness and Pentecostal movements that stirred the pot of sanctified lives and implied the Spirit might be a whirlwind to be chased and scattering new visions across the landscape.

At this dawn of the third millennium could we again reimagine a social gospel richer than the Protestant liberal version that left too much of historic Christianity and the church's resources behind, while embracing prophetic calls to social justice and "bringing in the kingdom"—a project Luther renounced, but accomplished. May we hope this time for a fuller gospel, replete with historic Christian orthodoxy, liturgical renewal, sacramentalizing the commons, liberation theology?

A new social gospel should come from a Christian witness (what in a particular historical situation the Church believes, teaches, and confesses) that would speak to the times and bring together every dimension of lived Christianity in America and including Christian historical theology and praxis, with each tradition speaking from its strengths and subject to correction of its weakness, summing the multiple dimensions biblical Christianity represents—all together amounting to social justice as the social form of Christian love unmistakably grounded in historic, uncompromised Christian theology. Of course what I am calling for emerges from deep resources in the Christian traditions. I am drawing water from Catholic, Calvinist, Lutheran, evangelical, and neo-Anabaptist wells.

Catholic social teaching is embedded in society through the principle of subsidiarity and the sacramentilization of life on earth. The Roman Catholic tradition imagines that the presence of Christ on earth can, in part, be institutionalized in society and culture, where it leaves abundant incarnational deposits, alongside and as extensions of its fuller and more explicit presence in the church itself. In this way religious values and instincts and indeed the material culture of Christianity can become a part of, can occupy, the public sphere. Ignatius Loyola, founder of the Jesuits, and many other communal traditions have kept alive the power of spiritual exercises and retreats as preludes to engaging society. The present pope has recalled and recommissioned the traditions of Catholic liberation theology and its startling mantra of the "preferential option for the poor," which so scandalizes the Christian Right and preachers of capitalism.

For Luther, it may be that just getting a theology of the cross right and highlighting the gospel (not, for example, natural law traditions that order creation with ancient prejudice) as the church's only treasure is sufficient. Lutherans have learned to ask one key question regarding every new thing that comes along: Is the gospel at stake? For example, is the gospel at stake if we honor and celebrate gay love and marriage? Or cheer the liberation of women? Luther's denigration of the theology of glory characteristic of the Christian Right and much else in the American civil religion is that it distorts the gospel, renders God's wisdom foolish, takes offense at the need of all for grace. More recently some Lutherans have tried to move beyond a history of "Lutheran quietism" influenced by Luther's two kingdoms doctrine, suggesting that the church, addressed in its own sphere by the gospel (the kingdom of God's right hand), may also set off small explosions in the realm of government (the kingdom of God's left hand.) In the same public land where Trump Tower looms I call for a resacralization of earthly life in its intended holiness, for the reestablishment of Christian humanism as a viable postmodern narrative. I call for the church to encamp, to set up shop in every earthly precinct, not accepting secularist exclusion. We look for spiritual presence in every matter.

Calvinism has often looked for cultural transformation with no sphere of public life left untouched. Calvinism imagines a common grace that covers the world, overlapping the saving grace of the gospel. So H. Richard Niebuhr called for "Christ transforming culture" and Abraham Kuyper saw God, even amidst church/state distinctions, as nevertheless sovereign over every sphere in which we must speak and act. There are no spheres in which God is not sovereign, he confidently insisted. In this vision the church is elected to take a place in the public sphere confident that every sphere of political and cultural life was created by God and that God still reigns over it, albeit in a different manner than in the church.

Wesleyan holiness of life methodically disciplined combined hearts "strangely warmed" by hearing the gospel with movements rooted in society like the Salvation Army. Methodists combined evangelical emphases on lives born again into discipleship and witness and distinctive Christian action. Evangelicals and Wesleyan holiness movements have rich traditions of revival and renewal, methodically pursuing both in their church life and in the life of the world.

Neo-Anabaptist traditions of dissent and nonconformity dared to "stand still in the light" as a way of being a colony of heaven. Staying on message precedes cultural transformation. Stanley Hauerwas has wanted to focus on "the church being the church" and telling its own stories in its own indigenous language and becoming those stories and thereby producing a moral outlook that requires vigorous insurrection.

Could evangelicals uncompromised by the Christian Right come on board? Consider the individualist approach of this statement, Baptist Faith and Message 2000: "Means and methods used for the improvement of society and the establishment of righteousness among men can be truly and permanently helpful only when they are rooted in the regeneration of the individual by the saving grace of God in Jesus Christ." In her book, *When God Talks Back: Understanding the American Evangelical Relationship with God*, Stanford anthropologist T. M. Luhrman, building on a year of participant observation, shows how evangelicals and Pentecostals are prone to believe that Christian liberals slight individual Christian piety and love of the neighbor and displace it onto government responsibility. At the time of the first social gospel, wedded to Protestant modernism, evangelicals who had a long tradition of civic influence, including abolitionism and the temperance movement, suspected that Christian modernists appealed not to the sanctified lives of individual Christians but shifted the sanctifying life to government programs—and compromised much of historic Christianity in the process. No doubt there would be serious debates about how to effect a social democracy/social justice embodying Christian vision, with liberals insisting on structural approaches to social sin and evangelicals looking to Christian charity from individual Christians. And yet, essential to early Puritan self-understanding, the early settlers of America had a twofold sense of calling: an inward call to redemption and a social vocation to the common good.

In a recent book which I read with some suspicion because it seemed utopian in its vision, *A House United: How the Church Can Save the World*, Allen Hilton calls for competing groups within Christian churches and competing Christian traditions like evangelical versus mainstream, and the pastors and theologians who lead them, coming together in the "divided states of America" and amidst rival prayers and righteous minds, move toward a deliberate and open-minded mingling through common mission, practicing courageous conversations, and saving the world.

For those committed to structural solutions to the good of the commons and for those whose first instinct is for individual sanctified lives of virtue and witness, it is entirely possible to unite a Christian humanism and an ethos of social justice all fed from historic Christian sources. Both together are driven by a religious vision of humans created and redeemed by God (as even the founding fathers nearly imagined) on a reenchanted earth. This requires a recovery and reinvigoration of biblical proclamation and historic theological, moral, and life-in-community deposits of historic Christianity displaying faith active in love.

A current, but not well-known, example is the attempt by some evangelicals in business to recover the Old Testament practice of *gleaning*, God's command that the edge of every field, of earth's bounty, be reserved for the poor. This is not merely a personal charity but a reimagination of how to think of one's business and the transformation of private enterprise into shared space and shared community. Always, this exemplary individual or communal practice is meant to evoke similar but perhaps more consequential practice in government and non-profit programs for the common good—as also in contemporary Christian attempts to mix public, private, and church-based efforts to give everyone enough food. Such efforts evoke both typical evangelical approaches that emerge from personal piety and practice and mainstream Protestant or Catholic lobbying for social justice as government policy.

But what will well-meaning secular proponents of social democracy say? How will social justice warriors who have written off religion and lie awake worrying about theocracy and the Christian Right respond? Consider David Bentley Hart's affirmation to the *New York Times* in 2019: "Democratic socialism is a noble tradition of civic conscientiousness that was historically—to a far greater degree than either its champions or detractors today often care to acknowledge—grounded in deep Christian convictions." Consider the prodigious scholarship of Gary Dorrien, one of whose books, *Social Democracy in the Making: Political and Religious Roots of European Socialism,* traces the roots of social democracy in European Christian public theology. Closer to home is Dorrien's book, *Reconstructing the Common Good: Theology and the Social Order.* This work draws on some of the most distinguished Christian theologians of the twentieth century who imagined a modern, non-Marxian, Christian socialism, like Rauschenbusch, Tillich, Moltmann, Gutierrez, and Miguez Bonino. They provide a unique context for addressing all the questions that need to be asked, both by secular idealists and public theologians—freedom and totalitarianism, sacralization and democratization, individual autonomy and the common good. Dorrien focuses on the differing conceptions of the common good that these major theorists have propounded, and explicates as well their theological arguments on the relationship between the kingdom of God and projects of historical praxis.

THE UNCERTAIN REEMERGENCE
OF THE SOCIAL GOSPEL

I don't want to get too far ahead of my readers. I am indeed calling for a sea change in the American social system, effected in part by a Christian vision and arriving in the trappings, at least for the churches, of a new social gospel. Mainstream Protestants and Catholics will need to regroup and re-enter the public square. This should also be a call to evangelicals to leave the Christian Right behind even while holding onto their historic strengths and with every right and responsibility to contribute from their own traditions. Secular liberals may deal with their anti-religious hostility, acknowledge that religion in general and Christianity in particular cannot be reduced to the Christian Right. Contemporary leftists may seek new alliances. The Democratic Party may overcome its decades-long retreat from all but black religion. Who knows, might the Republican Party go in search of the lost values of historic conservatism and find in a new social gospel a Christian humanism neoconservatives would celebrate?

A new social gospel may be the redemption of Christianity in our time. As we saw in the original social gospel in the early twentieth century, the social gospel was both the avenue on which Christianity could express itself and a test of the validity and scope of Christian public theology. As I keep saying, it is not a theocracy I envision. It is a multi-discoursed public square in which all can speak. It would be open to the historic mission of Christianity to proclaim and embody the covenantal theology of the Old Testament, Jesus' proclamation of the reign of God, and the New Testament normative insistence on the love command, expressed socially as justice across all communities with special attention to the lost and the least, the outcast and the poor and victims of majority prejudice.

In 1973 when most eyes followed the secular left, it was American evangelicals who called for a renewed social gospel in their Chicago Declaration of Evangelical Social Concern, highlighting racial and economic justice for the marginalized and the message and responsibilities of Christianity. They dared to argue that the Christian gospel spoke directly to structural inequities and not just to individualized sins. But when a few years later the new evangelical President Jimmy Carter echoed some of the same concerns in his "Crisis of Confidence" speech, the presidential Bible teacher and this unwelcome message crashed and burned. The tone of social justice made middle America feel bad about themselves and sank Carter's influence, though he had been elected in 1976 as the great evangelical hope.

By the '80s the Religious Left had lost currency and, coincidental with President Reagan's rise to power and influence, a new Christian Right ascended. The Religious Right was savvy, powerful, and influential, but it did not speak the language of social justice, perhaps partly because its Christian piety was individualist and because of its affiliation with and co-optation by corporate capitalism. From Reagan to Bush to the Tea Party to Trump, the Christian Right was insisting that social justice had little to do with biblical Christianity and was merely left-wing lingo. Only individual freedom—and personal piety—rang true. Both the Religious Left and Right wanted access and influence in the public square, but as an emphasis on class switched to culture or identity politics, the religious left gradually lost its ability to communicate with those angry and left behind. They were evangelized instead by oligarchs to believe that a looming socialism was the true enemy of God.

Meanwhile, American nationalist theology is too certain of the seamless continuity between American aspirations and the way God is. The Christian Right and Wall Street custodians devoutly say that God is the invisible hand of the free market. Self-congratulation and gospel-of-success worship go hand in hand. To a theology of glory, the cross is simply foolishness, the moral hazard of giving free lunch to poor school children and help to the needy, and the misguided and unrealistic attempt to turn corporate capitalism into the common good. Utopian! Unrealistic! Diverting from Christ in our hearts and our home in heaven!

READ ON

Which to choose, what to do, how to proceed, with whom to ally? This book's aspiration is *redeeming American Christianity after Trump*. If court evangelicals have moved into Trump Tower, where many other Americans have taken up residence as well, this book calls them out and appeals to Christians on the streets still rooted in historic Christianity to move vigorously toward a new social gospel. Biblical faith and Christian liturgies are filled with "re-words" like *repent* or *return* or *rebirth*. This book is an appeal in three parts. Consider the following:

Recalling God could mean remembering as if for the first time the God of the exodus and the prophets, who became incarnate in Jesus Christ and made earth capable of heaven. How is Christianity supposed to look? If you've brought something home from IKEA and the directions make you crazy, you look at the picture on the box to remind you what it's supposed to look like. And altogether, you proceed. Maybe a neighbor is called in to help. Maybe husband and wife come closer!

Reliving Christianity could mean recovering a genuine original experience, falling in love again, repenting, turning ourselves inward, reconsidering, reclaiming a lost inheritance. This may invoke the monastic option of *retreating, regrouping , renewal, and re-creation*. After letting go of Christ as an American icon, a reforming Christianity can project onto the social imaginary God's dream of a covenanted people living for the good of all and in peace with the earth. All this while being a new people "in Christ," as Paul kept saying in his letters.

Returning to and recontesting the public square from which religion has been vacated by court opinion or metaphysical abstention or an ideology of secular materialism. Aspire not to theocracy but to the language of the church. *All discourse is political, all speech comes from somewhere and is going somewhere.* Foster again a Christian humanism. Dare to imagine a divine economy that goes up against late capitalism. Perform the exodus. This book means to be an invitation and a manifesto for a new social gospel.

1

Exodus, Covenant, Prophets

AFTER EDEN

The garden of Eden had been magical, God and humans keeping company, *creation becoming*. But *unbecoming* came to be instead. Gardens run down. A new story about the human project and life with God would emerge. God experimented. God envisioned a new covenant with a people chosen to be a light to future nations.

This would require an exodus from human bondage, a long pilgrimage into a promised land. Led by Moses, the people escaped from Egypt, were tested in the wilderness, and would come to a promised land. Their evolution as a people of God was not obvious or easy. In a startling epiphany, God came down from Mt. Sinai, revealed the divine plan for their lives (as evangelical student groups used to announce on college campuses), and proposed a new way of living in community. It was called a *covenant* and it became their legacy from God in a land inherited as a gift of Creation.

To keep their faces turned towards the promised land and their minds on God, they moved forward with an ark of the covenant just in front of them, a holy symbol of themselves carrying God as the weight of their calling. *Let my people go* had been the magical incantation God taught Moses, and now they were supposed to keep going. Resolutely. Not looking back. This was no *Ocean's Eleven* heist from Pharaoh's casino. A fierce wilderness lay ahead, a difficult wandering, a rigorous preparation for being the new social order God had commissioned. They would not be able to make it on their own. They kept getting lost, often clueless. Again and again God sent prophets to them when they lost sight of the promised land, when their true

North needed resetting. They experienced the grace of repentance, exile and return, new chances when the weight of their inheritance became too heavy and they lost contact with the voice of God.

WALKING OUT OF EGYPT IS A RELIGIOUS CALLING, A PERFORMATIVE LITURGY

> I have heard their cry, I know their suffering,
> I have come down to deliver them;
> Let my people go.
> Exodus 3:7; 5:1

> You shall not oppress a resident alien; you know the heart of an alien,
> for you were aliens in the land of Egypt.
> Exodus 23:9

> When you harvest your land's produce, you must not harvest all the way to the edge of your field; and don't gather up every remaining bit of your harvest. Also do not pick your vineyard clean or gather up all the grapes that have fallen there.
> Leave these items for the poor and the immigrant; I am the LORD your God.
> Leviticus 19:9–10

> Sound the trumpet
> This fiftieth year is sacred—it is a time of freedom and of celebration when everyone will receive back their original property, and slaves will return home to their families.
> It is a Jubilee Year.
> Leviticus 25:9–10

> Hear, O Israel: The LORD is our God, the LORD alone.
> Deuteronomy 6:4

The exodus is a central meme in biblical religion. (I am following the interpretations of Walter Brueggemann here.) First told as Judaism's birthright story, the exodus narrative is then rehearsed a hundred more

times throughout the Hebrew Bible. Its endless ritual tellings and liturgical performances are etched in Israel's self-consciousness as witness to the
liberating God who called them out of bondage and into the promised land.
In America, black slaves knew the story best and were the first to decode
it for an American setting, since black liberation had not made it into the
American origin story. Consider these words, written in 1900, from what
would become known as the "Black National Anthem":

> Lift every voice and sing,
>
> Till earth and heaven ring,
>
> Ring with the harmonies of Liberty;
>
> Let our rejoicing rise
>
> High as the list'ning skies,
>
> Let it resound loud as the rolling sea.
>
> Sing a song full of the faith that the dark past has taught us,
>
> Sing a song full of the hope that the present has brought us;
>
> Facing the rising sun of our new day begun,
>
> Let us march on till victory is won.

*As if part of a catechism of the faith, or a pilgrim's initiation, or a map
for the road ahead, the exodus reprises God in one great celebratory liberation
and in the lineage of the Jewish people.* As often as Israel forgets and distances
itself from its origins story and in effect worships some other god, the God
of the Exodus needs to be decoded again and the inheritance reclaimed.
(America is past time for the recovery of a vision for people living together
interdependently amidst God's/earth's bounty, which may require a new
social gospel proclaimed and performed.)

The story is told in the book of Exodus, the second book in the Hebrew Bible, which became the Christian Old Testament. God is the original
protagonist of deliverance, but the prophet Moses is God's insistent earthly
voice. Here is the plot summary: God has been listening to a people's cries
and grieving over their suffering and is moved to come down and act.
God calls Moses to go before the king of Egypt, to whom the Israelites are
in bondage, and proclaim: "*Let my people go.*" The liberation from Egypt
will be preceded by the famous ten plagues, and then God will lead the
people through the Red Sea, while overcoming the horses and riders of the
Egyptian army in hot pursuit. (Are you thinking of a union strike hounded
by local police, or an occupation of Wall Street teargassed by the National
Guard, or activists at a city council meeting ushered out by armed guards,
or women who persist on the floor of Congress marched off by the sergeant

at arms, or local Christians ministering to migrants at the border hauled off into custody by the border patrol, or—much more hallowed and therefore safe—the Boston Tea Party?)

In effect God bid Israel to turn left after crossing the Red Sea, but this slow-to-learn people had first to detour through forty years in the wilderness where they learned to understand God's revolutionary turn and Israel's destiny waited to unfold. In what would become a powerful metaphor, *life in the wilderness* is where God and Moses (the original community organizer) gradually reshape the people into a new kind of community—and where Jesus and countless others would be tested at the beginning of their ministry. Every day God feeds them with quail and something called manna from heaven, so they get used to seeing all earthly sustenance as God's gifts for all. The turning point of life in the wilderness is God's self-revelation on Mt. Sinai. Moses comes down from that mountain with the ten commandments, which turn out to be *codes and covenants for the new community* God envisions, a *social contract* for a people's life together. So they won't quickly forget this formative story, a Sabbath is institutionalized in rehearsals that happen every seven days. When they finally have all this down, they enter the promised land.

The exodus becomes a chain story, told from one generation to the next. (This book urges another telling and calls it a new social gospel.) Ultimately, from the Jews to the Christians to all the world. If God were an old man this would be his last will and testament. Unfortunately, as happens in the grade school game where each student passes a message on to the next, the story gets distorted—sometimes completely garbled and sometimes totally forgotten and sometimes bent to someone's interest. In America the story got the pilgrims across the Atlantic but was subsequently narrowed to the bound vision of a young country. Over the course of political and economic evolution, the exodus becomes easy to forget. Sometimes repressed. The vision is astonishingly incompatible with the American enslavement of blacks. And incompatible with an unregulated capitalism that consists of commanding "more bricks with less straw" as the laborers' plight in the world.

As the story opens, God is moved to anger not by moral peccadilloes or affronts to religious purity, but by greed and economic oppression across the land—a story painfully familiar today. These are true affronts to God's intentions for earth. God is preoccupied with underdogs who are enslaved and subjugated. God displays the divine nature as compassion and nurture and dreams of an earth where justice and *shalom* reign in the land. God means to scatter these divine markers, this DNA at God's heart, into the communal life of Israel, so that generations to come will be able to follow the bread crumbs home. But humans often fail to tend to their own heritage, they lose the sense of where they came from, they forget that once they were in bondage in Egypt and are now freed for a new kind of life together. So God's liberation and the people's inheritance are to be *ritually rehearsed, morally performed, and socially reenacted* in the religious and political life of this people. No less today. The exodus becomes an ever-new social gospel. God's nature, as we have come to know it, is first expressed through the Jewish genome and witnessed in the Hebrew Bible. Christians pass it on as their inherited religious mission.

When there is famine in the land, when the poor are starving, when people are going broke from healthcare costs, those in power fear loss of control. Oligarchs tremble before scarcity and repress or disguise the peoples' unrest. God's idea for earthly good was bountiful land and food to sustain everyone. But economic forces reverse that teleology and turn food into wealth for the few and political and social control. Many in the Third World, and more than a few Americans, would understand today Israel's plight in Egypt. The story resonates, and could stimulate revolution *if God were perceived to authorize liberation.* Some modern historians claim that in the ancient world all revolutionary movements had a single program—*cancel the debts and redistribute the land.* And today? Who is in bondage to Egypt today? Who have lost their land and their freedom? Who is due redistribution? Whose social security has been stolen or borrowed away? Who wields economic power and who are enslaved? Christian pilgrims into the third millennium must learn again to seek this exodus God, to ask, Where is God today and who are the protagonists for God's liberation agenda? Is it us? The church? Can we hope for a new social gospel?

How are God's community organizers raised up? When people seek more earthly blessings than people in charge believe they are entitled to, legislation comes down to oppress the alienated with forced labor and denied benefits. Their lives are to be made bitter with hard service. Have-nots must not threaten the haves. Food stamp programs must be reduced. (President Trump proposed a special tax on retailers who accept food stamps.) As the Israelites groan under their oppression, their cries reach God's ears. (God's ears today can be reached in the church, some believe.) One poor boy survives to become Moses (as I write this, it is Martin Luther King Jr. day), the man God will call to organize the people and lead the exodus. Theophanies occur to the attentive, and so Moses responds, "Here I am." Divine interventions require the complement of human agency (think of the Virgin Mary in the New Testament); Moses is aroused to go before the king. He first tries to avoid his call from God, but God is insistent. If anyone asks who sent you, who has authorized this revolution, Moses is to say that God's name is: "I Will Be Who I Will Be." This is another way of telling the powers that be,

Don't try to constrain me, don't imagine you can shrink God to your own self-interest, don't try to dodge by declaring religious action off limits in the public square. Moses' most famous line is, *Let my people go*, and he speaks it in the king's court.

You can imagine how the story would read today. Oligarchs have created a monopoly of power and resources in the face of the weak and the hungry. They manipulate the economy in the interest of a concentration of wealth and power for the privileged. One percent rule 99 percent. Hard work makes wealth for the few and oppresses the many. Will American Christianity insist that a system like this is incompatible with the dreams of a liberating God? When the exodus inheritance is newly decoded today, liberation and revolution may follow. But "the system," often including religion, seems determined to keep God from hearing the peoples' grief. The powerful know how to use God too; they offer the self-serving religious admonition the rich tell the poor today: Work harder and earn the success we ourselves have merited. Your social security benefits may have to be postponed to heaven.

On the way out following liberation, God woos in the wilderness a not always grateful people, who may lack the heart for liberation and find themselves dreaming of the fleshpots of Egypt. Patiently and deliberately, God shapes a new life together in a covenanted community. Is this the way God shapes pilgrims over time? Is this in store for us who flirt with pilgrimage as our New Age mindfulness? The wilderness journey, as also for pilgrims like the readers of this book, is a deliberate social and religious construction, where people are schooled in God's dreams for earthly life. Religious liturgies are meant to perform God's intentions. Hebrew prophets came to call this Israel's honeymoon period with God—revisionist history, of course, since Israel was building a golden calf while Moses was getting divine revelation. Is the modern church eager to recover a honeymoon with God? In retroactive and redeeming memory, the grace of God in the wilderness becomes the formative motif that follows the exodus from Egypt, the gift that keeps on giving. The lessons don't stop. When God feeds the people and the greedy take too much, it rots. Bread from heaven becomes an expansive metaphor of life with each other and under God. Israel is *overwhelmed by God's capacity for generosity, which also redefines their relation to each other and to the land.*

TEN COMMANDMENTS ADD UP TO
A NEW SOCIAL COVENANT

Almost everyone knows that the Ten Commandments come from the Old Testament, and that God gave them to ancient Israel through Moses at Mt. Sinai. Many Americans, above all those who dream of theocracy, would like to see the Ten Commandments installed on courthouse lawns and in government buildings. Why are the Ten Commandments so esteemed today? Do people really get them?

After the exodus from bondage in Egypt, God intended to inaugurate a new covenant (social contract) that would foretell Israel's chosenness to be a light to the world. The early Puritans who came to America wanted to see the American experiment as a city set on the hill, as a witness to all the nations of the world. ("City on a hill" is a line from Jesus' Sermon on the Mount, and President Reagan added "shining" to it.) The commandments are more *covenant stipulations* than a moralizing list to be checked twice. The commandments instruct the children of Israel how to live on the land as a human family, how to organize public life for the common good. They begin by calling people to love, serve, and trust the God who brought them out of Egypt and slavery. The *exodus (a God who liberates) is the premise* of the commandments and of a covenanted people. And of our relation to God.

This is how the commandments work. Commandments one to three (God is Lord of all, Do not make idols of anything or anyone, Do not misuse God's name and authority to legitimize your own self-interest) announce a regime change that is to govern the peoples' consciousness regarding where ultimate authority lies. They declare under what point of view human society is to be constructed, not unlike America's founding documents, but far more radical—and including people of color. God's liberal grace, and not the king's economic and political power and not the survival of the fittest, is determinative of how this new community should live. Ultimately, human life is a gift, not a product of striving and acquisitiveness. Commandments five to nine (we'll come back to four) instruct how "the neighbor," which is to say everyone else and especially the disadvantaged, is to be respected and protected and not exploited. Honor your parents. Do not murder or bring harm. Do not commit adultery or ruin marital relationships. Do not steal or unfairly gain the property of others. Do not bear false witness or bring lying and deceit into human discourse. Neighbors are to be ends and not means. Commandment ten forbids the community-destroying, greedy acquisitiveness that governs so much of national life. Do not covet anything that belongs to someone else—house, spouse, goods. Do not spend your lives in gain at the expense of others.

So we must *unlearn* most of what we think we know well and *relearn* how the Commandments carry the DNA of a liberating God. If there's a problem, it may be that we have taught ourselves to trivialize the Commandments by making them God's checklist for bourgeois values. Or we pose them in front of court houses as public trophies that give evidence that we are God's favorite people. We have trimmed them to fit nicely into our present economic system, shaming the working class into showing up on Monday mornings and making the neighborhood safe for commerce, but betraying no concern for the good in common. These Commandments are not paeans to the nuclear family or authorizations for the culture wars, but the foundation of a new kind of life in community, a dike against all the predatory practices and aggressive policies that make the little vulnerable to the big and add up to unjust social systems. The Ten Commandments reset life in community from the rapacious system in which nobody's house or field or family or goods or inheritance are safe. The mention of Egypt in the preface is code for the exploitative system authorized to demand ever more—more control, more territory. Deliverance from Egypt requires us to move out of our quagmire and set up a society that is modeled after the generosity of God. Where is Egypt today? Inside the beltway? In the confines of Wall Street? If you're in it, start walking out. Are we part of the oppressive system or will we become the visionaries who see a life over the wall?

All the Commandments are embedded in the Jewish genome via the fourth (the third when counted differently) commandment. (I am again following Walter Brueggemann here.) You are to honor the Sabbath and keep it holy. That means a whole lot more than getting to church on Sunday or not shopping. The fourth Commandment institutionalizes an alternative to relentless striving and greed and the economic anxiety that drives it. The Sabbath deliberately requires *work stoppage*, and also worship, and also the enhancement of the neighborhood. The Sabbath provides *time to mend the world*. The Sabbath tempers economic productivity with acts of communal imagination and renewal. In effect, the Sabbath becomes the great equalizer, the sacrament of God's reordering of life, the one day when economic exploitation cannot happen, cannot drive human life, cannot determine everything else. Especially on this day, God-the-liberator is worshiped and God's designs for the commons are exemplified. It seriously distorts the fourth Commandment to frame it as "Sunday closing laws," a strategy that claws back from God the meaning of our life together as 24/7 commerce. Judaism at its best *turns Sabbath into an art form*, a sacred aesthetic of common life. And true religion.

The Ten Commandments and the social contract they authorize may be seen as the *first social safety net* in the history of the world. They guard the good of every neighbor and hem in every propensity of the rich and the powerful to render the neighbor a means to their own ends, a target for exploitation, a satellite of the free market. This social mandate of the God of the exodus is greatly expanded in the book of Deuteronomy (the Deuteronomic Code). There we are instructed that debts owed by the poor must be canceled after seven years so that no permanent underclass develops. (Ask your senator to propose this. Suggest it be written into the platform of your favorite political party.) Interest is forbidden, no collateral is required on loans to the poor, permanent hospitality is to be a communal norm, justice is extended to aliens, leftover abundance is reserved for widows and orphans. Always the reason is the same: Once you were slaves in Egypt and God delivered you and decreed a new kind of community. Ultimately the land is God's own, so there must be grain, oil, and wine available for all. Never is the economy meant to be a freestanding autonomous system—that would break the first commandment, devoted to God's priorities. Israel's God is a liberator, not a chaplain to the Chamber of Commerce.

AND THEN GOD CALLED PROPHETS

When King Ahab saw Elijah, Ahab said to him,
"Is it you, you troubler of Israel?"
1 Kings 18:17

The days are surely coming, says the LORD,
when I will make a new covenant
I will write my law on their hearts
and I will be their God and they shall be my people
I will forgive their iniquity, and remember their sin no more.
Jeremiah 31:31–34

Go down to the palace of the king and declare,
"Do what is just and right.
Rescue from the hand of the oppressor the one who has been robbed.
Do no wrong or violence to the foreigner, the orphan, or the widow,
and do not shed innocent blood in this place."
Jeremiah 22:1, 3

Let justice roll down like waters, and righteousness like an ever-flowing stream.

Amos 5:24

What does the LORD require of you but to do justice, and to love kindness, and to walk humbly with your God?

Micah 6:8

Consider the prophets. In the book of 2 Samuel (chapter 12), the prophet *Nathan* comes to court one day to tell King David about a rich man who had many flocks and herds and a poor man who had just one little ewe lamb that he raised and treated as his own child. When the rich man had guests to entertain, he did not want to take an animal from his own flock, so he took the poor man's lamb. Have you seen this story in the papers? As the king listened attentively, he grew incensed and demanded that that evil rich man be put to death and the poor man compensated fourfold. Then the prophet Nathan denounces the king, *You are that man!* The prophet challenges the king's course; the king repents.

Elijah, much better known, is the most revered prophet after Moses and a kind of Moses *redivivus*. (In a richly symbolic Gospel story, Elijah and Moses, archetypes of the prophetic genome, appear with Jesus on the Mount of Transfiguration, to stimulate the disciples' imagination and authenticate Jesus as a genuine match with God's visions.) To this day, pious Jews "set a place for Elijah" at their ritual tables to keep his memory alive, to keep the family aware of what might be missing from Jewish life.

Elijah flourished in the middle of the ninth century BC and his exploits are told in 1 Kings 17—19, 21 and 2 Kings 1—2. At this time, the Israelites were distracted by rival gods to the one who had called them out of Egypt. *True prophets, then and now, are always in the king's face.* Elijah has been denouncing the royal court for selling out the Sinai covenant to the claims of imperial commerce. As Elijah accuses King Ahab of blaspheming God, the king tweets that Elijah is a royal troublemaker. Can you think of any prophets who fiercely denounce America's sell outs to Wall Street, who take back God's bounty meant for the poor? Rev. Jeremiah Wright had been candidate Obama's pastor in Chicago, but was thrown under the bus on Obama's way to the White House. President Johnson and FBI Director J. Edgar Hoover came to think that Martin Luther King Jr. should go under the bus. A clever move to make against prophets today is to call them communists or, presently, socialists. Prophets are denounced who do not bless America enough.

When Elijah flees from the wrath of the beltway to hunker down in the country, God does not brook the sequestration of the prophetic vocation. (Pastors today are not meant to hide out in their pulpits.) Elijah is ordered to trouble the powers. When he comes back to town, the king greets him with the wonderfully ironic words: "Is it you, the troubler of Israel?" Elijah rejoins that it is the king who is Israel's ruin. In a classic duel, Elijah hurls thunderbolts against the royal chaplains to the king's court. (Check the newspapers for the professional outrage streaming from the president's evangelical court.) Before Elijah can be repudiated or assassinated, he is taken up to heaven in a fiery chariot (2 King 2:11), a scene American blacks have kept alive in communal memory and song: "Swing low, sweet chariot, coming for to carry me home." Some see in their celebration of Elijah an allusion to the underground railroad and the abolitionism meant to be their exodus from Egypt.

The prophet *Amos* had been a simple farmer, but was called to public life during the middle of the eighth century BC, a time of aggressive territorial expansion bought with gross inequities between urban elites and the rural poor. Wealthy landowners were accumulating vast estates by cynically manipulating debt and credit at the expense of small farmers. (Like New York billionaire lenders cheating taxi drivers out of their living and driving them to suicide.) At this time the smallest debt could become the thin wedge of foreclosure that separates farmers from their patrimonial lands and turns them into plantation slaves. Amos denounces the greed of the markets in words no man of God can say politely. He scorns opulence wrapped in decadent piety. He unclothes civic hypocrisy and redresses the commons in divine justice.

Imagine inviting a prophet to speak at a national Fourth of July celebration—rather than tanks displaying the president's ego. It happened. Early in his ministry, Amos (chapter 5) presided over a national celebration. He took his audience on an imaginary inspection tour of the lands bordering Israel, denouncing each one by one. The crowd went wild. "USA, USA!" Suddenly, the tour de force turned homeward and God's judgment was directed to Israel itself, for breaking their social contract with God and each other. Listen to these words as if delivered at the National Mall: "You sell the righteous for silver, and the needy for a pair of sandals; you trample the head of the poor into the dust of the earth, and push the afflicted out of the way." Then the betrayal of the exodus, the national story: "People of Israel whom I brought up out of the land of Egypt, you only have I known of all the families of the earth. Therefore I will punish you for all your iniquities."

Like any prophet, Amos can't keep quiet. "The LORD God has spoken; who can but prophesy?" he says (Amos 3:8), rather than, Don't bring politics into the pulpit. He disdainfully turns on wealthy women in a way that is impossible to imagine in a modern megachurch: "Hear this word, you cows of Bashan, who oppress the poor, who crush the needy." He closes his July 4 speech with a kind of funeral oration: "Fallen, no more to rise, is maiden Israel." When the religious establishment and the beltway hypocrites remind the prophet of their public religion (closing every speech on any topic with God bless America), Amos speaks for God: "I hate, I despise your festivals, and I take no delight in your solemn assemblies" (Amos 5:21).

The Sabbath had been instituted as a religious festival meant to institutionalize seventh-day "rest" as a way to tend to family and community, and honor God and the commons. So the prophet derides those who can hardly wait until religious observance is over so they can get back to trampling the needy and bringing ruin to the poor, making profits in the grain market, bankrupting the underprivileged, monopolizing the sweepings of wheat intended for the hungry. As a result of greedy attempts to evade the good of the community mandated by God's covenant, Amos sees a famine coming to the land. *God* will become what people are starving for. The true God will stop speaking in public life (as today). Amos calls this a *famine of the word of the* LORD. In an infamous lament speech at Harvard, the Russian exile Solzhenitzen accused the modern West of having forgotten God. Our status elites thought this simple-minded.

Think about the last time you heard someone who might be a prophet. They rub against the grain. They question the national mystique. In the '60s they were called the "hate America first" crowd. In Amos 7:10–17, Amaziah, the king's loyal chaplain, accuses Amos of treason. He admonishes God's mouthpiece that the government is "not able to bear the prophet's words." Get out of Dodge, prophets are told: "O seer, go, never again prophesy in the king's sanctuary, which is the religious center of the kingdom." Amos answers back with God's latest message, "This evil country shall surely go into exile." It did. Of course America in exile is inconceivable, so we don't have to worry. The Christian Right representatives to the president's court know which side they are on.

Some *writing prophets* left long collections of oracles and attention-grabbing stories for the next generation. *Jeremiah* flourished around 600 BC and he gave his name to what we today call a *jeremiad,* a denunciatory speech full of divine outrage. A bad marriage is what Jeremiah called the relation between the nation and God. Imagine this from the mouth of Billy Graham's boy: God is the aggrieved husband and America the cuckolding wife who decorates her skirts with the lifeblood of the poor (2:34) and throws banquets for the wealthy with food plundered from the tables of the peasants (5:25–28). Can you hear Jerry Falwell's boy chiming in at a Liberty

University graduation: "Woe to you who build houses by unrighteousness and upper rooms by injustice, who make neighbors work for nothing and refuse them living wages" (22:13)? Aren't there any prophets among those who wear red caps that say "Make America Great Again"?

Then there's this iconic scene. Imagine it captured on YouTube and going viral. Jeremiah (chapter 36) is writing down in a scroll all the words God was giving him to say. The president wants a copy for the Library of Congress, but fancies a private reading from the prophet would be nice. It goes downhill from there. As Jeremiah's lines are read out and the scroll unwinds, the king, increasingly infuriated, takes out his penknife, cuts off the prophet's pages one by one, and throws them into the fire. Fox News loves it but MSNBC releases a statement: *This is how the powerful regard the justice God demands for the poor.* When every last page from the scroll is burned up, the president tweets that the prophet must be arrested. Jeremiah goes back to his room and writes it down all over again. The internet goes wild—at least until the next spectacle comes to cable TV.

English-speaking Christians know the prophet *Isaiah* through his many quotations in Handel's *Messiah*. The form of the book of Isaiah is drawn from three different time periods, *pre-exilic, exilic, post-exilic*, from the eighth to the sixth centuries BC, as if from several periods in American history, say the revolution, the civil war, and today. Each epoch gets its own prophetic words. Imagine a pilgrim's souvenir with devotions for the archetypal stages of a life. Imagine if you *composed a life* using prophetic scripts. A "Book of Hours" for pious Americans.

Isaiah chapter 3 stages a "covenant lawsuit" in which God puts the nation on trial. Think of the Attorney General (if not a lackey) as the prosecutor, with a bill of goods from a contemporary prophet. Prophets are fond of bringing the public before the bar. Listen to the charges: The oligarchy has devoured the vineyard that is the land God provides for all, the spoil of the needy ends up in the mansions of the wealthy, who crush the people and grind the face of the poor.

It gets better: Wealthy women in their fashions walk before the cameras with outstretched necks, glancing wantonly and mincing along as they stroll across the national mall with tinkling feet. (These are quotes from the biblical prophets; no one would say them today, not even a leftist.) God, the original giver and the liberator of the public vineyards and the plots of the poor, is mad as hell. God threatens to cover the heads of the wealthy with scabs and expose their secret parts.

No medal of merit from the Arts Council will go to any such prophet, although we miraculously made Martin Luther King Jr.'s birthday a national holiday. But Cornel West, a black prophet not yet martyred, couldn't get a ticket to Obama's White House. Too much drama came with him. Always the *vineyard* is a metaphor for God's gift of the land to all. But instead of justice God sees bloodshed, instead of righteousness, God hears the people's cries. Congress busily and cheerfully writes oppressive statutes that turn aside the needy from justice and rob the poor of their rights. Widows are ruined and orphans are prey (Isaiah, chapter 10).

The Prophets constitute one of the three divisions of the Hebrew Bible, along with Torah and the Wisdom literature. A common characteristic of these prophets, initially, is that they all run away from God's call. They are reluctant and unwilling instruments of a God who wants to use them to scatter the divine seed across the land and raise up new crops of justice. (Is this what seminaries are training pastors for?) Isaiah 6 depicts the paradigmatic calling of a prophet. While the prophet-to-be is sitting in temple enthralled with the worship, he has a vision in which an angel takes a live coal from the altar fire and flies over to lay it on the prophet's lips. The prophet understands that his mouth is being cleansed and his heart commissioned to speak on God's behalf. This is almost never a welcome assignment—not for the prophet and not for the nation. Let there be no doubt. The dangerous holiness of the prophet's call does not play in the national cathedral where people hunker up to God with pious words while their hearts are far away (Isaiah, chapter 29).

In Isaiah's imagination, God wants to dream a world in which Israel becomes a light to the nations, but the people only dilly-dally and indifferently put in their time as the chosen people, eager for rewards and universal admiration, not sacrifice and social justice. In Isaiah 42, God imagines a whole community sequencing God's DNA: they become a servant people clothed in righteousness, they take shape as covenant neighborhoods, they open eyes that were blind, they bring out prisoners from the dungeon—until (chapter 49) finally God's right-making shalom reaches to the ends of the earth. When that day comes (chapter 58), everyone will offer food to the hungry and satisfy the needs of the afflicted, and that people's light will shine in the darkness for all the world to see. If only they do not run away from their calling, nations will come to their light and rulers to the brightness of their new dawn (chapter 60). Can you hear these words being sung from Handel's *Messiah*?

This expression of God's DNA is sometimes depicted as the "Messianic program." Which brings to mind, get with the program. It originates in the Jubilee Year prescribed for the covenant community of Israel in Leviticus 25. *You're not going to believe this.* Maybe on his best day ever Bernie Sanders dreams this, but of course everyone understands it would never work, and the moral hazards are astounding, and even leftist pundits say acidly,

"Get real," and everyone knows it would lose the election. Israel is to count off seven times seven years and celebrate what can only be called a divine utopia. In this time of freedom and celebration, a kind of apotheosis of an individual Sabbath, everyone will receive back their original property, slaves will return home to their families, and all debts will be forgiven—so that the community does not stray irreversibly far from God's original intentions as the giver of all we can have. This is like a periodic estate tax in spades. Get with the program is Isaiah's message, so that divinely chosen Israel becomes a light to the nations (Isaiah 61). Finally this re-echoes in Jesus' first sermon in Luke 4. This is how Isaiah proclaims it and how Jesus quotes it: "The spirit of the Lord God is upon me because the Lord has anointed me; he has sent me to bring good news to the oppressed, to bind up the brokenhearted, to proclaim liberty to the captives, and release to the prisoners; to proclaim the year of the Lord's favor." Imagine if every chaplain to Congress sounded this way. Imagine God escaping from the church's lectionary and running all over town.

ONCE THE FORGOTTEN WORDS OF PROPHECY PROVOKED NATIONAL REFORM

When King Josiah ruled the southern kingdom of Judah in the second half of the seventh century BC and foreign gods (evil forces) in the land were serious rivals to the God of the exodus, Israel was in the midst of national reform. But they had lost touch with their origin stories. Or the exodus had become, *like social justice, a discarded image*—written off as a tired leftist slogan having nothing to do with the economy or society. In a gesture of renewal, the High Priest was directed to take tax monies and apply them to the renovation of the Temple built by Solomon—soon to be destroyed by the Babylonian invasion. (Think: open up the ten commandments displayed in the court house. Take a peak inside the Bible used to swear on at presidential inaugurations.) Amidst the ruins there was found a back room where sacred relics of the past had been kept. According to the story in 2 Kings 22—23, the High Priest astonished everyone with the news: "I have found the book of the law in the house of the Lord." This seems to have been the book of Deuteronomy, the fifth book of the Pentateuch that elaborated the exodus legacy and its evolution into a social contract. When it was read aloud to the king, he tore his clothes because he understood the book to imply a condemnation of the people for wandering from the Sinai covenant, a rebuke of the present and a recall to the past. A local prophetess (say what?) declared that disaster would fall on the kingdom if the king did not immediately initiate a reformation across the land, a renewal of the covenant with the God of the exodus. The prevailing national DNA was far from a match with the God who had led Israel out of bondage.

King Josiah then arranged for public readings of the long lost book, the book that laid out the whole point of national existence. "Deuteronomic Reforms" were instituted to get Israel to recover its origins. In the twentieth century, the Christian apologist C. S. Lewis saw the decline of common life sure to come when the book everyone is reading has a missing chapter—the one that brings everything together. Amazingly, the king understands this and takes action to restore the lost story, the discarded images of Exodus and Covenant.

Myths of eternal return posit a perennial wandering far away from an original condition and then a return to the story of origins. Martin Luther (and before him, the Renaissance) called for continuous returns to original sources and hence new reformations. Just as the original book of Deuteronomy had come to ancient Israel as they were about to *enter* the promised land, now it is recovered by a people who are about to *return* to that land. The lost Deuteronomic Code had elaborately described how a new nation should behave in unfamiliar territory. The rediscovery and match with God's DNA provokes an astonishing re-creation. On the occasion of this Ancestry.com revelation, and to mark this return to origins, Judaism rehearses a basic confession for all situations ever since: *Hear O Israel: The LORD is our God, the LORD alone"* (Deuteronomy 6:4). This is an explication of the First Commandment: Always make your very being a match with God's intentions. This is the authorization today for a new social gospel for the churches to proclaim. (Of course we're not a theocracy, no government has to do what all the pastors unite in saying. But still . . .)

WOULD PROPHETS BE PERMITTED IN THE PUBLIC SQUARE TODAY

I've just told the stories of exodus and covenant and Prophets. I've implied these stories are still relevant in the modern world, otherwise what was the point. But do prophets, for example, really belong to today? Do historical religious figures who insist on flying out of sacred texts and appearing in contemporary contexts have the right? Of course, university courses in literature or religious studies offer courses in the Bible, but current attempts to teach the Bible in public schools worry people. What if students get converted (by mistake), take it seriously? What if it spreads to government and business? Evangelicals may carry their Bibles around, but few other

Christians do. That the Bible's voice should be part of the noise of the public square seems objectionable and especially the Old Testament, which seems to imply theocracy and strange directions for running a government. Maybe nearly every ancient civilization was a theocracy of sorts, but almost none today is except Iran—a scary thought.

Has the Old Testament then lost its legacy, its relevance, its voice? In God's eye, according to the prophets and reaffirmed in the New Testament, Israel was meant to become a light to the nations. And surely not all the nations would be theocracies. Contemporary Israel does not claim to be a theocracy, and 65 percent of its population claim to be either not religious or convinced atheists. Yet it seems to claim "election" or "chosenness," just as the Puritan tradition in America has done. If the subject of God is relevant to contemporary discourse about the meaning of life and about moral vision and religious humanism and virtue and ideals about living in community and whether there is an ultimate destiny built into our evolution, then surely the Bible is in the mix. Yes or no? In the university we say that a great play by Aeschylus or Shakespeare, a great novel by Melville or Dostoevsky, a great poem by Tennyson or Emily Dickinson carries weight, makes claims, invites us to consider whether we would live differently if we accepted their claims as relevant and true. The Bible is part of that mix too, only more so. There is no doubt that it wishes to be understood as making theological, life-altering, life-directing claims—though not everyone accepts them.

The legacy of the Old Testament is that it is part of what being the church means, part of the church's language, part of the church's story. If one wishes to posit a social gospel, a lived-religion, real-life-on-the-ground vision for humanity on earth, then the Old Testament will contribute some social substance to it, some earthiness to what Jesus must have meant when he proclaimed the arrival of the reign of God. Unless we choose to argue that the material/spirit binary is all over, that only secularism offers a meaningful and realistic account of life and our expectations of it, the Old Testament, at least for Jews and Christians, is part of the substance of God's vision, of Christian humanism, of the reign of God. If freedom of religion means the church has the right to be heard in contemporary public space, then the church's book does as well.

Which gets us to the point. If prophets come off ancient pages and appear on the streets today, or make their claims in houses of worship or motels or around the table in homes, their message will be either self-validating or not. So it won't do when coming upon them in the public square simply to say, "What are you doing off the reservation? Aren't you out of place?" But this hostile questioning may be more about our resistance to any interrogation about the way things are, or what our lives mean, than to the nature of the Bible itself. In the '60s, radical students were always asked, especially by California's Governor Reagan, "Who let you off campus?" Union organizers are equally out of place on a factory floor, disenfranchised by those who control capitalism, and sometimes beaten by the police. Beginning with women's suffrage campaigns, women were resented and sometimes arrested and yet they persisted. Martin Luther King Jr. was undoubtedly speaking as a revolutionary idealist authorized by the Bible; he led an entire civil rights movement and was also assassinated. If someone appears today to call for a new social gospel, on what grounds may she stand? And how will she fare? But she cannot be forbidden to speak in public, to boycott the commons, to sit in, block streets, to trouble people.

So true prophets, then and now, will move from page to stage and appear where they're not invited. You can't lock them in the Old Testament canon and throw the key away. (A similar attempt was made to lock up the Apostle Paul when he came to town preaching. Indeed, "lock her up, lock her up" still has a certain ring to it at political rallies. Or, "Go back to where you came from.") Prophets do not require official authorization. The Chinese say: "Better than the assent of the crowd is the dissent of one brave man." Pascal admonished: "Trust witnesses willing to sacrifice their lives." Martin Luther King Jr. and Mahatma Gandhi sealed their legacies with martyrdom.

But who talks like that? Aren't we entitled to insist on the American vernacular, which is materialist and secular and capitalist? It is not prophet-speak. Towards the end of this book you will read the phrase "divine economy." Do those words really go together? Surely it must refer to the church budget. Can prophets stick their nose into the free market, can they witness on Wall Street, can they call corporations to account? Can they insist every market comes encumbered—by the common good, by concern for the least, by earth-care? No corporate oligarch concedes this, so prophets must get noisier.

When pre-president Obama's Chicago pastor Jeremiah Wright opened his mouth to condemn America, the response, also from Bible-believers, was incredulous. Few could imagine anyone denouncing his own country in the name of God. Certainly not this country, the city God set on a hill for all to admire. Hillary said Methodists would never talk like that. J. Edgar Hoover had tried to segregate Martin Luther King Jr. as a communist. And President Johnson stopped admiring King when his rhetoric turned from garbage collectors to the Vietnam War. Because he was a prophet, King could see the connection. Because he was the commander in chief, Johnson could not.

Any college student who has taken a Religious Studies course on the Hebrew Bible or the Bible as literature will have read these prophetic oracles, but perhaps concluded they were speaking in an idiom lost to modern civilization, no longer relevant, or even intelligible. Business majors often cannot fit the humanities of the Western tradition into their thick enclosure of economic realism and money-making. Indeed, Republicans have recently proposed a surcharge on such courses because they do not contribute to the needs of the economy. Some American Bible-believers prefer a spiritualizing Jesus to an angry prophet with all that social justice language. Some say that fundamentalists want to keep Jesus on the cross and with few speaking parts. Many Christians invite Jesus into their hearts but not the economy. The spiritual-but-not-religious stick to nature but quickly return from Big Sur to Silicone Valley when the weekend is over.

To be sure, prophets are hard to live with. They especially grate on nationalist sensibilities and on patriotism as the common default. Americans, though not Europeans, cannot imagine a God who blesses social democracy while condemning the idolatry of free markets. Abraham Heschel, a great admirer, admitted that prophets always seem to sing an octave too high. And they do not sing for their supper with the 1 percent. The only solution to some is to cut their words about social justice from the Bible with a pen knife. This leaves the Old Testament full of holes in all the right places. For more than a century the Bible had nothing to say about slavery. The founding fathers were not enslaved to the prophets because they had developed "self-interested" readings.

COULD YOU BE A PROPHET

Christians speak of Jesus coming again. Can prophets come again—disguised as you? Here's how it starts: simple *seekers* with good eyes and ears and an inquiring spirit find themselves perplexed by all the things that have gone wrong in this world and look earnestly for the promised handwriting of God in history. Churning in their minds and hearts are biblical words. Then a call from God, almost always unwelcome, turns them into divine witnesses and social critics. They are deputized as voices for God's ambitions for earth and humanity. They slowly find their way as social critics and then actors in a society that has lost its moorings. Maybe they consider community organizing. Or preaching in churches and then on the streets and factory floors and city council meetings and then before Congress—as John Stewart famously did on behalf of the 9/11 first responders. They are determined to believe that *history has a plot and the religious agenda is to name it.*

In acts of guerilla theater they *play God's dreams on public stages.* They mean to disturb and captivate new audiences. Like Marx, commonly called a secular prophet, they are determined to change the world. Their plots may be taken from the exodus or the wilderness period, their style from those who got in the king's face and became a nuisance on national holidays. Today they are likely to be responding to the call of Christ, since there are 2.1 billion Christians in the world today. They decode a liberating God everywhere, announce God's intentions, call the oppressed or the deceived to march into freedom. They insert themselves into the vortex where the forces of prophetic ministry and the lives of the disempowered swirl. *Can you see yourself? Can you hear yourself?*

The *freedom of God to do something surprising and the American freedom of religion* can become the prophet's calling card, as it was when Pharaoh asked "Who's calling" and God identified as I will be who I will be. God is not a household idol kept at the Smithsonian, but an iconoclast on behalf of a new age. Today we say we prize "speaking truth to power," although the chaplains who just go along get the promotions. Prophets *bring grief over injustice to public expression.* The cries of the poor, amplified in the prophet's voice, portend a market crash. True religion echoes the pain of God and transforms the numbness of history.

Prophets, like poets, are "indicator species." What will happen to the rest of us first happens to them. They sound alarms, concentrate the mind, escape sentimentality, face evil, expose our hiding behaviors. In ages of assured sunshine, prophets retain the ability to see in the dark. Consider this touching poem "Games" by Jack Gilbert, who like the ancient prophets, does not speak in Hallmark verses:

> Imagine if suffering were real.
>
> Imagine if those old people were afraid of death.
>
> What if the midget or the girl with one arm
>
> really felt pain? Imagine how impossible it would be
>
> To live if some people were
>
> Alone and afraid all their lives.

2

The Risk of Incarnation: The Christian Sequel

IN CHRIST EARTH BECAME CAPABLE OF HEAVEN

In the beginning was the Word, and the Word was God . . .
And the Word became flesh and lived among us,
And we beheld his glory, the glory as of a father's only son,
Full of grace and truth.
John 1:1, 14

Where is the Child . . . For we observed his star at its rising,
And have come to pay him homage.
"Wise men still seek him."
Matthew 2:1–2

He has scattered the proud in the thoughts of their hearts.
He has brought down the powerful from their thrones, and lifted up
the lowly;
He has filled the hungry with good things, and sent the rich away
empty.
Song of the Virgin Mary, Luke 1:51–53

> The spirit of the Lord God has sent me to bring good news to the oppressed,
>
> to bind up the brokenhearted, to proclaim liberty to the captives,
>
> and release to the prisoners;
>
> to proclaim the year of the Lord's favor.
>
> (Isaiah 60:1–2) Luke 4:18–19

> Jesus came to Galilee, proclaiming the good news of God, and saying,
>
> The time is fulfilled, and the reign of God has come near;
>
> repent, and believe in the good news.
>
> Mark 1:14

In the Old Testament God led an exodus out of bondage and into the promised land, inaugurated a new covenant with a chosen people, and voiced the prophets to speak God's vernacular in every time and place. Eventually, the prophets came to imagine Israel as a light to the nations and foretold a Messianic program open to all peoples. The Christian New Testament proclaims that a new reign of God on all the earth has been initiated. Jesus Christ comes as the universal *paradigm of earth capable of heaven*. The story of Jesus, of the early church, and of lived Christianity ever since also became a story about the *risk of incarnation*.

The opening lines of the Gospel of John connect Jesus, the divine Word, to the Word God first spoke at creation. The Word from the mouth of God that constituted the earthly Jesus is understood as none other than the Word that first announced, "Let there be," the Word that said to Pharaoh, "Let my people go," the Word that was good news to the oppressed from the mouths of the prophets. Jesus and early Christianity—and now we today—are the sequels to a long tradition that carries the DNA of a liberating God. Was God mapping salvation into our genes? Humans are on a pilgrimage to realize their true nature. A Christian humanism will include a vision of a just society for all, lived on a reenchanted earth, and for those who can see set into a Christian cosmology of universal meaning. We are called in each age to extend the incarnational vernacular, to enact a new social gospel that renders earth and us capable of heaven.

The theological implication of the New Testament gospel is that heaven has emptied and God come to earth, fully aligning divine nature and human nature. To keep your eye on God, Martin Luther admonished, keep your eye on Mary's baby. Christianity (and Judaism before it) implies a divine politics of identity—God identifying as human and humans identifying with God.

But this is a fraught story, inescapably conflicted. *If earth is to become capable of heaven, there will be contested ground*—just as when the church enters the public square. Worldly leaders are not amused by anyone called *Lord*. Early on, Jesus becomes a refugee condemned by a king and hunted by his army. The powerful who acknowledge no universal covenant that takes precedence over their social and economic arrangements resent the undocumented—all those with rights and identities and futures not yet recognized. Born into an imperial world order, the Christ child is carried into the maelstrom of powerful political and economic forces and eventually experiences the violence that comes from all systems whose dominion is threatened. The early readers of Matthew's gospel account of the annihilation of the babies in Bethlehem and the holy family as escaping refugees were themselves experiencing the hostilities being visited upon their Christian movement towards the end of the first century.

Perhaps first-world Christian hearers were not astonished at the Gospel's politicizing message, but modern tellings of the Christmas story easily slip into sentimentality. *Cross-class readings* of what the Bible must be saying are difficult if not impossible. American Christians do not typically see what Central Americans see when they hear Matthew's Christmas story and what the good news is and who the refugees are. But the oppressed can recognize good news when it comes; they name it and claim it.

Having decided to take the risk of incarnation, God chooses for a mother an unmarried girl in a land occupied by a colonizing empire. Jesus will be subject to every oppression that cries for exodus and will raise a prophetic voice that threatens every political jurisdiction. Jesus touches the untouchables, reaches out to ostracized women, befriends despised foreigners, associates with public sinners, and heals, in particular, the socially stigmatized. All in all, the disturbing implication of the New Testament is that this Jesus is in fact *God on earth as a new liberator who sets us free and calls us to follow.*

"CHRIST PLAYS IN TEN THOUSAND PLACES"

I say more: the just man justices;
Keeps grace: that keeps all his goings graces;
Acts in God's eye what in God's eye he is—
Christ—for Christ plays in ten thousand places,
Lovely in limbs, and lovely in eyes not his
To the Father through the features of men's faces.

Gerard Manley Hopkins, "As Kingfishers Catch Fire"

While John's gospel offers a "Christology from above" that traces the voice of Christ back to the mouth of God at creation, Matthew, Mark, and Luke begin with "Jesus from below," Jesus fully on earth in first-century Galilee and Judea. This is also the trend in Gospel studies today.

There is a predilection among middle-class Christians to spiritualize Jesus away from everyday eating and drinking, from mundane involvements, to locate Jesus in one's heart but not on the streets, to make following Jesus a prim moral walk more than a neighborhood demonstration. But the New Testament ties God, through the coarse life and death of Jesus, to a troubled social location on a gritty earth. In *The Message: The Bible in Contemporary Language,* Eugene Peterson paraphrases John 1:14: "The Word became flesh and blood, and moved into the neighborhood."

It would not occur to most modern Christians to look to the posters of Amnesty International or Human Rights Watch or "Missing" flyers at the Post Office or in the IRS booklet—to find the face of God. But consider this famous parable at the end of the Gospel of Matthew (25:31–46), in which judgment day poses a litmus test of how true religion has gone on earth. All of humanity is lined up, to determine who will face the eternal absence of God and who will go to eternal life with God. How is this to be decided? Sitting in glory as the sovereign of all, Jesus says to those pilgrims heading for life eternal that when he was hungry, they gave him food; when thirsty, something to drink; when a stranger, welcome; when naked, clothing; when sick, care; when in prison, a visit. Astonished, they say they do not recall ever specifically seeing Jesus hungry, thirsty, a stranger, naked, sick, and imprisoned. And he answers them: "Truly I tell you, just as you did it to one of the least of these who are my brothers and sisters, you did it to me." Some contemporary "social justice Christians" have taken to calling themselves "Matthew 25 Christians." In medieval art the scenes from this parable are commonly depicted as the "works of mercy."

Brace yourself. Now the story shifts to those in line for the life without God they have effectively chosen. While they are claiming a right to heaven based on the picture of Jesus carried in their wallets, they never actually saw him anywhere on earth. They are outraged and incredulous when they are told that their religion was bogus, that they had spent their religious lives looking for God in the wrong places, while determined to avert their eyes from the most promising places. In *Les Miserables,* Victor Hugo portrays French society looking at poor women and orphans *"as though they were on a planet much further from the sun than we."*

JESUS' PARABLES OPEN SPACE FOR GOD

Jesus was in the habit of turning life into teachable moments that disarmed his hearers or even tickled them with unexpected insight. He spoke in parables. In captivating and disarmingly familiar stories, the kind we all know, Jesus lures his hearers into houses built of their own assumptions, and then once the door is closed pulls the roof down with surprising punch lines. As in the musicals *Godspell* or *Jesus Christ Superstar*, Jesus blows peoples' minds. He pries open public space for the staging of alternative worlds—worlds of good news to those whose circumstances oppress and confine. He envisions new forms of community where God's DNA can reproduce and multiply. He grants little validity to commonly accepted truths, yet his new tellings seem uniquely convincing. New wines require fresh wineskins. Old Reaganesque stories about welfare Cadillacs and the undeserving poor, so beloved by those in power, are now turned upside down.

God's reign announced by Jesus starts small, with all those who lack a vote, but portends immense consequences. Jesus first challenges the stories told by the religious establishment. Mocking them in Facebook memes that go viral, he portrays them as arrogant upstarts who have taken over God's vineyard and betrayed the intentions of the master wine maker. Jesus has the audacity, in his breakthrough story of God, to claim that those who come to hear him have come into the presence of a life-changing reversal of the world's course, not a safe place for the risk averse. He tries to provoke his audience to radical response, to join him on the God-stage he is constructing. A crisis of decision ensues. Should we take our place with Jesus or not? The script includes genuine joy in heaven when the poor get good news—not a Wall Street intuition nor the platform of any known political party.

At first, the coming of God to start the revolution seems as insignificant as a mustard seed, not like the great cedars of Lebanon. Will trees become shrubs and shrubs trees? Will mustard plants attract birds that disturb nicely cultivated fields? Does God aim to reverse the world's course? In the parables of the Lost Coin and Lost Sheep, Jesus appears to be a bleeding heart for all who have missed out, who never got called on in life, never chosen for the team. God takes no delight in a banquet from which some are missing or deliberately turned away. In the parable of the Good Samaritan, Jesus suggests that humans are obligated to anyone in need, but more than that—it's an undocumented alien not a respectable citizen, who actually steps up to help, while the purity-obsessed religious avoid social contagion by walking on the other side of the street—no doubt wafting "thoughts and prayers" to the wounded man in the ditch. In the parable of the king who gives a great feast and nobody comes, Jesus may be saying that if the officially religious do not show up for God's party, then God will go out of the way to seek the lost and neglected, who become, in God's plan, "replacement guests." Imagine strangers lined up at the great cathedrals today identifying themselves as replacement guests, unforeseen pilgrims. Or, perhaps, the hearers are just to exclaim: How odd that a man is throwing a party with the entitled absent but unkempt strangers welcomed!

In the parable of the Prodigal Son, the elder brother represents the self-congratulation of the pious and of every self-made man expecting his proper recognition. But God, in the form of the prodigal father, bewilders the hearers of this parable with unhesitating love for the lost son. The father (God) is depicted as a proud man who gives up his dignity to run through the streets robes flying to greet a loser—never an American presidential campaign strategy, never a Horatio Alger story.

In a story about building one's house on solid rock instead of shifting sand, Jesus suggests that all the reality commonly thought solid is, in fact, insubstantial and undependable. *Parables make space for the unexpected.* They give God room (an act of moral imagination), shattering the structures of the accepted world and puncturing holes in the stories by which most people live. In place of defensiveness, they create vulnerability to God's initiatives.

Early Christian communities came to see that *Jesus himself was a parable*, the parable of how God's DNA would fare on earth. Imagine the relatives who show up on Ancestry.com if Jesus' own DNA is being traced. Jesus is a demonstration project of humanity opened or closed to God. Jesus undermines the accepted lines, challenges assumptions that have turned into bad news for the 99 percent, and proclaims open space where God and humanity could become a new community. Jesus leads to the promised land.

The Gospels recount Jesus' healings and exorcisms. There is leprosy, paralysis, hemorrhage, deafness, blindness, epilepsy, and death, that make Jesus' stomach hurt (the literal meaning of the Greek word translated as *compassion*). These maladies are occasions for human degradation and social ostracism, and Jesus, fulfilling the vision of Isaiah, nevertheless comes with good news for all in their captivities and exclusions. The exorcisms are difficult for the modern mind to grasp, but they seem to be symbols of the profound "domination systems" whose grip is so powerful that it takes supernatural force to be set free of them. Think how much power today the 1 percent have over the 99 percent. Release from bondage is the point, just as in the exodus. When Jesus arrives at the sites of oppression, people can walk out of Egypt. Every Sunday's liturgy invites such a performance.

The healing stories, then, can be seen as *enacted parables,* in which what happens is more than meets the eye. Social and not just physical forces are challenged, and a larger conflict comes into view. Un-preoccupied with his own purity or boundary markers, a typical religious obsession, Jesus touches an unclean woman, and makes her whole in body and soul. Kierkegaard saw that making no claims to importance and holding no entitlements, this woman nevertheless resolved to come close and touch—making her a "knight of faith." And she modeled that role for everyone. (Maybe she could be ordained too.) Jesus intervenes in the social world, refusing to accept diseases' ritual uncleanness and social ostracism, thereby impugning the claims of society's boundary keepers. When he heals blind men, he plays with religious definitions of who actually can see and who cannot. All who long for exodus come to see, and all who enslave them do not see—what a liberating God's intentions are. Wait, does God approve of universal health care, as if in the vernacular of a Scandinavian social democrat? What Jesus can see puts him on a collision course with religious authorities who claim to be the doorkeepers of God's presence, with political authorities terrified of moral hazards if Jesus reigns, who guard what they presumed was God's DNA stored in the Smithsonian. The true miracle of Jesus' healings is the picture that emerges of human wholeness in a liberated world.

When it is time to eat, Jesus deliberately seeks out the company of the excluded and makes a point of sitting at table with them. He enlarges the family of God. He breaks bread and boundaries. He models *divine commensality* and calls humans to imitate it. He abolishes customary rules to make way for love. He is criticized for feasting indiscriminately by those who fast to gain ground with God, but Jesus provides food prodigiously as a pointer to a new age banquet to which everyone will be invited and no one excluded. At a single wedding, a foretaste of divine-human celebration and abundance, Jesus turns 180 gallons of water intended for foot-washing into wine. What an imagination! Really, if this is just about thirst, it's way too much. Go easy. Use the water in the jars for servants to clean up for the middle class, not to celebrate with abundant drinking.

GOD WAS THERE IN JESUS' DEATH AND RESURRECTION

The terrible climax of Jesus' life is his death. Like Martin Luther King Jr.'s death or Gandhi's, for example, Jesus' death is the outcome of risks taken on behalf of love and justice, carrying out God's intentions in the face of an often hostile world. Christian theology is bold to say that in Jesus' suffering and death we see a crucified God. We see God as if a bleeding-heart liberal dying for the world's illiberalism. We see how God's DNA fares in a hostile environment. Much of the ground is not ready for the seeds God sows. In the incarnation, particularly in the death and resurrection of Christ, Christianity sees a coming and going. God descends into humanity and in Jesus' death takes back into God's own being the dark power of the world's rejection. When God fully identifies with the crucified one, the very negative powers (religious? political? economic?) that put Jesus to death are absorbed up into the life of God—for transformation. So even God changes—when God-present and God-forsaken are joined together. So that something new can happen. And people looking on must decide what it means and what to do about it, whether they will participate in God's becoming that implicates them too. This could be a new social gospel for our times. This would be worth a pilgrimage.

Religion that wants to imitate the story of an exodus-God told in the life of Jesus tries to stay close to all these things Jesus said and did. The well-known admonition "What *would* Jesus do?" can become the far more concrete—and uncomfortable—"What *did* Jesus do?" In Jesus God portrays God's own gentleness and vulnerability. God really does head straight for the marginalized, once arriving on earth. God really does evince a compassionate love for all, demanding no initial proof of having earned it. God really does call into question all the things we are certain of, for example, the law of the market and the high calling of every human to become a consumer and get rich. If what is said of Jesus can be said of God, then we are seeing, in the pages of the New Testament, God suffering persecution because God will not bend to the inexorable evil from which the human condition requires exodus. Jesus' crucifixion gives evidence of the willingness of God to suffer and to die with and for us. His resurrection is the assurance of the tenacity of God's involvement with the world and the coming victory of God's way. How we handle Jesus is how we handle God. (For a "theology of the atonement" that works all this out, look in a coming chapter. It's not about an angry Father; it's about a self-sacrificing Son.)

PAUL AND A HARVEST FOR THE AGES

> If anyone is in Christ, there is a new creation, everything has become new.
>
> In Christ God was reconciling the world to himself.
>
> 2 Corinthians 5:17, 18

In Christ Jesus you are all children of God through faith.

There is no longer Jew or Greek, slave or free, male and female,

for all of you are one in Christ Jesus.

Galatians 3:26, 28

In the telling of the Christian sequel to the primal story in the Hebrew Bible, God is fully present on earth and active in the life, death, and resurrection of Jesus. To register this claim, early Christians confessed: "Jesus Christ is Lord." Which is to say unmistakably, "We do not recognize Caesar's claims as all-encompassing." How far did the early Jesus Movement take the reality-bending confession, Christ is Lord/*Kyrios Christos*? Already towards the end of the period of the Hebrew Bible, some teachers and sages were asking whether God was the God of the Jews only. Centuries earlier the prophet Isaiah had begun to claim that the ultimate mission of Judaism was to become the vehicle through which the God who had liberated Israel would become a light to all the nations. That vision, that sequel to the call of Israel, that tradition of Messianic Judaism, would become the Christian mission.

As early Christian communities began to take shape, they were at first populated mostly by Jewish Christians, and thus seemed a rival movement to establishment Judaism. The person who became the Apostle Paul was at first a fierce advocate for traditional Judaism against these new Jewish Christians. Even the Jewish Christians themselves at first assumed that the influx of Gentiles into the Christian movement must first be routed through Judaism. And so it was at first expected that the new Gentile (non-Jewish) converts would have to accept circumcision and other Jewish cultural markers, and place themselves under the traditions of the Torah and become ethnically religious just the way Jews did. When some Jewish Christians attempted to open an alternative path for the new converts that did not require Judaism as its entry point, or the Temple as its epicenter, fierce controversy broke out. The Apostle Paul would take up the painful transition of early Christianity beyond Judaism in his letter to the Romans 9—11. Paul was becoming certain of two things: "Jesus is Lord" (Romans 10:9) and "There is no distinction between Jew and Greek; the same Lord is Lord of all" (Romans 10:12).

This is the setting for the call (sometimes called the conversion) of Paul, from fierce persecutor of Jewish Christians who were seen as apostates from Judaism to universalizing Christian missionary to the Gentiles. On the road to Damascus (Acts 9) Paul experienced a powerful vision of the risen Christ making a belated appearance and calling Paul, as prophets of old had been called, to a special mission on behalf of God's new initiatives. Paul, who had been present at the stoning of Stephen, the first Christian martyr, would eventually become in Rome a Christian martyr himself.

In a series of extraordinary letters (to the Thessalonians, Corinthians, Galatians, Romans, and Philippians, and several more probably emanating from a Pauline circle) Paul developed an early and determinative Christian theology, not as a dogmatic system but as a new way of thinking and responding to the diverse contexts and challenges of the early Christian mission to the Mediterranean world. Certainly the most creative and influential personality in early Christianity, Paul honed the central message about Christ and salvation, or at least an influential version of it. (Later on, Luke, the author of Acts, would offer his own version of the life of Paul and how his missionary journeys *took the early Christian movement public*, from Jerusalem to Rome.)

Paul had been a Hellenistic Jew, born in the diaspora. He believed himself uniquely called by the risen Christ, authorized and commissioned for the missionary venture that would *make Christianity a universal religion*. In the debate over whether Christianity would remain a special form of Judaism and whether all new Gentile Christians would have to become, in effect, ethnic Jewish pre-Messianic Christians, Paul fiercely contended for the opposing view, the view that decisively won out by the end of the first century. The route into Christianity would not have to pass through Judaism. (Today there are about 15 million Jews in the world and 2.2 billion Christians.)

Specifically, Paul developed the theological justification for an uncircumcised Christianity not defined by Jewish ethnicity, and deliberately cast on a world stage. *God's DNA is carried far beyond the Jewish genealogical line.* For Paul, the entire Christian proclamation revolved around a cosmic, universalizing Christ as the new paradigm for God's relationship with humanity. The living, dynamic God of the Hebrew Bible was now releasing, through Christ, a new power of salvation, a gracious bestowal of God's righteousness (right-making) upon the entire human race. Giving away divine particularity and prerogative, God comes to earth in the person of Jesus. An old creation (the "old Adam") becomes a new creation, by being incorporated into a new life in the cosmic Christ, a life upon which the liberating Spirit of God is poured out. That life is driven by gratitude to God (religious) and takes the form of love for the neighbor (ethical)—what Martin Luther will call faith active in love and what Christians who get it today might call faith active in social justice. *From this grace bestowed a new social gospel emerges,* which is to say the word of grace takes root in earthly soil and human societies. If we do not see it growing in the churches in our time, we must ask why. The entire new creation, in its reality and its purposes, is seen as the body of Christ extending across the entire world with welcoming engagement with the entire diversity of all peoples. Paul wrote: "In Christ God was reconciling [friend-ing] the world to himself" (2 Corinthians 5:19). This was the text for the first sermon I ever wrote. While home from seminary, I practiced it aloud upstairs while my mother stood nervously eavesdropping downstairs.

Paul's opponents tried to reverse Paul's missionary theology. To this day there remain sharp disagreements over how to read Paul's understanding of Christianity, and of grace and faith and justification. In the view taken here, Paul's missionary efforts became *a contest between ethnocentric particularity and Christian universalism,* or as some of the prophets had begun to envision, between Israel as God's only chosen people and Israel as a light to all the nations. Today the agenda would be, "How do we demonstrate that the Christian social gospel is in fact good news for all the peoples, not merely an artifact of the American middle class?" The New Testament proclamation of God's good news for all, and especially the lost coins and the lost sheep, begins in the Magnificat, the Song of Mary quoted at the beginning of this chapter, and continues in Jesus' proclamation of the reign of God arriving, and is then worked out as a public offering to the world in the letters of Paul.

Modern commentators unfailingly notice that Paul seems disinterested in the particularities of the earthly Jesus, but that he develops his universalizing Christology from Christ's death and resurrection. No doubt Paul's intent is to dramatize God's grace and human response on a worldwide stage, not limited to a particular "holy land." (Could contemporary sub-Saharan Africa be a Christian holy land? China? Homeless encampments? Prisons and poor houses? Enclaves victimized by the American way of life?) That Jesus was an ethnic Jew with a public ministry in Palestine was not the final and definitive point. Or that Jesus was a dark-skinned Middle Easterner. Or male. Rather, as in the prophet Isaiah's vision, Jesus would become God's light to all the nations, all tribes, all classes, all parties. Paul opened up early Christian preaching and worship to their full implications across the Mediterranean world. And then everywhere. If it is not too crass to say it, Paul brokered God's Initial Public Offering.

Every neighborhood, every class, every nation could become a holy place. (Later European Christianity would have to learn this as well, and with great difficulty.) Paul's sense of being called to, and a participant in, momentous historical developments facilitated his vision of Christianity as a worldwide new movement of God. In Paul's view, *Christ cleared the way for a time in which there would be neither Jew nor Greek, slave nor free, male nor female, but all co-existing in a new humanity on a new earth* (Galatians 3:28). All walls of separation, social or political or economic, are to fall. Paul's vision was inclusive, not exclusive—a daring viewpoint that very many modern Christians still decline to accept. The power and love of God are freely available to all, not held back for insiders, or the privileged, or the entitled. Paul saw himself founding across the Roman world *colonies of heaven*, which is to say, God's dreams for a new humanity springing up and rooting across the earth. The breadth and mercy of God's love and its fruit-bearing in any and every society constitute the social gospel Christians today are called to make new and specific again. Will American soil, so seeded with political and economic pesticides, be ready for it?

PAUL'S ETERNAL SONG: AMAZING GRACE

Some people love to be annoyed by Paul. But he's worth a pilgrimage. To some he is the one who ruined Jesus by turning his eloquent peasant's life into a dogmatic Christology. Or he comes off as a disgruntled Jew, or a guilt-ridden and sin-obsessed Protestant (sometimes Augustine or Luther are blamed for this). But Paul's much-vaunted doctrine of justification by grace through faith means God's free conferral, no prescribed religious or cultural trappings required, of friendship on the entire human race. God offers the divine DNA to all. An unexpected inheritance is read out to everyone in every gathering. Paul saw Christ as a worldwide icon of God's dreams for humanity, and himself as the one who would *initiate the eschatological harvest of God's new age*. Paul envisions a cosmic Christ with a new gospel for every people, for all of a new creation. That Paul's vision carried the day is shown by the radical assertions in the possibly post-Pauline epistle to the Colossians: "Christ is the image of the invisible God, the firstborn of all creation . . . For in him all the fullness of God was pleased to dwell, and through him God was pleased to reconcile to himself all things" (1:15, 19). And the early Pauline letter to the Galatians has the most radical religious and social claim to come out of the first century—or the last two millennia: "There is no longer Jew or Greek, there is no longer slave or free, there is no longer male and female; for all of you are one in Christ Jesus" (Galatians 3:28). Paul's universalizing and inclusive legacy is a modern Christianity, however flawed, with worldwide adherents.

The only religious call, to which every seeker is invited, was to live *in Christ* (Pauline mysticism), to become a part and play one's part in a new creation. Paul famously reminded his hearers (Philippians 2:1–11) that God had held nothing back safely in heaven, but freely brought all of God to earth and gave everything away to all, in the coming of Jesus Christ. God's DNA was spreading and available as an inheritance all were invited to claim.

Earth became capable of heaven—a fundamental assertion of Luther's Christology, and redolent with Catholic sacramentalizing theology as well, though Calvinists make a different point by having God holding something above and beyond in heaven. (So that we do not too readily imagine that even our best social programs do not add up to the entire will of God.) Now the *earth is full of God*—every class, every neighborhood—because God has emptied out heaven and made earth home. Calvinists love to assert that there are no spheres in which God does not reign. This is an assertion of such immense proportions that most Christians fail to think and see it through. And fail to consider how large are the circles of inclusion they must draw. It is for many beyond all imagining that all the earth is called to imitate this divine servanthood and become a new kind of human community. The pilgrim's task is not just to seek, to walk the road, but to draw the circle larger.

It is a curiosity of contemporary America, and perhaps especially of many American Christians, that Paul's breakthrough message is again being challenged and a different kind of good news is put in its place. Just as the emancipating God of the exodus was later challenged by those who wished to hem such free-wheeling acts of liberation by stipulating ethnic markers and purity codes and religious worthiness or the refinements of earthly sovereignties as ways to determine who was deserving the good news, so many Christians in our time are *not willing to let Jesus' paradigmatic self-giving define what Christianity is about.* (They prefer to take away the word social from "social gospel" and define the Christian message as an individualizing, personal relation to God in one's heart and not spilling over into neighborhood demonstrations or marches against cruel governments or good news for the poor.) As Paul laments to the Galatians, these people are stuck in "another gospel"—falling far short of the central New Testament proclamation. According to this other gospel, people must earn their place at Jesus' overflowing table where food and drink had been offered to all, people must meet the criteria stipulated by a religious establishment whose point of view is far more constricting and exclusive than is the imagination of God. The laws of the market and the purview of government are independent and free of the reach of a social gospel. And middle-class American Christians, of course, sit at the head of the table and assert special privilege. These religious tenders are determined to contain and restrain God's DNA and keep it from spilling everywhere. Keep it uncontaminated. Keep it from becoming hybrid. Keep it away from everyday assumptions about how things are and must be.

It is very hard for people in every age, but especially for self-made men or women, to accept that *Jesus seems to reverse the expected religious sequence of repentance first and fellowship second, conversion and then communion.*

But in Jesus' ministry the first offer is the amazing commensality of God: contact (grace), communion (fellowship), then conversion (repentance and new life). God's DNA seems to reverse the orders of creation we have come to insist on. God first meets us in our old clothes.

Just as Paul's opponents argued that entry into the new community cannot possibly be as easy as "justification by faith" or "grace" seem to make it, so contemporary proponents of American exceptionalism want to insist on a moral and religious worldview populated by self-made men, by those who worked hard enough to succeed, by those whose virtue is unambiguously rewarded with wealth—or soon will be. For them, *Pauline grace is a moral hazard.* It cannot be squared with the laws of the market. It might encourage lethargy. It might dishonor overachievers or encourage freeloaders. Every Congressional vote on food stamps or healthcare or education is salted with pious-sounding and even explicitly social gospel-denying sentiments. The idea of God's bounty needing to be distributed to all, and certainly the biblical interest in redistribution, are cursed ideas, cut out of the Bible with always available pen knives. Paul and Christ and the prophets before them need sanding down. And some additions are required as well: caveats for enslavement, something about American hegemony, unregulated markets as additional revelations (and markers) from God.

In 1934, at the outset of what would become Nazi Germany, the "confessing Christians" (where are they today?) insisted in their Barmen Declaration that there is only *one* word from God, and that is the gospel of Jesus Christ, not blood, not territory, not standing for the flag, not national destiny. (Not the Chicago school of economic conservatism, not trickle-down theories.) Making America great again is a current competitor to Paul's vision. Around the world today there are many who make gender binaries or the control of women by men, for example, rather than the gospel the definitive word from God. Sensible people want to add something to Paul's gospel, in addition to grace, perhaps insisting on the proper positions in the culture wars. One even hears the implied claim that no one comes to Jesus except by embracing free enterprise as God's way of life, as Jerry Falwell's Liberty University mission statement seems to assert. Recently, famous evangelicals claimed that God has anointed Donald Trump as the prophet of this new dispensation, or at least as a secular and perhaps even unwitting foreign king who becomes God's agent for the good of a free-enterprising world.

That the God of the Hebrew Bible and the God of Christ and the God taken public in Paul's theology might enact true religion on earth by *grace,* that that God could be a radical redistributionist, that God turned left after creation, that the entire earth is God's possession to give away or redistribute, that God lends the divine DNA to the entire human family and holds nothing back—all that is horrifying heresy to many American Christian ears, and to many non-believers as well. In a profound reversal of valences, that liberal God of the Bible is thrown under the bus and the ruthless god of social Darwinism, the survival of the fittest, the stand-in for the American way at least since Reagan, is set up as America's golden calf. How hard it is for every age, but especially the American age in which so many are just so proud of their can-do individualism, or of their whiteness or maleness or entitlements, to accept that every good gift comes down from above, that it takes a community to nurture the new creation, that we live by grace. The only payback grace inspires is fervent gratitude expressed in the joy of mutual existence and service to the neighbor, including the very earth—a joyous interconnectedness. These fruits of the Spirit have come into short supply in modern America, so distanced has it become from the biblical God who proclaims exodus.

As this book sees the light, Americans will find themselves in an election year. Will any candidates dare to imply a new social gospel as what the country most needs? Will the churches come together around this message as the means to their own redemption? The recalling of the strange liberating God of the Bible? A relived Christianity? A return to the public square with something to say, something nonconforming, insurgent, revolutionary?

Where does all this leave you? What do you want to do about it? God waits for new auditions, in new theaters, in new neighborhoods, with new audiences, and new actors. As a universal Christianity extends the risk of Incarnation, pays God's DNA forward, the earth is reenchanted and the divine presence hangs low over every neighborhood.

3

On Not Letting the Religious Parade Pass You By

PARADING CHRISTIANITY

No one thinks of a parade when contemplating American Christianity. The First Amendment right to freedom of religion does not typically stimulate marches through town. Parade seems a counterintuitive metaphor when describing the role of religion in culture and society. Most people, including Christians, would consider it gauche to parade God around. Secularists would be astonished at the breach of the modern contract that relegates God's appearances to church and home. Professional God-decriers like Richard Dawkins would object to any return to pre-modern civilization, and celebrity atheist Christopher Hitchens would return from the dead to prophesy darkly.

But Time's Up women and Black Lives Matter people of color and Gay Pride celebrators readily parade in the streets because the times require it, and the press dutifully counts their numbers and compares them to President Trump's inauguration numbers. Movement activists are accustomed to demonstrating they have a dog in the fight, an oar in the water. In Latin America, crowds cried *Presente* when the names of "the disappeared" were called out at rallies of remembrance. They gave voice to the marginalized, a good reason for a parade. Christianity's proposal of a new social gospel would be one of the most conspicuous validations of its presence in society. In universities Greek societies parade through the campus as part of their recruitment rituals—celebrating their traditions and attracting new members, without annoying the larger student body.

But parading religion isn't mostly done, perhaps because good manners accept exclusion from the public square. You don't belong here, say all kinds of people, from nones to hostile secularists to church/state patrols, to people turned off by Christianity's bad reputation. So a recent best seller, *The Benedict Option*, proposes that Christians declare the culture wars lost, concede victory to secularism, call Christians to retreat and regroup, *and then* return to the creation of new communities characteristic of fifth-century monasticism as Roman civilization was going under. Take back the streets—at the right time. *Reliving* is the point of chapters 3 to 5 of this book, and it's always what the situation calls for. But did you know that a larger percentage of the 2018 Congress is Christian than the general population? If they were charged with identifying as Christian, would there be enough evidence to convict them?

In the Old Testament ancient Israel was directed by God to construct a gold-covered wooden chest called the ark of the covenant and pack it with the material culture of Israelite religion. According to an account in 2 Samuel 6, King David, dressed in a linen priestly garb, famously "danced with all his strength before the LORD," as the entire house of Israel brought up the ark of the covenant with shouts and loud trumpet blasts. (His wife was scandalized at David's exuberance, since his private parts were exposed in the enthusiasm of the dance.) In 2019, some Hispanic Baptist churches would sometimes sing a song called "Danzo Como David," which is to say that "when the Spirit of the Lord falls on my heart, I will dance like David danced." Hindus take their gods out of their temples to go for a walk, parading them before pilgrims to *see and be seen*, as the word *darshan* connotes.

In the New Testament, Jesus announced the arrival of the reign of God at the beginning of his public ministry and then, in effect, led a march through Galilee, accumulating followers one by one along the route. Eventually, at the beginning of what Christians celebrate as Holy Week (today more words than action), Jesus mounted a donkey and led a parade into Jerusalem, as the gathered crowd threw down palm leaves to celebrate the way. The most dramatic parade, however, is the one Jesus led carrying a cross from Pontius Pilate's court to the crucifixion grounds at Golgotha. This is the parade Catholic Christians call the *via dolorosa*, and they replicate it during Lent as they move devotionally in their churches, pausing for meditation at each of the fourteen stations of the cross. That the road to Golgotha should be the ultimate Christian parade points to what Martin Luther found at the heart of the gospel—a theology of the cross. In a startlingly inclusive parade celebrated only in the Eastern Orthodox tradition, the rising Christ of Easter pauses for a march through the netherworld where he gathers up the righteous lost since the beginning of time and leads them upward toward a resurrected life. Some Orthodox art dramatically depicts this scene, sometimes called the harrowing of hell and obscurely alluded to in the New Testament in 1 Peter 4:6 and in the ancient creeds.

In a sweep that astonishes historians of religion, the early Christian missionary movement paraded across the Middle East, North Africa, and the Roman world—taking Christianity public as stock traders might say, and by the fourth century Christianity had become the official religion of the empire—not a wholly felicitous accomplishment.

In the fifth century St. Patrick paraded Christianity across Ireland and left a permanent residue of Catholicism in Irish culture and society. In the eighth century St. Boniface paraded eastward across the Anglo-Saxon Germanic lands, contributed Christianity to the unification of Europe, and sealed his legacy with martyrdom. In 1170 the Archbishop of Canterbury, Thomas Becket, was murdered in his cathedral by agents of the king, in a contest between church and state. Shortly thereafter there began a parade of pilgrims to Canterbury, which continues to this day, to honor his martyrdom. I have kneeled in Canterbury. In the fourteenth century the greatest early English poet Chaucer chronicled this unending parade in his *Canterbury Tales* as one of medieval Europe's most popular pilgrimage routes. Along the way he noticed and described one of the lasting effects of a pilgrims' parade—an "accidental community."

In the thirteenth century St. Francis paraded simple Christians before nature and nature before the eyes of Christians, for example in outdoor manger scenes. One of his legacies today happens on his feast day in early October, when many churches sponsor a blessing of the animals and parade their pets up the aisles of churches to have them acknowledged and blessed at the altar. An animal parade in a fussy church alters the perception of holy capabilities. What else might be brought into the church's precincts—the homeless? Folk art? Popular culture? Guitars? Churches without the nerve gather the community's pets outside on the lawn but do not risk bringing them inside—such segregation is a pity and the opportunity for evocative ritual movement is lost.

In the sixteenth century, following his excommunication by the Pope, Martin Luther was called by the Holy Roman emperor to give an account of himself. He and his entourage famously paraded westward from Saxony into the city of Worms on the Rhine, unfurled the banner of individual conscience, professed faith before church and empire, and rerouted the course of Christianity and the Western world. On the way home agents of Luther's German protector kidnapped him and hid him away in the Wartburg

Castle—where he idled away his time monumentally translating the New Testament from Greek to German. Making God speak in the vernacular is a worthy goal of the church's parade. A new social gospel would be an example of God's vernacular; look at the incarnate Jesus Christ for the invitation. If God can speak German, then an American social gospel is also possible.

In many Anglican and Catholic cathedrals there is a procession around the church and up the central aisle every Sunday, led by a cross-bearer, and a Bible held high, and incensors (smells and bells accompany high church worship), then the choir, and finally the clergy dressed in beautifully embroidered vestments displaying the colors of the season, blue or white or green or purple. Why not take the procession outside? To carry religion into the streets is not to play Taliban, or stop traffic. No guns. No threats. It's entering and occupying public space in an obvious and by-your-leave way. Maybe even with a permit, like a St. Patrick's Day parade. It's the church in motion, evoking God in motion. Like Jesus did.

Not everybody gets street theater, even after the '60s. Or even liturgical *movement*. At the beginning of Jesus' public ministry, the Gospel of Mark posts a placard: "The good news of Jesus Christ, the Son of God, is soon to appear." The intention is that you *consider the e-vite, RSVP, fall in line, accept the good news, and change your way of living*. But in the face of the Christian parade, you may say "Been there, done that." Or if you decline all religion (I'm calling it metaphysical abstinence), you can call yourself a "none," meaning I don't do parades. Or you could follow another parade. President Trump thought he was elected to lead a parade called "Make America Great Again." Its tone and message do not resemble biblical parades, though some churches have fallen in line and named Trump God's grand marshal.

The first day we drove in to Prague years ago, we happened upon a spectacular commotion as we were heading towards the city square. We had accidentally arrived the day Catholic Christianity celebrates Corpus Christi, a movable feast that typically falls in June, manifesting the real presence of Christ in the Eucharist and, by extension, in the life of the city. It is said that a medieval Czech priest inspired the feast of Corpus Christi when he experienced the literal blood of Christ drip from the host as he offered Mass. Such a vision gathered momentum. Catholic Christianity is not unaccustomed to parading Christ through the world, dense with the material culture of religion. A crucifer holding high the cross and elaborately vested . clergy take the lead. Then acolytes. There are banners flying, images of saints precariously carried, and elaborate floats that display Christian pageants. A band plays. People cheer. Deacons swing their censers and the fragrance of incense floats in the air. The whole city has turned out. (In the *Godfather* trilogy, Francis Ford Coppola astonished theater audiences by juxtaposing religious movement with targeted assassinations. Rituals get things done, he seemed to be saying.)

Even little Protestant parades can occur when church members, reminded the week before by an email from the church office but largely unnoticed by the wider community, gather outside their churches on Palm Sunday morning. Palms are handed out by gleeful children and all happily greet each other. Then the choir begins leading the procession singing "All Glory Laud and Honor, To Thee Redeemer King/To whom the lips of children made sweet hosannas ring," and all march into the church. The little crowd waves its palms, everyone feels they are really doing something noteworthy, that a real occasion is happening, especially for Protestants whose words are usually better than their movement, and it's going to be an exciting event. Of late a farmer who owns a little pony brings him to the church grounds in early morning, ready to lead the procession, evoking Jesus riding into Jerusalem. Everyone is making a video or snapping selfies that they will post on Facebook to show it really happened and Christians are cool. If a Protestant parade catches on, it may occur to some to "take it outside"—to the streets.

During graduate school when we bought our first house ever, in the little suburb of El Sobrante a few miles north of Berkeley in the East Bay, we decided to stage a house blessing to consecrate it. I enlisted a number of clergy friends who kindly arrived fully vested, we borrowed a processional cross from our Lutheran Church, we invited all the friends we knew, and we processed around the house. It was a wonderful time, and the neighbors seemed to find it quaint. I presume God smiled. The next day a woman who lived next door was telling me she had just been recruited to be a bus driver for the Sunday school program of her evangelical church. "What is your route, how many children will you be picking up?," I asked. "I don't know," she answered. "That's my assignment—to find the kids, get them on the bus, and make a route." In a way unimaginable to Lutherans, she had been commissioned to recruit and produce her own parade and carry Christ and the Sunday school children through the neighborhood to the church.

In the Psalms of the Hebrew Bible "God is lifted up on the praises of Israel." An ancient religious mandate was to write God atop history. Holding up the faith as street theater could be the beginning of that commission. If the Christian parade streams through the town, with those at its head catching sight of those at its tail, as in the winding streets of a medieval town, then it will become evident that religion can move, that ritual is performative drama, that faith can come alive, that the church can parade the presence of God through the neighborhoods, that guerilla theater can insinuate the arrival of God in earthly precincts. Christianity gladly, or timidly, would be going public, occupying public space, the theme of the last three chapters of this book.

Modern Christianity mostly lacks the imagination for street theater, or for installation art. The Belgian abyss Juliana of Liege spent nearly half the thirteenth century dreaming up the full contours of the Corpus Christi festival that would parade the presence of Christ through medieval streets. She helped write it into the culture of the Christian calendar, where it is marked to this day. Groups of holy women took up the task in those days and *brought an incarnate Christ to contemporary embodiment*—an obvious woman's task, some might say. Who today assembles, under religious auspices, in a public park, heads down through town, past fancy shops and restaurants, alongside the enclaves where homeless people camp, past the Jesus Center where the hungry are fed and warmed? Is this a Christian calling? Is this an announcement and an invitation?

Depending on what the times require, on the extent of the decimation of the commons and the lives of the poor by a rampant market economy and reigning greed, the parade could take on a quite different mood. Following Jesus' parable in Matthew 25, the parade may go looking for the poor and the forgotten, in order to find Christ in them. That would be a social gospel parade, through perilous streets. Indeed, a famous hymn in the requiem mass chanted by processing medieval monks is the somber *Dies irae* (Day of Wrath), whose fifth verse goes: *Liber scriptus proferetur/In quo totum continetur/Unde mundus judicetur*. Which is to say: "Lo, the book, exactly worded/Wherein all hath been recorded/Thence shall judgment be awarded." The conceit is that our lives, and perhaps the history of the world, are books carried through our times and now to be opened for inspection. This will rival a military parade evoking national patriotism or, more recently, playing as the president's self-aggrandizment.

What precincts would welcome a Christian parade? Newspaper offices, college classrooms, halls of congress, market streets? It is not uncommon to hear thoughtful people, including scientists, say that we seem lost on an aimless planet, homeless in the universe. The big bang set us in motion, but where are we going today? *Teleology* is the word for ultimate purpose and direction, but evolutionary biologists are suspicious of the word. No meaningful parades run through their laboratories. Not a trace of the Old Testament notion of radical amazement. When I was in college we thought ourselves very clever marking elegant despair by quoting Shakespeare's lines from *Macbeth*: "And all our yesterdays have lighted fools. The way to dusty death. Out, out, brief candle! Life's but a walking shadow, a poor player. That struts and frets his hour upon the stage. And then is heard no more: it is a tale. Told by an idiot, full of sound and fury. *Signifying nothing*." Naturally, ersatz fraternities imagined rechristening themselves in Greek letters, SIGNIFY NOTHING. Let it never be said that Christians march through the commons carrying banners that say "Signify Nothing," though some suspect it.

In chapter one I decoded the great exodus narrative in the Hebrew Bible as the parade out of Egypt led by a liberating God. I say "decode" because only black slaves seemed to understand the exodus as a religious dream. The great theologian of black liberation James Cone made it his life's work to restage the Christian parade and lead it in new directions. *Whose exodus*, he thought to ask, as he articulated God's identification with American black people. In portraying Christ's blackness, he took over a parade led by white theologians and redirected it to themes of liberation from a white racist society. He boldly claimed that "the gospel was identical with the liberation of the poor from oppression" and that it "is necessary for the language of theology to be derived from the history and culture of black people." Sounds like a new social gospel. There are now counter parades, led by white supremacists.

In what I have called the Christian sequel, the New Testament claims this Old Testament inheritance as God leaves heaven behind and incarnates in the paradigmatic life of Jesus, who emerges as God's chosen phenotype. *God wagers all of divinity on earth.* God resolves to take the risk of incarnation. Then the Apostle Paul takes God's DNA public in the early Christian mission and freely offers God's markers of reconciliation to the entire world.

E-VITES

A parade is always a public event and an invitation. To assemble and take it in. And perhaps to join it. As we have seen, the New Testament Gospel of Mark opens with a broadside: "The good news of Jesus Christ, the Son of God" (in theaters near you) is soon to appear (Mark 1:1). As the drama begins, Jesus meets John the Baptist on the banks of the storied river Jordan for the event that will inaugurate his public ministry. Even Protestants today can make a Holy Land pilgrimage and bring souvenir water home in a bottle. Perhaps like Hindu pilgrims they could parade through their home villages carrying holy water in their bottles and pouring it out to make sacred ground. We might call it christening public spaces in preparation for a parade route.

After the practice of John the Baptist, later martyred by King Herod when his daughter Salome danced him into it, Christian baptism came to be associated with renunciation and confession. In Jesus' own initiation, Satan appears and offers him the world if he shows off, plays to the stands, dazzles the crowd with fake miracles, and—oh yes—bows to the dominion of prevailing world systems. Brushing Satan off, Jesus turns in the direction of a new creation. It features a parade of people made so new that Karl Marx or Chairman Mao, always hoping to evoke the "new socialist man," would be filled with envy.

Test taken and passed, Jesus proceeds to Galilee and announces: "The time is fulfilled, and the kingdom of God has come near; repent [turn your life around], and believe the good news" (Mark 1:14–15). When Jesus spies the first potential company of the kingdom, the fishermen Peter and Andrew, he says: "Follow me and I will make you fish for people" (Mark 1:17). The New Testament Gospels tell stories about the kingdom of God as a high-stakes parade led by Jesus, who seeks followers who might be convinced that this is a parade not to miss. Don't let the parade pass you by is Christianity's message even today, as many "parables of decision" illustrated in the Gospels. Wager on God. "Thy kingdom come, Thy will be done, on earth as it is in heaven." Kierkegaard admonished, become a knight of faith.

REGRETS

You can say no. You can let the parade pass you by. No is in, as we know from Pew Research data on the *nones* (none of the above) and the *dones* (been there, done that). How many today are waiting for the parade that hoists Christ on a new platform and carries him through the city? Do you think the poor, those without adequate food stamps, those without shelter, those looking for a sympathetic ear, are waiting to see a new social gospel coming their way? It's said that about a third of Americans would like to see Christianity established as the national religion and are fevered with theocracy, though the DNA lines in the Bible may not be what they are looking to match. Meanwhile the secular world chokes on religious fumes. In America today, whether among Bible-believers or secular naysayers or the majority who have lost their heart to cynicism about Wall Street and Washington, the news that God is mounting an exodus seems an unlooked-for surprise. When the church commences a religious walk-out of Egypt, will many join in? What street did God go down when the incarnation sacramentalized the world? Conservatives don't want to hear about a revolutionary God, and secularists don't want to hear about any God at all. Has it become hard for many to even *think God,* just as it's hard for many to *think the state* or to *imagine the commons.* Or meaning. We are on our own, without God, without a covenanted community.

This book's title was almost *God's Long Pursuit: American Christianity*. God is not a new idea to Americans. We've seen this parade before. Exodus from the Old World, fleeing across the Atlantic as our own fearful Red Sea with European kings in pursuit, was a story Americans once loved to tell themselves, but it failed to turn into a national mythology about social justice and new creation. Eventually the founders allowed a new Egypt to develop in the promised land, and entire populations were excluded from the codes and covenants originally envisioned. Promises came true to people in power, but most were left out. And although we do tell ourselves stories about Jesus, they do not seem to come from a book whose cover displays a God of the oppressed and the outcast. A Gideon Bible dressed in liberation and social justice would startle people who open it up from the bedside drawer in their motel.

Consider the present state of American religion and irreligion. Because loud-mouthed and obnoxious Christians are the worst possible advertisement for God, many citizens withdraw from *any* religious discourse in order to insulate their lives from religious fanatics and their overreach into the public square. The devoutly secular thought they had been promised that the "death of God" was guaranteed by modernity. Yet religion of some kind flourishes, far more in the United States than in Europe.

But what are the chances in American life that a God who frees the captives and sides with the poor and undocumented gets a parade along our borders? In what election year will such social gospels be part of stump speeches, installed in party platforms? Of course, as we saw in the black gospel movement and the emergence of Martin Luther King Jr., the churches can march their own visions through town—asked or unasked, welcomed or driven back. For status elites and for much of the common culture of buying and selling, God is out of mind, while the evangelical God who is a best-selling accoutrement of the (what?) purpose-driven life does not mostly disturb bourgeois entitlements. Silicon Valley entrepreneurs who go to Big Sur to practice mindfulness only stay for a day and then reliably lose their minds again on Monday morning back in the city. Aren't the Ten Commandments meant to confirm bourgeois values? The fervently religious seem to lack a chastening, ascetic experience. No seekers are going out to the desert to meet the strange God of the Bible—because God is already an honorary American, living in the suburbs.

Just before Jesus' time, a sect of Judaism, the Essenes, had gone into the wilderness to prepare themselves for the return of God from exile. They thought they would see the new dawn of a Messianic age. They hoped to disencumber their lives, pay attention to spiritual things, and tune their ears to God's voice. They believed that a sufficiently purified community could coax God into a millennial reappearance. Already during the sixth century BC exile from their homeland, Jews had hung their harps on the willows and lamented, "How can we sing the LORD's song in a strange land?" No parades in exile!

It may seem odd to suggest that God is in exile and without a parade when the media report a superfluity of religious activity in this country. There is, in fact, God-a-plenty, but the religious establishment's sermons are full of patriotic bluster, economic aggrandizement, and well-worn prejudice. While the story of the exodus can be decoded by slaves, it is unknown on Wall Street, where Goldman Sachs claims the franchise, or among the many who believe white supremacy is their covenanted entitlement. Once yellow ribbons bespoke the missing; once north Europeans at winter solstice lit bonfires to coax back the sun; once ascetics sought to create a vacuum that only God could fill. But who today worries over an empty seat at the American Thanksgiving table? Who orders a chair for Elijah from Amazon?

In the musical *Godspell*, the prophet cries to the masses, *Prepare the way of the Lord*. And onlookers dance enthusiastically and the music plays. If this is the perennial ambition of true religion, it is a task for which we just now may have lost the imagination. Dante likened his age to being lost in the forest, yet through his poetry he ingeniously *turned his experience of loss into a locus of transformation*. He staged his own parade. He put Paradise together from a renewed Christian culture while placing local losers in the Inferno. In post-Christian modernity, too, poets attend to *presence* where others notice only *absence*. How many people are saying, listlessly, "Have you seen any parades lately?"

COMPETING PARADES: "MAKE AMERICA GREAT AGAIN"

Of course there are always rival parades. Already in the Hebrew Bible the primal story of the Exodus soon enough became a *contested narrative* when its original intent of liberation no longer served the new devotees of wealth and power. Cosmopolitans outgrow the need for a God of the oppressed. Today, too, we see competing narratives about American ideals, political debates about government for the common good. Besides the constraints of Enlightenment rationalism or skeptical detachment and gated communities that separate the privileged from the rest, *the most remarkable challenge to the biblical story of a liberal God may come from within contemporary American Christianity itself.*

While *grace*, which is to say the divine self-gifting, is foundational to the exodus, renewed again by the prophets, paradigmatic in the ministry of Jesus, and the key to Paul's universalizing of the Christian gospel, it has always been problematic. "No free lunches" is the world's wisdom, and conservative Christians are dubious. This is why the previous Speaker of the House of Congress, Paul Ryan, thought he should fire a Jesuit chaplain. There will be no daily prayers in Washington for the poor, and certainly no "preferential option for the poor," which lurks in the contemporary Catholic DNA. It was always a slog to convince ancient Israel that the land really belonged to God and that their liberation from Egypt came with serious implications for the kind of covenanted community they should build. Libertarians do not believe that it takes a village to shape a conscience. Already in early Christianity Paul, the apostle of grace, was fighting off "another gospel" that found grace unsuitable for the masses. Paul's opponents were sure they knew what religion should look like. Sheer grace was not one of its constructs.

Today, a God who overturns the furniture in the national living room runs contrary to the American self-regard that makes of our wealth and power the reward for our virtue and the evidence of our election to be the greatest. *A God who "gives it away"* provides too little to do for those who monitor food stamp recipients, too little warrant for national self-congratulation, too great a moral hazard for the American way of lifting yourself up. That's why much of American Christianity has ended up with quite a different *social contract* from the one issued at Mt. Sinai. That's why President Reagan liked to tell wry and mocking stories about people who want to live by grace, about old ladies driving welfare Cadillacs. (There was one.) Already by 2017 cartoonists were picturing President Trump as the golden calf that Israel worshiped after deserting the God of the Exodus.

Starring on Wall Street is the God of the Washington Consensus who rewards the 1 or 2 percent and admonishes the masses to wait in line for the trickle down. *A God who gives benefactions away is going to have to come from off Broadway.* Of course, everyone purrs "God bless America" on every state occasion. But the Wall Street parade does not lead us out of Egypt but into it. Already when Thomas Jefferson made some God or other the authorization of a new social contract for colonial audiences, the God of the exodus was not one of the contenders, although Jefferson did fear the rise of billionaires. "Good news for the oppressed" did not disturb Monticello, and the American founding story made room for slavery. The "equality" of the French Revolution's *liberty, equality, fraternity*, which subconsciously takes a page from an Old Testament covenant, did not rub off on America. Can you believe this: in 2018, a French farmer who smuggled an immigrant into the country out of compassion was acquitted by a judge who declared *fraternity* an objective and absolute constitutional value. Television preachers who claim the founders had theocracy on the mind offer no briefs on behalf of the strange God of the Bible, neither the primal stories of the exodus and the prophets nor the God whose freethinking is poured out in the life of Jesus Christ. Many American parades take a detour. Now is the right time for reconsidering the Christian parade

Opportunities to reclaim the biblical traditions and redeem American Christianity, as this book is titled, are scattered through history, including contemporary history. A remarkable opportunity occurred fifty years ago when Cesar Chavez, accompanied by a presidential candidate, brought together their Catholicism and issues of race, labor, poverty, and politics. Chavez was having success with his protests and boycotts on behalf of the farmworkers' movement until things got away from him and looked to turn violent. And so, at risk to his frail body, he began a hunger strike to retake control of his movement. When the principle of nonviolent resistance seemed reestablished, Chavez brought his twenty-five-day hunger strike to an end by publicly breaking his fast receiving the Eucharist in the fields. This Eucharist in the fields in which the body of Christ became the bread to break a fast, in which hunger for God and for social justice came together, was performative liturgy at its most exemplary. It became the most famous reception of the Eucharist in California history, with Bobby Kennedy famously in attendance. Within three months, Kennedy would be assassinated, the hopes of the farmworker movement for a liberation from their exploitation would seem to die with him, and Nixon would emerge to champion the rights of the growers. The achievements of social justice across the land, a new social gospel, would take many more marches, new parades. Many are still waiting.

The grape boycott had been going on for two years and workers often adopted Catholic symbolism in their marches through the fields. Hunger was transformed into fasting. Marches through the California valley to the state capital were called pilgrimages. Banners featuring the Virgin of Guadalupe sanctified the lead. Chavez's movement was a march decorated with Catholic Christianity. Will proponents of a new social gospel after Trump succeed in equivalent symbolism, equally suggestive performative liturgies, new unions between those who cry for justice and those who proclaim the Christian gospel? Will people think to look to the churches? Will the churches think to look to the streets?

The grapes at the center of the labor struggle were themselves full of Catholic meaning. Wine occupies a sacred place in the Catholic faith, transforming into the blood of Christ. And the UFW campaigners were masters at using the grapes as symbols. As the union switched tactics from asking farmworkers to strike to asking consumers to boycott grapes, they made buttons that read "Grapes of Wrath," referring to John Steinbeck's epic novel about Okie farmworkers who had hopefully journeyed to California. The title of Steinbeck's book was taken from a line in the "Battle Hymn of the Republic": "He is trampling out the vintage where the grapes of wrath are stored." The biblical imagery of a vengeful God had been appropriated for a song written for America's deadliest war, a war over the future of an agricultural society that had built itself on the exploitation of a racial "other."

The time of the grape boycott resembled the post-Reconstruction South, when the law enforced the boundaries between growers and workers, and Jim Crow defined the social system—a time that cried for the exodus promised in the Civil War. Agricultural labor had been excluded from the New Deal, in order to gain necessary support from Southern Democrats. In March 1968, when Chavez's famous eucharistic celebration occurred, the Jesuit editors of *America* wrote: "Is it too much to hope that Mr. Chavez's suffering may also inspire a change in those who are denying justice to farm workers and thereby creating conditions that invite violence? Practically all farm strikes have been caused by refusal of farm owners to recognize the moral right of their employees to organize and bargain collectively. Nor if violence comes can the U.S. Congress escape responsibility. It could very simply remove the chief ground for violence by extending coverage of the National Labor Relations Act to farmworkers." It was not to be. Although such legislation eventually came to California, it did not prevail across the United States. Violence returned. Justice denied still awaits "Matthew 25 Christians" to appear in new parades through the fields and the cities. These days injustice has moved from farmworkers to the urban poor and to immigrants. The exodus waits. In Delano, California, a rich man Kennedy and a poor man Chavez had come together to receive the Eucharist. "New occasions teach new duties," as the hymn verse goes, and await such celebrations. But many states passed "right to work" legislation, which is to say right to be free from exodus ambitions and covenant aspirations. In California Chavez's birthday is a public holiday, but elsewhere nobody knows his name.

We cannot keep waiting for just the right time for taking up radical scripts, for God to appear on opening night at the opera and call the well turned out audience into the plot. Two opportunities for groundbreaking experimental theater have come and gone. After Soviet communism became the god that failed, the time seemed ripe for alternative and post-Marxian revolutionary narratives, ambitious stories about new worlds and just societies. But all people could talk about after 1989 was the triumph of Atlantic-style capitalism. And not just in the United States. East Germans

auditioned to turn themselves into West Germans, but neither West nor
East auditioned to become some new kind of Germany. A little later, as the
year 2000 was dawning and there was space on the appointments calendar
for new mythologies and we were starting to pronounce the "third millennium," we learned instead to reduce our hope to computer programs that
would not stumble over three zeroes. The elation at the beginning of the
third millennium was that the old world had not stopped working, not that
we had imagined a new future.

But we cannot give up simply because the public is tired or unimagina-
tive or holding season tickets only for old hits. One could argue that *putting
God on stage (which is to say into the national conversation), displaying God
in public, projecting Exodus motifs into political platforms, sponsoring a "Matthew 25" float in the Rose Bowl parade* is the quintessential religious task of
the age. The prophets kept God in the public mind and in the king's face.
The Apostle Paul anticipated that ever new vernaculars, all authorized by
the incarnation, would declaim human revolution on world stages. Where
is the grand ambition to follow a parade into the third millennium—or, for
a start, the first few decades of the twenty-first century?

Know-it-all skeptics glimpsing the parade from a distance will pon-
tificate that all parades, no matter what their religious pretensions, are just
made-up human constructions. Nothing to see here. Skeptics are inoculated
against change of mind and heart. God, you see, liberal or otherwise, is a
projection of human yearnings, the sophomores fresh from their first Religious Studies class confidently whisper to others into their popcorn. But
when that knowing insight becomes accepted logic, it sucks the revolutionary dynamism out of religious drama and eliminates the disturbing possibility of transcendence in everyday existence. What if this parade matters? No,
we are allowing no surprises, we've been down this street before. It may be
that artists and seers know about radical amazement, but where are they?
The crowds know all about being jaded.

Parades can be radical theater that insistently expects something of
us. (Join in.) Parades can draw *indrafts of meaning* onto the theater of the
streets. So thought Antonin Artaud, a theorist of radical theater. In an age
of indifference or ignorance, powerful images on a stage, or in a passing
parade, can draw existential meaning onto the stage and rivet the audience's
attention. The idea is that the audience should not skip out on the questions
that haunt, not miss the point of the play. True, ecstatic prophets made God
the subject of every transitive verb, but they also counted on audiences to be
alert and take up residence in the scripts. Radical prophets out in the market
place will try to get their audiences to rush the parade as it reaches city hall
and occupies the commonwealth. Will you be on hand to notice?

New times require parades taking us in new directions, hoisting banners that feature discarded images newly recovered. Students, blacks, women, and gays got this at various times. Promising stories put God on stage, think God out loud, and give equally good lines to the audience as well. A good parade coaxes the audience to fall in line with the rhythms of movement. My own belief is that life on earth has an upper side that is transparent to the ultimate direction of the universe, a cosmic drama. The point is not to put things upside down but to *keep that upper side up (think solar panel), so that incoming light can energize it.* The churches need solar panels to keep themselves going. When only turned downward, human life becomes opaque and people die longing for light. But when Martin Luther King Jr. preached at the Washington Mall, he was dreaming God into the end of the second millennium. Christians are to face the light of the incarnation, because in Christ God shines a light on us that cannot be extinguished (John 1:4–5).

On the stage of a declining Roman Empire, Augustine set out to write his autobiography, and his *Confessions* established this genre in the West. But though he was intending to write his own story, *he wrote in God in order to get his account of himself right.* He wrote, "What can anyone say about you, God? And yet, woe to him who says nothing." Our lives, like Augustine's, hide a drama—"Our hearts are restless until they rest in you."

4

From Parade to Pilgrimage

PREMONITIONS OF PILGRIMAGE

In the middle of the seventeenth century, while imprisoned for religious nonconformity, John Bunyan wrote *Pilgrim's Progress*, the most influential religious book ever written in English. For a long time it was second only to the King James Version of the Bible as a constant best seller. It was an allegory about humanity's course through the world on the way to its ultimate destination in God—amidst beguiling distractions and shady characters meant to throw pilgrims off course.

When Bunyan was writing, everyone knew life was a pilgrimage. It was just a question whether or not they would falter along the way. At this beginning of the third millennium, it cannot be assumed that everyone accepts that the human prospect is a pilgrimage towards ultimate meaning. Kierkegaard imagined seekers (parade watchers) could become knights of faith tantalized by taking the leap into belief. Pascal thought the unlived life is the one in which you fail to see God as the ultimate wager. Jesus said the good news about the reign of God on earth is like treasure in a field: when you find it, you sell all to gain it.

At the dawn of the New Testament period, ancient Israel, which had periodically traversed the promised land in the Old Testament, is again pictured as wandering and looking for a sign from God. One of the prophets had called a time with no religious parades a famine of the Word of the Lord. So in the Gospels Jesus appears to lead a parade through the holy land and gather a following. The Gospels make this encounter between a friend-making God and an often recalcitrant earth a crisis of decision. This book intends to make the time after Trump into a moment for redeeming American Christianity, for performing a new social gospel. Sometimes God is imagined as someone who has made a very long pilgrimage to earth and we are the destination. Or is it vice versa? The Christian parade would be a way to process this drama through public space.

WHERE IS PILGRIMAGE HEADING?

The parade route is not irrelevant. Jennifer McBride's *Radical Discipleship* claims that Christians must assume Jesus will be found in the neighborhoods of social concern, of profound human need, and this will be a good place to meet him. True discipleship parades among people hungry, suffering, lonesome, rejected, alien, on the borders of life, people disacknowledged and undocumented. And among the powerful who make them so. The Christian parade comes to reduce distance between opposite ends of the socioeconomic spectrum. Oppressors and oppressed, brokers and the broken, are meant to "pass the peace" just before the eucharistic celebration.

One idea of a Christian pilgrimage is to show up in unexpected places. To surprise people. In the early 1970s I studied a motley crew who called themselves the Christian World Liberation Front. This band of pilgrims, who helped change the face of evangelical Christianity at the end of the 1960s, returned to Berkeley fifty years later to compare notes. Nearly everyone was still Christian. Many were still evangelicals, but a small number had become Orthodox. Their list of accomplishments, from worship renewal, to street theater, to Christian publishing was remarkable. Imagine contemporary start-ups ("church plants") calling themselves Christian World Liberation Fronts. *The point of pilgrimage is to follow the reign of God wherever it takes you, from Jerusalem across the world.*

WHICH GOD ARE PILGRIMS HEADING FOR?

If there is going to be a wager on God's direction, the parade route, and the ultimate destination of the American Christian pilgrimage, which God would Americans, Christian or not, likely *option*, to use capitalism's mother tongue? Americans try everything, and their history abounds with wide experimentation in the religious market from covenanted communalism to fierce individualism. Unencumbered individualism or libertarianism has won out. What kind of divine DNA is most likely to flourish on American ground? If we set out to sow a new social gospel, how and where would it flourish?

Doesn't everything grow in America? The sociologist Rodney Stark posits that religion in America is more vigorous and pliable than in Europe because we have a free market and no noncompetitive state church. After 1776, religion gradually became a free choice, and religious and no-religion movements of every stripe would arise as voluntary associations in niche markets. With such prospects, America would seem to be the ideal place to sow God's seed. On one hand, progressive religion strives to embrace the liberating God of the exodus, the prophets, and Jesus. On the other hand, economic, political, and cultural resolve has domesticated the strange God of the Bible into a cheerleader for national purpose and has made divine providence the invisible hand of the free market. Which God-narrative should be woven into the national mythology? *Would Americans become more godly or God become more American?*

Consider the staging grounds for possible parade routes today:

- Religion, to be authentic, must demonstrate the fervor of fundamentalism, so sophisticated people must choose agnosticism or atheism.

- Secular agnosticism makes itself the last best hope, but its fundamentalist style of absolutist certainty is troubling. Particularly ridiculous is its naive certainty that *losing ones faith is all it takes to stumble onto the meaning of life.*

- Triumphalist conservative religion denounces "progressive religion" as anemic, half-hearted, and a sell-out.

- The Roman Catholic hierarchy adopts the fixities of gender as the meaning of religious life. No gays. No women priests.

- Conservative evangelicals insist they own the values agenda, and only they should be taken seriously regarding American religion. Meanwhile, progressives have a serious religion problem on their agnostic Left and their religious Right, so that Democrats without religion are reprehensible and Democrats with religion seem uncertain, hypocritical, or cynical.

- Pollsters regularly find that independent thinkers who express strong interest in spirituality have nowhere to go with their searching and they see few welcome signs on the streets and airwaves. The new self-identifying "nones" assume that *none of the above* is sufficient for a cosmic wager, and they take pleasure in not being joiners. And yet the aftermath of Trump has produced social media stories on the revival of a religious left as a genuine Christian alternative to Trumpian self-aggrandizement.

- Many people of good will feel bad about the state of American society and their own complicity in it. But they have not found *a way to live that makes them feel good and responsible, rather than guilty and empty.* Forms of resistance, however, are afoot, and they come in multiple varieties, often connected to identity politics or social justice warriors.

- Just four years before Trump's election, the *New Yorker* analyzed the American religious electorate as follows: "Fox News friends, Limbaugh dittoheads, Tea Party animals, war whoopers, nativists, Christianist fundamentalists, a la carte Catholics (anti-abortion, yes; anti-torture, no), anti-Rooseveltians (Franklin and Theodore), global-warming denialists, post-Confederate white Southrons, creationists, birthers, market idolaters, Europe demonizers, gun fetishists." When polls suggest that this coterie mostly identifies as Christian, enthusiasm for the brand falls off. The 2016 election of Trump made all this official.

Arguments about which parade is true, which takes you somewhere, become noisy and fractious at the Thanksgiving table, if not barred for the sake of congeniality. Already after the victory of George W. Bush was arranged by the Supreme Court, urbanites on the coasts quit inviting their relatives from middle America to family celebrations. Imagine God in the table talk of American gatherings. First, consider the Jewish ritual table, a place made for questions and conversation, in which Jews show they are like the rest of us, only more so. From time immemorial, Jews have set a place for Elijah at Passover. Often, no doubt, they were not in the mood to do so, but they did it because tradition required it. Often, no doubt, they did not deeply reflect on how the dinner conversation would shift if Elijah actually showed up, but they set the place anyway. Perhaps they sang a half-remembered song of welcome to Elijah, who would usher in the Messiah. The vacant place setting for Elijah became, if noted at all, an eschatological overhang on the celebration—and on the family conversation. Ideally, it lifted the tone of the meal.

Christians believe the Messiah has already come. The New Testament reveals that the God of the Exodus and the Hebrew prophets has now become a paradigmatic human presence in the life of Jesus, who distills God's liberalism on earth. Will this God be coming to dinner, invited to dinner? Will Christian thanksgivings turn into a social gospel for all? *The rest of this book depends on the answer to this question.*

WHY IS THERE A CROSS ON CHRISTIAN PILGRIMAGE ROUTES

Theologians once imagined Jesus' suffering and death as the price demanded to appease a demanding Father and offer a fit ransom for the world's sins, but this legalistic view of the "atonement" as expiation before an angry God no longer prevails. Instead, the *risky experiment with divine self-giving on earth* is the lead story. The cross bespeaks human suffering and God's suffering on our behalf. The cross counters worldly wisdom and gospels of success. This New Testament God-story is dramatic because it is set amidst the forces that still today threaten authentic human life on earth, that still interpose powerful political and economic forces between a giving God and an earth waiting to live in a covenanted community

But there is something new as well as old about the cross. The black liberation theologian James Cone took up this theme in his book, *The Cross and the Lynching Tree*. Despite the obvious similarities between Jesus' death on a cross and the death of thousands of black men and women strung up, few people, apart from black poets, novelists, and artists, have explored the (dangerous) symbolic connections. The cross and the lynching tree are the two most emotionally charged images among black Americans. When they are brought together, blacks can discover liberation and redemption, and whites must repent of the violence of endemic racism. Cone transforms a central category of the Christian faith so that the cross can no longer readily be coopted by whites in the face of their own historic transgressions. The cross as lynching tree nails the white conscience. What is at stake is the credibility and promise of the Christian gospel and the hope that we may heal the wounds of racial violence. Christianity must be inserted in parading lynch mobs and must reawaken repressed memories today. And this would be another dimension to a new social gospel—even as the powerful still openly proclaim white racism in the most offensive possible manner.

WHERE CAN PILGRIMS GO

Across all times and places religion names what people experience and believe, and how they act, when pursuing, usually collectively, questions of ultimate meaning, mystery, connection. Religion initiates, frames, enlarges, and complexifies any conversation about betting the farm. Religion enables and organizes the quest for God and also complicates it. At least in the West, religion suggests a purposeful, ordered, and often institutionalized pursuit of God and all the God-questions. But religion also carries a long list of negatives—dogmatism, self-serving institutional behaviors, obsessive boundary-tending, conflict, intolerance, warfare, excessive certitude, hierarchy, priestcraft, hypocrisy, sexism, racism.

The American founders most influenced by the eighteenth-century Enlightenment were cautious about religion because the memories of European wars of religion following the Protestant Reformation were still fresh, though this had not weakened Puritan resolve in the seventeenth century. By the end of the twentieth century the legacy of the Enlightenment, and of Jefferson in particular, played in endless arguments about the role of religion in public life and especially in public schools. While nearly all—except the overly confident celebrity atheists—consent to religion in private, many fear its encroachment on the public square. Even those loudly tolerant of many things and more than tolerant of pluralism may believe that religion is best quarantined from the commons, that society and certainly public policy should be kept free of the intrusion of religious motivations and reasoning. The absence of religious language in the Constitution is taken by enthusiastic agnostics as nothing less than a quarantine.

But as the twentieth century wore on amidst many challenges regarding religion in public, the Supreme Court began to lean toward free speech in its decisions more than free exercise (whose rival twin was the establishment clause) and so decided that religion cannot be excluded from public venues where all other kinds of free speech are welcomed. (If people can shout in the Congress that free markets must rule, others can insist that social justice must prevail.) The present Court seems to be leaning towards decisions that favor the free exercise clause over the establishment clause.

To help religion go down easier and not taste like castor oil, consider this metaphor: religion involves *pouring molten gold into iron vessels*. So any parade is not a perfect vessel, nor is any social gospel equal to what it points toward. The spiritual search for transcendent gold inevitably involves the use of iron vessels to hold the gold and transport it. If religion is the iron vessel, it sometimes produces a bad taste, or an aftertaste. Enough to make some people leave the table or refuse to imbibe. They want their gold without the iron container.

But religion tracks the bread crumbs that lead back, or forward, to God. The Catholic novelist Walker Percy wrote: "The search is what anyone would undertake if he were not sunk in the everydayness of his own life. To become aware of the possibility of the search is to be on to something. Not to be on to something is to be in despair." This is also Bunyan's point in *Pilgrim's Progress*. Not every religious experience is your mother's. Such shifts include changes in the way we reason and process contemporary reality. One generation says "because the Bible says so" and the next says because *this story is better than others* in accounting for the mystery of the human condition. Changing times and deeper thoughts spice religion, so the way it tasted when you were thirteen is not enough to go on for the rest of your life. Marcus Borg liked to say: listen to your life, your heartbeat, when in the presence of religion. Bill Moyers has said that in seminary he learned *the answers to the questions, but in life he learned the questions to the answers.*

What about atheism? Atheists are impolite and lately militant, they don't fit the American mode of tolerance, and their over-confident nihilism is tiresome at parties. No politician admits to it. Atheists are often—confidently—guilty of a category error. They announce over drinks or in academic forums that they have discovered there is *Nothing.* But nothingness is not the new grand narrative that comes as the final replacement for all those somethings by now deconstructed by postmodernism. *Nothing is in fact just another something,* another belief, another competing grand narrative. There is no grand nothing; there are just a lot of somethings. Atheism is one of the competing somethings in a postmodern time. Losing your faith does not guarantee you have found the meaning of life. Some atheisms have a militant side, especially if they are bent on displacing all rivals. The Soviets launched militant atheism as the necessary legitimation of the new state their revolution was achieving. *Enforced secularism would eliminate religion as the supply side of alternative worldviews.*

MAKING THE PARADE YOUR LIFE
PILGRIMAGE IS THE ULTIMATE WAGER

The seventeenth-century scientist-mathematician Blaise Pascal troubled himself over the relevance of Christianity to early modern Europe. He made the Christian parade high stakes. He believed that human potential involves a struggle between greatness and ruin and lamented that his countrymen were content with expedient diversions from ultimate questions. Against such evasions he proposed that to live authentically means to *allow oneself to be confronted by God,* to watch the parade, hear its call, fall in, become a pilgrim. Humans should not be chatting over drinks at sidewalk bars while human misery and possibility go by. Because "the heart has its reasons which reason does not know," we should consider the possibility that wagering on God is the best course for settling the human dilemma, the ultimate resolution. Because we cannot finally avoid the choice between religion and irreligion, because we cannot spend our entire lives suspending judgment, because there is no final joy in metaphysical abstinence, because new iterations of social gospel are required after Trump, we ought to wager on God, take in the parade, join it, and begin just societies.

Jesus told stories about lost coins, lost sheep, and treasure buried in the field. Often it is a woman who won't let life go on until the lost are found, who discovers a treasure in the field and sells all she has to receive it. *We should bet the farm* to claim lasting treasure. If life is a choice of stories to live by, a story with God parading through it is the better story, as Yann Martel claims in *The Life of Pi*. T. S. Eliot said Pascal is the evangelist to "those who doubt, but who have the mind to conceive, and the sensibility to feel, the disorder, the futility, the meaninglessness, the mystery of life and suffering, and who can only find peace through a satisfaction of the whole being."

Risking God has little to do with the idle existence-of-God-arguments engaged in college dorms and letters to the editor and cheeky commercials from Ronald Reagan's son on behalf of Atheists United, on whose behalf he announces he has no fear of burning in a hell he does not believe in. No serious theologian, or mystic, thinks that God belongs to the category of *one among many things, take your pick*. Kierkegaard argued in the nineteenth century that the wager on God is *the* existential leap, the leap of faith that can initiate humans into authentic existence lived in community. If you stumble on treasure in the field, run back to town, sell all, acquire it. Pascal and Kierkegaard saw the wager on God *as the ultimate human vocation*—the life calling to find, watch, join the parade, become a pilgrim through your neighborhood and town. Existentialists were big on decisions that define and create who we will be, rather than easy essentialist assumptions about who we already most likely are.

But many why's follow the ultimate wager. Due diligence is not improper. For example, does wagering on God necessarily involve reconsidering what counts as *religion*? *If we're going to bet the farm we are entitled to consider certain questions.* Keep reading. What would it be like to live among the community that regularly stages the parade? What would it take to make the parade keep happening? Do pilgrims always discover an accidental community on the way to their destination? Are we going to end up in church? Turn to the next chapter.

5

It Takes a Church

PILGRIMAGE BECOMES THE CHURCH

The Christian parade becomes a pilgrimage. *Pilgrimage becomes the church.* *Pilgrimage is becoming to the church.* I mean that it turns into the church and also that it reflects back the church and is the church's most important characteristic. To call the church a parade is to keep it moving, through public space. The point of pilgrimage is to stay on the journey, to keep moving towards an ultimate destination while being mindful along the way.

Central to this book's message is the proclamation of a new social gospel after Trump. The church as an institution and a pilgrimage must demonstrate a "carrying capacity" for such a gospel. Influenced by progressive Christians and others, the state may answer the call to operationalize social justice in the land and even nurture a new humanism with the values a healthy commons requires. But it is the church that must proclaim and embody such a social gospel, arising from its own origins, its own charter, its own belief in the God of the Bible. The church urges social justice on the government just as the environmental or civil rights or workers' rights or women's movement urge their visions and causes upon the government—calling the government to be an instrument for social good. Pilgrimaging towards a new social gospel is the task the times require if we are not to continue our descent into Trumpism—white racism, resentment, selfishness, a rapacious free market, and government in the interest of the 1 percent.

"It takes a village" is an African proverb that shows up in Hillary Clinton's children's book, and libertarians held it against her forever. People internalize society and culture via institutions that develop, embody, and pass on communal traditions. It takes an institution to plan a parade, to invite the world to the parade, to be the parade. The church has a rich reliquary of material culture to display, accumulated as it sacramentalizes the earth over time. When eighth- and ninth-century Eastern Orthodoxy lost confidence in the validity of icons, of externalities, it resolved this crisis of representation by seeing anew that God's incarnation in Jesus Christ left an embodied religion as its legacy.

Inside the parade a life of faith happens, tempered by humility. People in the parade practice caring for each other and model the life of Christ before onlookers. Diverse people achieve unity walking together. A Christian parade wants to reach out and "pass the peace" to the crowd, just as they do every Sunday right after the prayers in common. Those who walk the parade and those who watch catch sight of a salvation demonstration. They carry banners, but not only what you would think. To remind themselves of Jesus' parable in Matthew 25, Christians might carry photos of children that say "Missing," Amber Alerts, Amnesty International pleas, announcements of meals for the homeless, pleas for prisoners, proposals for social justice through workers' unions. All together they constitute a social gospel. The marchers keep looking for people on the edge waving, who might need a friend. This is what God visiting earth and making friends with all the people looks like.

To call the church a sacramental demonstration means that wherever the parade leads, including city council or congressional chambers, they make sacred what was profane ground and effort, which is to say they make visible God touching down. Something holy happens, as when you are walking through a redwood grove and experience an epiphany. The parade happens because the world wants to be touched. Or the oligarchs do not want to be touched and you nevertheless persist in touching them anyway. A new social gospel after Trump will be performative and not just propositional.

When the church is moving it can be amazing, because not everything is conveniently laid out and expected. Pilgrims are open for course corrections and detours, for God's directions. The church is more than memorized answers to questions on a religious test. Sometimes the parade looks unwieldy and unpredictable as everyone with their instruments are running to keep up. Jesus, in his final commissions to the disciples, anticipated the parade would be led by the Holy Spirit who blows the church in new directions, off designated religious maps. Hence *new* social gospels.

WHY THE PARADE MUST BECOMES A PILGRIMAGE
AND THE PILGRIMAGE THE CHURCH

In his *Canterbury Tales* Chaucer watched a band of pilgrims become an accidental community. In the New Testament Paul's vision of the church is more intentional than happenstance. The church is a community of resident aliens called out by God and designated the body of Christ, a colony of heaven. Across history churches carry Christian traditions (and failures)—an elaborate material culture, a sacramental life, a rich body of teachings, the very treasure of the gospel and ever new instantiations of a social gospel, passing them forward through generation after generation, the extension of the incarnation in ever new vernaculars. This is not a matter of a group of people thinking too much of themselves, but the collective instantiation of the Greek word for church, *ekklesia,* people called out and appointed by God. Consider whether you have this calling, this religious vocation. In the church as a historical institution, Christian lives are composed as people let themselves be formed by the gospel of Jesus Christ. Stories tell Christians. Socialization into the life of God and into Christianity's living legacy takes an institution, a living family of God. Institutions take care of and tend the commons, which is why they are often dispensed with by libertarians, who prefer to be a barn full of feral cats. People who post on Facebook that they're into Jesus, but not the church, don't get it.

Good institutions are intrinsic to good societies and worthy endeavors. They are the facts on the ground that religion deposits and depends on. The church called out by God occupies the world culturally and socially and institutionally. But occasionally the church separates itself to create nonconforming *sects* at fortuitous moments that open themselves to the new mutations the times require; other times the church produces mystics who independently swim through the world to channel the stream of Spirit. Ernst Troeltsch famously imagined the church taking three different forms: institutionalizing *church*/separating *sect*/individualizing *mysticism.*" (Examples would be Catholics, Anabaptists, and free-thinkers.)

Our age of hyper-individualism is not a good time for noticing, appreciating, and relying on institutions, including good government that does good things in society. "Mediating institutions," of which churches are prime examples, are held up by sociologists as a bulwark against the overwhelming power of the state or economic forces and also a balance over against atomistic individualism which can become the only alternative to the state, leaving a vast middle space empty of human constructs. Mediating institutions provide opportunities for community and support as people move through their lives. As "plausibility structures," churches also provide space in which the meanings and beliefs and moral actions of religion can be tried and practiced in communities that carry them forward and nurture them over time. Schools are another example of institutions in the middle. I often say that religious individualists, not to mention "nones" and "spiritual but not religious" devotees, who make a point of rejecting institutions, fail to see that they themselves are living on *borrowed capital*, that the traditions that have fed them have been carried forward as living deposits of social capital made available in each age by committed people occupying institutions. (A devout mother I know well would like to tell her sons-in-law, so self-confidently dismissive of religion, that a good deal of what they love about her daughters is their fervent Christian upbringing. Their marriages are living on borrowed capital.)

The church, and good government and other institutions, must be the opposite of the *unencumbered self*. Or in the case of libertarians, the *disencumbered self*. Wide awake people see and aspire to earth-and-human interconnectedness, and therefore the necessity of new other-regarding social gospels whose time has so clearly now come.

But the theologies of the Hebrew Bible and the New Testament are not content to justify religious communities merely as *socially necessary* mediating institutions. The community that is Israel is called forth by God as a covenant people who offer up praise, authenticate the covenant, and become a lighthouse to the world. Israel, the aggregate of Torah and prophetic witness, rises up to be God's partner, God's chosen people on earth, God's presence on the ground. In the New Testament Jesus quite deliberately calls and commissions disciples as a group. The Apostle Paul especially imagines and nourishes a called-out community that represents and becomes the body of Christ in the world. First Peter imagines the church as the household of God where strangers and resident aliens can occupy a new life. Communal Israel and the communal church are indispensable theological constructs. The Bible emerges as the witness of and to those communities. The Bible constituted the church, and the church the Bible. Well before it accepts responsibility for proclaiming, embodying, and effecting a new social gospel, the church—and ancient Israel—were called first to their own mission of lifting up and embodying the God of the universe, the God of a covenant with earthly peoples. Sacred stories that purport to reveal the point of life on earth require a community of people who will tell the story, interpret the story, follow the story, *become the story*.

Here's a story about Christianity as a living institution. During World War II when Nazi Germany was occupying France, orders came down to round up Jews and deport them to concentration camps. In southern France there was a little Protestant village called Le Chambon. Protestants had mostly been expelled from the country when the political arrangements that followed the Reformation fell apart in France, but this village, with a Huguenot heritage, had endured. It faithfully told its story. Gradually it became its story. When orders came to ring the church bell on Nazi political occasions, they simply said no—because they had learned nonconformity over time. When everyone was ordered to turn over any Jews lurking in the countryside, they simply said no—because they understood religion as resistance. Over the centuries this tiny group of Protestant Christians had learned to be dissenting, undomesticated, resident aliens. Much practiced in saying No to the state, they simply kept saying No when orders came to hand over the Jews. Resistance was part of the story that constituted them. It came naturally. It will take such self-understanding for American churches to proclaim and promote a new social gospel in a society and government addicted to ignoring the commons.

IS CHRISTIANITY THE BEST WE CAN HOPE FOR?

In this book urging a new social gospel and the redemption of American Christianity, I have occasionally paused to take up the more preliminary question of religion itself, in an age that keeps postponing or even rejecting the God-question and has a tendency to question the validity of religion. If I succeed in reopening the discussion of religion, it may be inevitable that potential converts may inquire, But why Christianity? I pause to address that question.

Worldwide Christianity reflects the diversity of the Christian sequel of God's DNA and the risks of incarnation as well. To some, it is the elephant in the room when discussing the gracious God of the Bible. Christianity is the religion secular Westerners love to mock—when they are not preoccupied with Islamophobia. For what it did to the Jews, or to rationality and science, or to women and gays, or for making everyone feel guilty about sex. The rest of the world doesn't always like it much either, suspecting it is less a religion than an imperial enterprise, used to inflict Western colonialism as God's will.

Paul's dream of taking God's liberalism public came true. Christianity, the Christian sequel to Exodus and Prophets and the mirror of the incarnation, is the largest of the world religions, with Catholics numbering 1.1 billion and Protestantism and Orthodoxy adding another 1.1 billion. In its evangelistic mission it purports to be a universal religion, proclaiming and uncovering (not bringing) God everywhere, even if its adherents often fail to achieve an ecumenical mind-set. Its sins are many, and educated people know them by heart. They include absolutist certainty, a remarkable lack of humility about its grasp of the very being of God, and a confident superiority to all other world religions. American Christianity has a tendency to fashion God in its own nationalist and capitalist image.

But not all is ill. Many Christians feel called to an ecumenism that recognizes all fellow Christians as brothers and sisters and all the *world religions as repositories of other faces and moods and incarnations of God*. The parade welcomes all. Progressive Christians attempt to live fully, believingly, and meaningfully within their traditions about Jesus Christ, while warmly acknowledging and celebrating every other search for God and a just and peaceful world. In this book I mostly look at religion and the world through a Christian lens because *Christianity constitutes the glasses I cannot take off and because it is the religious tradition I must accept responsibility for*.

Does the Christian sequel, or *any* story about God, require joining up? (Fraternities and sororities call this pledging, and they make a point of ritualizing it at the beginning of every semester to keep the Greek spirit alive on campus. Parade first, then pledge.) Imagine Christian mission in the community living by such a semester system. Old Testament writers would not have understood the question whether you should join, since God embraced Israel as a covenanted community, not a set of philosophical ideas appealing to individuals who might sign up. Indeed, God *married* Israel and accused it of idolatry/adultery when it broke the relationship and flirted with other gods. In the New Testament, Jesus' proclamation of the reign of God provokes a crisis of decision—I am calling this "betting the farm" or wagering. In the Christian sequel, being born into the reality of dying and rising with Christ, to a new openness to and embrace of God, is typically a communal experience, involving and requiring reconciliation with all other humans—and with the earth as our adoptive mother. Such followers are on the way to personal but also social transformation, liberation, reconnection. Within the Christian traditions one enters a *great conversation*, a community of memory and ritual and moral practice. And learns to pass it on.

The contemporary situation presents new opportunities and new problems for the Christian sequel. A post-Christendom age offering no special privileges to Christianity is a challenge, but it may also present the right opportunity to retell the Christian story about God free of past compromises with state, society, and economic powers. The contemporary interest in spirituality, to some, portends a new "great awakening" in which Christianity lets go of acquired religious trappings that turn so many seekers away. (But which should be treasured and which let go?) If Christendom has come to represent a heavy yoke, post-Christendom may free Christians (and others) for new efforts to follow and embody the exodus God of the Bible and re-encounter the Christ of the New Testament.

WHAT DOES A LIFE OF RELIGIOUS FAITH LOOK LIKE?

Religion, and perhaps any paradigmatic worldview, begins and ends with that well-worn and much-abused word, *faith*. Faith can refer to the entire content of what someone believes, as in the *creeds*, or it can refer to that human receptivity that apprehends and trusts and bets the farm on something. (Scientists bet the farm on the always self-correcting scientific method.) Faith as the sum total of what has historically been believed, e.g. "the Christian tradition," is experienced by some as mystifying, authoritarian, hierarchical, anti-modern, irrational, dogmatic, even enslaving. Or liberating and enriching and foundational and "saving." Faith is distrusted by liberals because fundamentalists have turned it into rigidity and self-righteousness. Even believers who confess their faith in creeds every Sunday morning in words hammered out over 1,500 years ago are often not sure what they're saying, or why, and so they may stand with fingers crossed behind their backs. (Then there's the old line that Anglicans confess the creeds but don't actually believe them, while evangelicals abstain from creedal confessions because they're too liturgical and not made up on the spot—but believe every word of them.) Periodically, courageous Christian groups attempt to revise or write new creeds in the belief that those who simply keep repeating the same words without change may be losing the point of what was originally intended. Only in the sixteenth century did God learn to speak German, so the Lutheran Confessions could emerge. Theology helps the Christian tradition rethink and reframe and explicate faith in every new age and culture. The twentieth century saw new Christian confessions and creeds, across the world, in attempts to offer a Christian witness adequate to the times. A famous example in English is *A New Zealand Prayerbook*.

While faith has sometimes implied content on which there will be a test, it is also prized as openness to and trust in God. (I am following Marcus Borg here.) Faith as a way of believing can become a new way of being. *Credo*, the first word of the creeds, means I give my heart to, more than I cognitively subscribe to, these truths. So faith is *more performative than propositional*, something that atheists and agnostics always miss—and the religious often forget. Faith means a set of commitments more than a set of cognitive assertions, even if the latter underlie the former. Faith includes head and heart and disposition, evidencing itself differently in different individuals. Faith is a way of life that centers on a basic trust in God's good disposition toward humanity winning out over the anxiety and mistrust everywhere at hand. Faith is about grace and gratitude. It is common in the Trump years to assert that his evangelical supporters are in search of a strong man to recover a lost and privileged past—less a life of faith, grace, trust, and service than of guaranteed power and privilege. Or guaranteeing the courts will outlaw abortion and gays.

A dilemma of faith in the modern world is that *some believe too little and some believe too much.* While tempted to jettison everything thought to be inconvenient, irrelevant, or difficult, progressive religion instead rethinks, reclaims, redevelops, readapts what has historically been believed to new situations. The most difficult task is to determine what of faith is historically and culturally conditioned, admire it for what it accomplished in its time, and either let go of it in favor of new affirmations or hold on to it, with a second naïveté, as a truth entrusted from the past. There can be rich reward in "living within the tradition." It's the instinct of my anthropologist wife. The content of faith is partly a product of its times, since lived religion (and even God) always *appears in cultural clothing.* New immersions of faith in culture are required of every new generation. What will the new social gospel after Trump look like? What will reconstitute Christian humanism? Will it play in public life?

Given the human propensity for self-delusion, or over-assertion, caution about one's own creeds and over-certain faith always seems in order. (I am partly following Charles Kimball's *When Religion Becomes Evil* here.) The insufferable arrogance of many fundamentalist Christians (or Muslims or Hindus or Israeli settlers) is the argument that seems to count the most against modern religion. So religious faith is stronger, with more to recommend it, when it is tempered by humility. Humility is the best antidote to spiritual self-righteousness and religious fanaticism. It does not imply moral relativism or mindless tolerance. Humility means we can believe in absolute truth but not in the absoluteness of our own theological and moral definitions. *Our* writing is not precisely *God's* own handwriting. We can never capture God or pin divinity like an exotic butterfly, confined in our own cabinet of curiosities or on carefully typed pages. Indeed, to claim absolute truth for a rational concept of God is to corrupt the religious stance and turn our aspiring formulations into idolatries. There's a slippery slope from certitudes, to arrogance, to total self-delusion, to persecution of others— and it is a slope well-traveled by religious people. Humility recognizes the difference between God talking and us talking—sounding like we are certain how God would sound if God could learn our language. (If God talked, he'd sound like me; if God wrote a book it would be like one I'd write.) Humble doubting means that we temper spiritual obedience with rational reflection and consultation with the larger community of faith, and with the historical traditions from which we come. This makes us much less likely to drink the Kool-Aid offered us by overconfident leaders. Humility keeps us from writing God's appointments on human calendars and demanding that God arrive on time and do what we've scheduled. Humility means we don't spend time drawing boundary lines that define which side God is on and who is excluded from God's presence. Humility means we do not identify God with our country, our time, our place, our self, our class, our gender, our sexual orientation. Humility is the readiness to hear God's voice from unexpected lips and to see God's presence in unexpected faces, honoring God's presence elsewhere in all the world. Humility puts off the confidence that we have fully arrived. Humility keeps us from insisting that our last word is God's last word. Humility does not assume that the "institutional church" is the final stage of God's earthly visibility. *Humility avoids assuming that current Christian definitions are the only language God has ever learned.*

Another check on the oppressive certainty of religious faith is to devote it to ever greater *inclusiveness*. Will a new social gospel be expansive enough? Devote our religious energy to drawing larger circles? Jesus surrounded himself with victims of social exclusion—women, foreigners, public sinners, tax collectors working on commission, soldiers of the Roman occupation—and ate and drank with them. In the early chapters of the New Testament book of Acts, the Apostle Peter has a vision from which he concludes that ethnic boundary markers and circumcision and food fetishes must be left behind as Christianity opens itself to the world. In the eyes of a prodigal God, everything is clean, everything pure, everything capable of heaven. The entire missionary activity of the Apostle Paul took God's liberalism public and made it available to all comers across the Mediterranean world, from Jerusalem to Asia Minor to Greece to Rome. To emulate a gracious God is to extend the circle of God's love far beyond our own comfort zones. *The divine guest list is always larger than the church's imagination.* Many Christians haven't received that telegram.

Ecumenical specifically names the movement in the second half of the twentieth century that sought to bring all Christians together as members of the same family of God. The World Council of Churches was an attempt to give expression within history to the transcendental unity of the church and to respond to Jesus' prayer that all those who follow him "may be one" (John 17:11). All churches could be reimagined as a fellowship of the Holy Spirit in which diversity rather than divisiveness was celebrated. Protestants, historically given to fragmentation and vilification, learned to call each other brothers and sisters. A little later Catholics tried it too. Though most lay Catholics found it quite congenial, Popes John Paul II and Benedict

XVI found it necessary to clarify that only Roman Catholicism is the one true visible manifestation of Christianity on earth and Protestants must be marked off as disturbingly imperfect relatives. Now Pope Francis I is working on the equation again.

Although ecumenism began as an intra-Christian venture, it soon became an *interfaith* movement as well. Representatives of world religions began engaging each other. Minimally, a typical American city may have an interfaith council in which Protestant, Catholic, Jewish, and Muslim (and sometimes Buddhist) clergy come together regularly for dialogue and, often, mutual projects on behalf of social justice or the environment. Conservative Christians, of course, would not be seen in such groups, lest their claims to be guardians of exclusive truth that they alone have captured be weakened. Missouri Synod Lutherans stay away in case there is a common prayer that would compromise them. In recent decades, however, conservative evangelicals have joined with conservative Catholics to fight the culture wars and with Jews to maintain Israeli exceptionalism and to confirm Zionism as a biblical bequest and requirement. And a preparation for apocalyptic endings.

One way in which ecumenism flourishes is in finding things to celebrate in common. People of many different minds can seek and share spiritual paths together, sing together, eat and drink together, march together, go on pilgrimage together, pray together, serve together, picket the government together, dream up, argue for, and come to embody a new social gospel together. Third World theologians have tried to reorient the churches to belief-full praxis in contemporary contexts instead of preoccupation with the fixities of the past. The North practices learning things from the South, the West from the East.

A common misnomer of ecumenism is the assumption that its etiquette requires that everyone pretend, or make themselves believe, that we're really all the same and believe the same things. This is like saying to a black person, "Let's ignore your blackness and focus on the fact that we're both human." Or to a woman, "Let's ignore your gender and emphasize our common humanity, understanding that male pronouns of course include you as well." A mature ecumenism celebrates difference, encourages people to be themselves and to speak and act eloquently from their own traditions and occasionally to risk sharp disagreements. One way of thinking about this is that Christian theologians, no matter how ecumenical, must tell their own story because it is their story and one for which they must accept responsibility.

Once, Christians knew for sure that entire populations, *of all the other world religions,* were going to hell. When that notion became impossible to sustain, the choice was not to think about them at all. Now we know too much and our experiences are too wide for that option. "History of religions" has been a university discipline since the nineteenth century. Today, any college student may take a course on world religions from East to West as a General Education requirement. Many Americans have met representatives of the world religions, as fellow students, as co-workers, as neighbors, on their travels. American Jews and Christians estranged from their own traditions but still committed to spiritual seeking have sometimes turned East, especially to Buddhism. Others pick their way back amidst the ruins of Celtic religion or attempt to revive Druid rites. Still others are resurrecting goddess religion, or creating nature religions.

Many thoughtful people, including adherents of any of the world religions, try to imagine a God, the same God, who lies behind them all. (If representatives from all world religions came together to propose a just society, sharing God's bounty with all, free marketers would still oppose it.) Some scholars previously championed a "perennial philosophy" that underlay all religions, seeing differing dogmas in the foothills but one mountain on the distant horizon. Some find the commonalities of peace/love/understanding at the heart of every religion. Several decades ago there were attempts by scholars and others to distill from all the world religions a common body of belief and ethics, but this attempt is no longer in fashion. There simply were no religions that looked on the ground like the common denominator that well-meaning scholars invented. This attempt was also rooted in an Enlightenment predilection for rational abstractions that would supersede the messy particularities of individual religions.

So now pluralism or diversity are mostly prized. Postmoderns are comfortable with multiple realities, even disdaining any imposed grand narrative common to all peoples. Many things are true. By the end of the twentieth century, pluralism and diversity had become the modern prism under which world religions are to be viewed. Multiple religions run parallel with multiculturalism.

Not really a world religion, New Age spirituality is a visible part of the cultural mix in a postmodern age. New Age movements have been around for the last fifty years. They include Wiccan spirituality, inner healing, yoga, shamanism, redwood consciousness, Native American borrowings, alternatives to world religions, and the cultivation of self. Maybe even Burning Man or dancing naked in the woods. They are responses to global social and ecological crises and to a postmodern crisis of spirituality. They seek new ways of feeling and thinking and acting in every sphere, including science, politics, ecology, diet, self, and their response may be condensed as a holistic spirituality. They respond to problems and opportunities neglected by much institutional religion. When dominant religious institutions locate God within carefully gated precincts and ignore, trivialize, or forbid the journeys of many seekers, then those seekers will invest new pilgrimage sites with ultimate meaning and sidestep hallowed institutions. Today's New Agers are likely to constitute a global cultural network of those who self-consciously cultivate an intellectual and aesthetic stance of openness toward divergent quests for meaning and multicultural spiritual experiences.

New Agers are critiqued for their perceived flight from social responsibility, and their spiritualized individualism makes a virtue out of abandoning institutions. In this, they seem *more symptom than solution* to the spiritual vacuum of a rapacious capitalist society, just the kind of religiosity one might have expected a materialistic civilization to invent as a self-help cure. They are capitalism's favorite spirituality because it changes nothing on the outside and does not question the economy. But they see themselves as reversing the shrinkage of the sacred in a modern scientific age, of reviving the practice of the numinous that atrophied through the legacy of the Enlightenment. They are creating new frameworks, new structures for the numinous.

Across all the religious movements mentioned above are human beings making the great wager on God, on the universe coming to self-consciousness, on the aesthetic and perhaps ontological possibility that God and humans are wrapped around each other in an upwardly moving double helix. Two steps after Trump would be a new social gospel and a maturing Christian humanism.

FUNDAMENTALISM: WHEN FAITH AND RELIGIOUS CERTAINTY GO WRONG

Fundamentalism seems a uniquely American style of conservative Protestantism, exemplified politically by the Christian Right and flourishing especially in the South. But in style and motivation it is in fact a worldwide phenomenon that includes Judaism, Christianity, Islam, and Hinduism—and perhaps lately Buddhism. Fundamentalist religious movements are typically seen as regressive or oppositional social and cultural responses to modernity.

At the beginning of the twentieth century, American fundamentalism stood against religious modernism and its accommodation of evolutionary theory and the culture of the university, and explicitly took a stand on behalf of historic Christian beliefs like the deity of Christ, his virgin birth, his bodily resurrection, his substitutionary atonement for the sins of the world, and his bodily return at the end of the millennium. In a misguided response to the Enlightenment and modernity it turned Christian faith into rationalist, literalist, cognitive propositions, often losing the gospel dynamic of the New

Testament in the process. Its crucial presuppositions were the inerrancy of the Bible and dispensationalism as a key to interpreting world history, but the good news of the gospel was less clear. It took a lone stand against what it named apostasy in American churches and decay in Western civilization. In the name of religious individualism and personal freedom and personal ethics as the demonstration of faith, it also opposed—and still does—the early twentieth-century social gospel. In the first decades of the twenty-first century and sometimes aligned with conservative Catholic bishops, fundamentalism made ever more militant declarations against LGBT people and insisted that male and female, and manhood and womanhood in monogamous relationships, are unquestionable "orders of creation" that God has instilled in the human community and that departure from them is non-negotiable. Some leaders even proclaimed that natural disasters like floods and fires were God's punishment for homosexuality.

After beginning as a rearguard and isolationist movement against religious liberalism and indeed in opposition to the modern world, American Protestant fundamentalism eventually moved beyond its early theological agenda to become a cultural and political movement, exemplified for example in the New Christian Right and its protest against the eclipse of religion in American life that was driven by Supreme Court decisions. It added to religious awakening and moral outrage against selected topics an anti-intellectual, populist, right-wing nationalism, playing as patriotism, militarism, white racism, and a deregulated free market economy. It annexed itself to, or nearly became an indispensable base for, the Republican Party, and defined political activism in moral and religious terms. (Some scholars are now saying that it was economic conservatives who annexed white fundamentalists.) With its emphasis on abortion, homosexuality, and a secularism that is displacing prayer and creationism in the schools and the presence of Christianity in the public square, the newer movement found energy far beyond the earlier theological fundamentalism that had become irrelevant to politics and culture. Though ostracized by status elites, it created its own media presence and found a new sense of confidence and superiority. Its well-funded media messages implied privileged information regarding God's plans and it lured audiences with fantasies of revenge against colonizing secular elites. It was well adapted to a know-nothing, paranoid style that had always been part of American public life. From championing historic Christian truths against modern doubters, it moved to guarding Christian morality, and especially the sexual purity of young women, in a nation specially chosen by God. Protestant fundamentalists have lately been joined by conservative Catholics, at least on abortion, homosexuality, and freedom of religion from government intrusions (or the right to have government enforce conservative religious morality). American fundamentalism does not notice that its obsession with moral gate-keeping, America-first theocracy, and alliance with market capitalism has distanced it from the New Testament Gospel, perhaps, it is recently being argued, because its white conservative longing for an idealized past is more fundamental to its self-understanding than what used to be called the four evangelical markers: absolute authority of the Bible, conversion of the heart, responsibility to evangelize, and substitutionary atonement through the cross. So now the current trappings of the Christian Right appear to conceal a major mutation from the original Christian DNA. The fundamentalist covenant is that of a repressive national security state and a capitalist worldview, not the Old Testament ideal of the people of God called to embody social justice and covenant righteousness. The fundamentalist "battle for God" was an effort to fill the void at the heart of a society rooted in scientific rationalism and secularism. Its ideological self-confidence is evidenced by the sign often waved at 2012 to 2016 political rallies: "A liberal is not a Christian." Of course liberals return the favor.

Today, snarky critics believe that American fundamentalism is driven by fear of liberals, fear of women, fear of homosexuals, and the need to feel specially chosen. Evidence can be found for this appraisal. Commenting on the tragedy of 9/11, the Christian Right leader Jerry Falwell said: "I really believe that the pagans, and the abortionists, and the feminists, and the gays and lesbians who are actively trying to make that an alternative lifestyle . . . I point the finger in their face and say, 'You helped this happen.'" Pat Robertson, the highly visible anchor of Christian Broadcasting Network and a onetime presidential candidate said: "The feminist agenda is not about equal rights for women. It is about a socialist, anti-family political movement that encourages women to leave their husbands, kill their children, practice witchcraft, destroy capitalism, and become lesbians." The Pentecostal evangelist Jimmy Swaggert preached to a swooning crowd: "I'm gonna be blunt and plain. If a homosexual ever looks at me like that, I'm gonna kill him and tell God he died." Such assertions, including slightly less offensive declarations during recent Republican primaries, are met with rapturous applause. Under Trump, the goal of such assertions is to become more offensive and to claim to be making America great again.

Religious fundamentalists, especially in America, resent the constitutional trick that seems to have been played on them in the modern world. *A secularism that does not admit to making religious-like claims has made of itself the only appropriate mind-set for a post-religious age, and in fact displaces historic religion and establishes itself as a kind of rival religion, an enforced system of ultimate meaning that is constitutionally privileged in the United States—precisely because it is not taken as a religion.*

SALVATION: EXPERIENCING AND NAMING FRIENDSHIP WITH GOD

What do Christians mean by salvation? "Jesus died to save us from our sins," Sunday school teachers drill. Redemption is in the blood of the lamb, revival preachers shout. Blood atonement separates true Christianity from faint-hearted versions, fundamentalists claim. What do these phrases mean today? Most Christians learned them as children and they think they understand them—until asked to explain. Surely some version of Christian salvation lies within, or motivates, or seeks to express itself in a new social gospel. Salvation is the good at the heart of the church's proclamation, what motivates a new social gospel. And the ultimate outcome of a social gospel.

Jesus saves. For Christians, what was happening in the life, teachings, death, and resurrection of Jesus was a paradigm of God's full intentions to befriend the world and take up residence on earth. Hence, Christians produce Christ-centered interpretations of salvation. What's the problem? "Jesus saves" is meant to be the answer to the human dilemma, but to many people it sounds peculiar or even ridiculous. What Jesus saves means is likely to correlate with what we perceive to be wrong with us or what the universal human dilemma is.

How does Jesus save? In the Christian view, salvation must mean a new status between God and humanity and among all peoples of the earth—and perhaps interconnectivity with the universe, even worlds unknown. The Hebrew Bible does not envision individualistic salvation apart from a community—it takes a village, an entire people. The New Testament does not make individualism a theological concept, as very much of the culture of the United States does. At the beginning of American history, utilitarian individualism and covenantal communalism seemed to balance each other. Individualism has clearly won, which is why most Americans cannot even imagine north European social democracy, voting for, demanding, living out a social justice covenant. Already in the Hebrew Bible salvation included the liberation experienced in the exodus, the gift of a new land on which the entire community had a claim. In the New Testament, salvation means Jesus' proclamation of a new time of God's self-disclosure and the invitation to accept and claim it, a new life of freedom and reconciliation, a dethroning of the powers that work against full human life, a deliverance that is experienced communally, already now and still not complete.

To say this in contemporary language, the New Testament proclamation about Jesus means that a self-giving God wants to share Godness (God's right-making goodness), but that proclamation is situated in "Christian realism" about the world. God seeks to friend humanity and the earth, even amidst much reciprocal un-friending, viral jamming, cyber bullying, and an *unbecoming* that reverses the vision of God. As shown in the crucifixion, God takes human rejection and earthly tragedy up into God's own divine being. Played out in Jesus' ministry, God's identification with the suffering, misery, and abuse of the world becomes *a dramatic story in the revelation of God's character and in a new dynamic with the world.*

Soon enough, early Christianity tended to define salvation in terms of the incarnation. Salvation meant a human existence redefined as deeply touched by the coming of God-in-Christ. Salvation through incarnation meant, in the language of early Christian theology, that "what God fully assumes, God fully saves." Or, "God became human that we might become divine." This robust view of salvation applied to all of creation. Another view emphasized Christ triumphing in a world caught in the grip of powers unfriendly to the human condition (a modern demythologization might emphasize deliverance from the powerful domination systems of empire and the national security state or global capitalism, whose forceful claims we cannot manage to escape).

But the medieval Catholic view, embraced by many modern Protestants as well, emphasized *judicial satisfaction*, in which God's son pays the penalty to an angry father for our sins. This crucifixion-centered view paid less attention to Jesus' actual life or teachings. But today this judicial view seems to imply an angry God who must kill his son to appease his anger and, in the process, to authorize a "redemptive violence" that seems to justify the use of political violence and valorize human suffering, especially of women, as an imitation of God. In this view of the atonement, the goodness of the world emphasized in creation and incarnation gives way to an evil world symbolized in the crucifixion. Modern critics, including very many Christian theologians, are horrified to find in this picture the idea that *God became a divisive, guilt-giving, punishing being whose desire for justice is satisfied only by the torture and crucifixion of his own son.*

The American evangelical version of salvation can lose the cosmic and communal nature of God's dealings with humankind, in favor of an extreme individualism that invites a "personal Savior" into one's heart—a concept unknown to the New Testament and much of Christian history. Progressive religion wants to emphasize not a deliverance from God's punishing wrath, but the *conferring of a human wholeness that overcomes a fragmenting, selfish, destructive, violence-ridden ways of living.* Jesus saves by incarnating God's presence among us. In Jesus God makes friends (reconciles) with the earth.

Salvation means authentic human life in the world, fully transparent to the presence of God and fully integrated with the earth and all its peoples. The human longing for salvation emerges amidst human anxiety and insecurity about finitude, guilt, and meaninglessness, about greed and ruthlessness instead of an interdependent human family, about the destruction of the earth, our mother. Salvation occurs at the crossroad where the world confronts God's offer to reconcile with the whole human race and decides how to respond. A diverse, abundantly plural God graces the earth, consents to a further divine Becoming in mutual relationship with humanity, and in this divine-human partnership the universe comes to its fullest self-consciousness. Salvation means all the stored-up good of the universe beginning to happen.

Jewish mystics imagined that before creation, when God filled all that was, God stepped back to make space for earth and humanity to be and to become, and to participate in God's own Becoming. God wanted company. God deposited the divine DNA in the midst of earthly life. (Think the Virgin Mary.) When everyone sees this and names it salvation, the universe comes to full self-consciousness.

SACRAMENTALIZING THE EARTH AND SOCIETY IS THE FOUNDATION OF A NEW SOCIAL GOSPEL

Abbot Suger of St. Denis in Paris, an early patron of Gothic architecture, famously said, "The dull mind rises to God through material things." Orthodox Christians believe God shines through holy icons and, more radically, that the earth itself can be experienced as God's body. Martin Luther proclaimed that in Christ God emptied heaven and took up residence on earth, making earth capable of heaven. The twentieth-century Protestant theologian Paul Tillich thought that the *holy of being* precedes the holy of *what ought to be,* that we should seek and find earth as the sacrament of God's presence. (This is a clue to what must underlie and found a social gospel.) The (Lutheran-tinged) writer John Updike said the world is like a eucharistic host that must be chewed. It wants describing, it wants transubstantiation by writers. The earth is spirit and matter, not one-sidedly to be reduced to materialism and brain chemistry.

The first white social gospel movement in America, grounded in liberal Protestantism, was somewhat anemic and intellectualizing, light on liturgy and sacraments and the material culture of Christianity, even though committed to social activism and perhaps even moral utopianism. Then and now, American evangelicalism has emphasized the state of the believer's heart, and individual religious freedom, and individual love for the neighbor, but it is very light on sacramentalism and suspicious of social structural recognition and response to God's initiative. Thomas Aquinas thought that we do not understand the human meaning of food until we have grasped its eucharistic depth, finding God lurking within the earthly business of meals, waiting to be disclosed. This is the consciousness that underlies a Catholic soup kitchen.

In the Hebrew Bible God is held high on the praises of Israel. In the New Testament Christians begin gathering every Sunday to make present the bodily resurrection of Christ (Easter) in acts of praise and prayer and proclamation and find themselves becoming, in fact, the body of Christ in the world, an extension of the incarnation, pilgrimaging to and from God. Every religion requires ritual to embody and act out its beliefs, emotions, experiences, and hopes. As we saw in exodus and Passover, which are *ritual movements*, liturgy is performative. Go forth, on Sunday, and feed on the Eucharist, experiencing yourself as one with the body of Christ. Go forth, during the week, feed the poor and experience uniting with them as the body of Christ. In liturgical action and music worshipers find their memories and their deepest longings settling into their very bodies as repositories of their religious lives. Guerilla liturgies play religious imagination in the streets, and they begin in a worship style that joins theological drive to social justice activism. Eventually, it is said, *believing is seeing*. Remember Cesar Chavez and the farm workers' union receiving the Eucharist in the fields and leading the Christian parade through the California valley.

But there is always the urge to achieve an exquisite religiosity by fleeing the material world and merging with God in mystical embrace. There's a place for that. Because earthly life can go wrong and become a distraction, there can be truth to the mystical aspiration. But what if earthly life itself can be the locus of transformation, the place where God's Becoming takes human form? And the universe comes to self-consciousness beginning with the earth and the human community as the locus of transformation, as Dante implied in the *Divine Comedy*.

To keep this in mind, Christianity celebrates sacraments—two in Protestantism and seven in Catholicism. The earth itself can become a sacrament of God's presence because God in Christ emptied heaven out on earth. Baptism, occurring in the sight and sound of abundant water, induces earthlings into the friendship of God's family in a sensuous way. Holy Communion is the weekly reclaiming and practicing of the presence of God in which bread and wine and the constituting Word of God make Christ fully present in the lives of the worshipping believers. Luther liked to think of molten iron, which is to say both metal and fire, as an image of the Eucharist. It's not just the satisfying miracle of bread turning into body. If you sit in church and watch long lines of people coming forward to receive the Eucharist, you see in your Christian imagination the body of Christ forming in the aisles to greet the catalyzing body of Christ at the altar. There are two constitutions occurring, a divine exchange. After I have received Communion and returned to my seat, I like to reach out and touch people going by up the aisle to the altar (though not in a Joe Biden manner). Sacramentalism is a materialism filled with spirit. A suspicion of sacraments has not served much of Protestantism well and keeps it cautious about the world.

Sacraments may be seen as a planned running into mystery, a ritualized enactment of the play of spirit and matter, the holy and the ordinary, God and earth, humans in their heavenward side and their earthbound side. The so-called "high church" traditions, like Orthodox, Catholics, Anglicans, and Lutherans, ground their sacramental practice in the "real presence" of Christ himself, whom they see as the original or paradigmatic sacrament of God's presence in the world. *Christ gives body to God on earth.* Look there, and see God. From that understanding, move to the sacramentalizing of all creation, in which earth and its peoples are openings to the presence of God. In the church's seeing (if it does not deliberately look away) this comes to be. See there, on that Amnesty International poster—a face of God. Look at the Bethlehem assembly, icons of God and creation. Believing is seeing. Liberation theology especially finds in the neighbor or the oppressed the sacrament of God's presence actualized through an engaged church. Orthodoxy imagines the earth itself as a kind of sacrament—a vital but missing dimension in the rapacious West, for which earth too often falls into something to be conquered and controlled. Mainstream Protestants and evangelicals find their own ways to concretize their Christian lives and evoke a new social gospel.

Sacraments are something to receive, something to do, something to see by. They *perform God's ways* in the life of a religious community, and they are a lens through which to see mother earth and all her peoples. Already established in the New Testament, they make the exodus God fully present. And moving. Material and spiritual, they invite and require the community to participate, to "offer consent" (as Mary did) to the movement of God over creation and into the community. Social justice religion might envision baptism as the inauguration of a life of resistance, under the sign of God who calls us to bury the old life and begin a new one—a point we return to at the end of this book. It sees the Eucharist as an eating and drinking that takes in the very grace of God, that must happen in community with others, and that actively anticipates a day when everyone in the world gets to sit down at a very large table and be fed. (Longer tables instead of higher walls is a contemporary Facebook meme.) The church's vision is supposed to extend the table to accommodate God's commensality.

From worship and sacraments is supposed to issue a pervasive social justice in covenanting communities. The commandment to honor the Sabbath already mandated a work stoppage on behalf of worshiping God, *mending creation*, and attending to life in the family and the village. Imagine taking off work to sweep the streets, tend to the park, nurture the family, feed the poor, work in a field hospital—only on a larger stage. A "Sabbath economy" would set people free from the enslavement of constant commerce as the meaning of human life. Is the Lord's Prayer suggesting forgiving *debts* or just *trespasses*? Building on the foundation of the Sabbath but employing far more encompassing social capital is the (utopian) notion of a Jubilee Year that appears in Leviticus 25, again at the end of Isaiah, and then as Jesus' inaugural sermon in Luke 4. Everyone can be released from debtors' prison and be welcomed home. Everyone reimagines the whole earth as a gift from above. Everyone recovers their original blessings. Everyone gets the land back God originally bequeathed. Debts are forgiven, land redistributed.

It is a telling sign that the oppressed and enslaved have always been quicker to decode God's radical intentions than the entrenched 1 or 2 percent. The nineteenth-century abolitionist, William Lloyd Garrison, wrote:

> God speed the year of jubilee, the wide world o'er!
>
> When from their galling chains set free,
>
> Th' oppressed shall vilely bend the knee
>
> And wear the yoke of tyranny, like brutes, no more—
>
> That year will come, and Freedom's reign
>
> To man his plundered rights again, restore.

Ancient Israel, at least in its theological imagination, stretched the logic of the Sabbath out across the economic landscape and turned it into a Jubilee Year that would be a great celebration to be marked every forty-ninth year (seven times seven), in which all creation would return to the "original position" (to use a term from the philosopher John Rawls) of its arrival fresh from the hand of God. From the original grace of the land as God's possession, human differences would inevitably have created uneven socioeconomic results. Every forty-nine years God would dismantle these inequities, people would be released from their debts, forfeited land would be returned to its original owners, and debt-slaves would be freed. (Capitalism's nightmare, God's good dream.) God's redistributionist visions far out-Marxed Karl Marx. In Jubilee, a liberal God institutionalized the divine dream in communal memory. A subversive God steps in periodically to dismantle the company store. *God's liberalism far exceeds our own.*

If all this never happened, or is a utopian vision, or completely unrealistic and indeed impossible in the modern world, could we perhaps just reread the story periodically as we contemplate the contours of a new social gospel? But surely the New Testament has left all this behind and a spiritualizing Christianity has set religion free from entanglements in politics and economics? Toward the end of the twentieth century, beginning with President Reagan, a blinkered Christianity seemed to go along in providing the market with a get-out-of-jail free card, a moral pass from culture wars scrutiny, which is saved for abortion and homosexuality. But consider the embarrassing fact of what Jesus actually did. In his first sermon (Luke 4:18–19), he makes the Jubilee vision of Isaiah his own, proclaiming that the time has come for the prophetic legacy to become God's light to the nations: to "proclaim release to the captives and recovery of sight to the blind, to let the oppressed go free, to proclaim the year of the Lord's favor." Perhaps early Christianity, as portrayed in the book of Acts, had Jesus' sermon in mind when the wealthier sold their goods and people held "all things in common." Isn't it odd that Bible-toting, Bible-quoting Americans never, ever punch such lines as these to the rest of the country: "They [the fresh born-agains] devoted themselves to the apostles' teaching and fellowship, to the breaking of bread and the prayers. . . . All who believed were together and had all things in common; they would sell their possessions and goods and distribute the proceeds to all, *as any had need*" (Acts 2:42, 44–45). How can Christians go public with this?

TAKE UP THE BIBLE AND LET IT READ YOU

I've saved the Bible as the last dimension of living in the church, of the pilgrim's progress, but as an heir of the Reformation's *sola scriptura* I consider it all-important for shaping a Christian humanism and evoking a new social gospel. The 2017 500th anniversary of the Reformation may have missed what was *most central about the Reformation*—not Luther or Calvin but *sola scriptura*, the gift that keeps on giving, the central and dominating presence of the Bible. The most important act of a reformer is to open you to the Bible and let it read you. (In what follows I am influenced by the treatment on exegesis and interpretation in Walter Brueggemann's *Theology of the Old Testament*.)

Why take up the question of the Bible now? The heart of this book and the foundation for its entire argument about the meaning of a liberating God come to earth are in chapters one and two and the practice of exegesis connected to them. In the exodus God revealed a remarkable DNA as a legacy for humanity. Carrying that genome, the prophets made God's intentions for justice throughout the land the foundation of Israel's life in covenant—what we might call a social contract. In the New Testament God's self-giving and reconciling move towards humanity disturbingly come to incarnation, with Jesus as its walking paradigm. Then the Apostle Paul takes this will and testament public and makes of the Christian sequel a universalizing religion. Open-minded secularists are likely to be happy with the message of a liberalism at the heart of the human world and maybe even built into the universe, but they don't want to think it has anything to do with God or the Bible. The point of the Bible is that it is tethered to what God began in exodus and prophets and what God finished in Christ. If you like to say *sola scriptura,* Scripture alone, there are several more terms that come in the package: *sola fide* (faith alone), *sola gratia* (grace alone), and of course *solus Christus* (Christ alone). As they say, if the Bible isn't delivering Christ to you, and you to Christ, then you have not been letting it address you, call to you, change your life.

Judaism, Christianity, and Islam are called "religions of the book." Their sacred texts brim with rituals, legal codes, prophetic oracles, divine revelations, visions, ecstatic poetry, theological proclamation, and great stories that witness to divine-human encounters. But religions of the book also have a tendency to make their sacred texts vehicles for priestly aggrandizement, proof-texting, weapons for heresy hunters, a suit of armor for the self-righteous, ammunition for the culture wars. Then there's the Bible's use to press dried flowers, write family history, and swear on. Pocket New Testaments carried over the heart sometimes deflect bullets, especially during war.

The Bible becomes the Holy Bible only as people respond to it as the Word of God. Here's a clue to keep you on the right track: *Let the Bible read you.* Sacred texts are relational and contextual: they become what they are through the role they play in historic religious communities. If no one visits the oracles, they cannot speak. The Bible is read aloud in worship, is expounded in preaching, and serves the purposes of personal study, devotion, and spiritual journey—or assigned reading in religious studies classes. Periodically, religious communities renew themselves by urgent return to their sacred sources, as the European Renaissance did by returning to the fountains of the classical age. I propose recovering lost stories and discarded images as what the times most require. There will be no new social gospel without the periodic recovery of its biblical foundations.

Sacred texts (like the American Constitution) require contemporary interpretations, and struggles over their meaning are part of every tradition. Some legal scholars believe that Constitutional *originalism* (the insistence that the Supreme Court must only determine what the language of the Constitution meant in the late eighteenth century) may have been inherited from American fundamentalist treatment of the Bible. But the history of Judaism or Christianity (or even Islam) could be written as a succession of new, recovered, contested meanings of the biblical message. God keeps learning new vernaculars. Luther famously made God speak German (and Germans speak God), and coincidentally produced a monument of German literature.

But what is the use of a sacred book? It is first to be experienced and lived, and then handled. Many Christians hawk the Bible as a divine product with a divine guarantee, a Wikipedia for looking up stuff about God and telling the neighbors where they're wrong. Biblicism refers to arming the Bible (and Christians) against the assaults of the modern age. Just as late nineteenth-century Catholicism made the pope infallible to guarantee religious certainty in a fast-changing world, fundamentalist Protestants at the beginning of the twentieth century made the Bible inerrant, a paper pope, so it could not be challenged. After the Bible became an error-free, historically and scientifically accurate manual for all times, it could be transposed directly into any situation to dispense its freeze-dried texts. One stopped looking in the Bible for theological metaphors, poetry, prayers, parables, and existence-changing good news and *taught oneself* to expect marching orders and straight answers to all the questions. Any view of the Bible is probably in service to some interest. "Never question the Bible" usually means never question the establishment that is quoting it. The antidote to this mishandling of sacred texts? Let the Bible read you.

Is it possible that the more inerrant you make the Bible the less likely you are to derive a social gospel from it? How or why could this be? Is there evidence? How is it that the Christian Right, with its evangelical paragons of biblical literalism and inerrancy, can find Christ in Trump but not on the border, in the free market but not in food stamps?

It is always difficult to go back in time and apprehend an ancient text. Or to make it new. Literature professors and their students know this. Some moderns assert that religion belongs to the world of children or that it cannot survive being read in a scientific age. Capitalism and other isms abduct texts that proclaim good news to all the people and turn them into bad news, as when the Christmas story becomes a sacrament of consumerism not offered to the poor, or the heart of the Bible is a gender totalitarianism on which Christianity stands or falls. Middle-class churches may doctor explosive texts to make them collectibles safe for passing around without blowing up in your face. If the glasses we wear are made in the present social, economic, and political world, they may imprison us in our modern context and *determine in advance what can be seen and heard.* As you sit on your hotel bed and withdraw a Gideon Bible from the nightstand, an entire cultural world shapes that moment and may stimulate or foreclose self-discovery. And yet, genuine surprise—something new is still possible, as we know from countless Gideon testimonies.

What if a sacred text could stand as God's free act of communication—from God's voice to your heart? What if the text in front of us, not the (American or middle class or white or free market or male) presuppositions behind us, offers a radical account of the one and only real world? What if the text is happening now? If this is a possibility, then *stay in the text* as it generates new worlds to live in. Paul Ricoeur advised giving up "the founding self" that arrives in charge of an open text and engaging instead in a "radical self-divestment." Consider *surrendering* to an alternative world when reading and being read by the Bible. Stay with what is in front of you, an alternative story not subject to prior restraints or external validation.

Biblical proclamation can be taken prisoner by the reader's "location." For example, "commonsense readings" by white slaveholders adjusted the biblical message to current social and economic conditions and choices. Even today, it is easy for "feels right exegesis" to commandeer a radical text and adjust God's intentions to fit your own. Jesus' audiences, and especially the religious establishments, were determined not to hear anything new when he opened his mouth. Central Americans are struck by political oppression and dying babies and the holy family as refugees in Matthew's Christmas story, while North Americans hear authorization for a consumer holiday. Down through the ages, the Bible creates its own responding audiences and gather its own faithful followings, what English departments call *reader response theory.*

The Bible can be unpredictable. It may need rescue from a pious certainty that literalizes human words as the very mind of God. It is better to see sacred texts as an ever-expanding repertoire of divine-human encounters than frozen truths. The Spirit blows through the words and unsettles received interpretations, fluttering the meanings across the pages of fixed type. It is not safe to assume ahead of time what a book would be like if God wrote it. That it surely would be like a holy book that *you* would write.

Luther admonished that if Christians are not finding Christ at the center, then they are misreading. Some contemporary theologians say that the *Bible must be held accountable to Jesus Christ.* For example, in the whole Bible there are about six verses that reference homosexuality in some way, while over a thousand verses obsess over the poor. Just as Thomas Jefferson deleted all the miracles from the New Testament because they offended his Enlightenment rationalism, many conservatives drill social compassion and justice out of every sacred page—leaving a Bible full of holes and no surprises. *Like Ancestry.com with the essential genes scissored out.*

What happens when a reader enters into a relationship with a sacred text? The so-called "hermeneutical circle" refers to the possibility that the text being handled turns around and handles you. While scrutinizing God, you experience God scrutinizing you. You may run into a different Jesus than the one you thought you knew. Fresh readings can "de-familiarize" texts that have been sanded down to normal comfort levels.

Beware also of the *hermeneutics of privilege,* in which some American Christians assume that the text is *automatically on their side.* And reads white. Or male. Or middle class. Or *America First.* It may be necessary to call for a "guerilla exegesis" that reads the Bible against the grain, wrests its texts from official custodians, unlocks their captivity to comfortable assumptions, disturbs their utility for the middle class, recovers biblical hope as liberation for the poor, opens up a new social gospel. Once, when a whole nation was reading the same Bible, only American blacks decoded the exodus and heard the call to march out of Egypt

While the Bible is reverenced too little by some progressive Christians who pride themselves on how little they believe, and while the Bible is smothered by fundamentalists who hold it so tight it can't breathe, the crisis of secular modernity (begun with the Enlightenment) is that it created a thought world in which the Bible simply was *no longer allowed to speak.* Don't quote the Bible in the public square because there is no public validity to *any and all* religious stories. Actually very many Americans believe this is the only way to protect the state from the church. They may be well-meaning but this position *brings the Bible into new captivities.* It is not allowed to speak in public. This may be part of a larger cultural move from spirit to matter, from religion to secular materialism.

But those who want to make claims in the public square, for example regarding a new social gospel, may appeal to the view of postmodern "critical theory": *there are no innocent texts and no innocent readers.* Feminists, for example, are leery of patriarchal texts that claim objectivity. People of color are suspicious of viewpoints that imply white privilege. A current example would be all the people who automatically know that slavery may now be wrong but reparations are out of the question. No text, no public speech, no belief system exists outside the traffic of social conflict and contests over power and place. Every argument is loaded. Christians arguing for a new social gospel after Trump should be ready to admit that *theological*

*texts, in particular, portray earth-shaking, existentially loaded struggles be-
tween God and humans.* The strange world of the Bible, also when alluded
to in the public square, is one of the stories, one of the God-stories, on offer.
The world you are living in before you come to the text does not necessarily
determine the world you might discover within the text. The *text can say
something new and unexpected to you*—and you to your neighbors.

What happens in Vegas does *not* stay in Vegas. The exodus narrative
and the prophetic imagination and Jesus' parables are all meant to desta-
bilize the givens that hem us. The religious agenda of a sacred text is to
generate alternative worlds that arise from within the text. Recovered sacred
stories, the very ones that C. S. Lewis thought had gone missing and without
which we were left clueless about the meaning of the larger story, become
capable of construing and evoking life-changing realities. Sacred texts may
require new life pilgrimages, new iterations of the social gospel, and these
may find their way through the public square.

People who enter the church with a colonizer's mind-set, and who
therefore know all things ahead of time, may encounter unexpected claims.
The point of a serious encounter with a sacred text (or Dostoevsky or Tolkien or Dickinson) is *not to ward off the power of the text but to engage it
existentially and possibly submit to it.* Will you be able to enter the public
square or join public discussions betraying no hint of your new convictions? Didn't Jefferson argue for "self-evident truths" bequeathed from the
Enlightenment? Didn't abolitionist claims get carried into public?

Biblical texts—and all great works of art—are saturated with what is
odd, hidden, dense, inscrutable, mysterious. In the case of the Bible, its texts
are self-construed as theological discourse replete with theological claims.
Luther said if you're not meeting Mary's baby, and I am saying that if you
are not hearing gracious good news for all peoples, you haven't come to
the New Testament. *Of course, that assumption too can be challenged.* I am
claiming that the account of God as a liberator, played out in the exodus, the
prophets, Jesus, and Paul, is the so-called "canon within the canon" of the
entire Bible. In its light, all the hiddenness and darkness of the text comes to
understanding. *Can this canon within the canon play on an American stage?*
Of course reason, too, will enter the debate, but the postmodern world is
less confident than the Enlightenment was that a cool rationality is the answer to all the questions. The heart has reasons . . .

If new social gospel scripts were to gain ground and pass American
auditions, then the audience would be struck by the partisan news, by the
normative claim, that God comes to the world as free gift, as does all the
bounty of heaven, and that this is liberating news for all the human family.
From within the world of the text as testimony to a liberating God come

new worlds this side of the text. The Bible may unsettle the received wisdom of the American way, of all political parties, of all economic classes, of every social location.

You can imagine how these newly claimed texts would give modern preachers something to say. Postmodern preaching is not a dirty word, a disreputable practice, but a new rhetorical possibility. Some materialist readings of reality have left people devoid of mystery and starved for metaphor and anesthetized by cognitive certainties and freed from the historic habits of the heart that once constructed a Christian humanism and a social vision. *Nothing to see here.*

But now the sermon becomes the rhetorical play of a reconciling God's self-communication with the human family. Sermons born in this context do not announce comfortable ideas but wrestle with symbols that unsettle human life. Biblical texts are not judged on whether they are historically factual but on whether their theological strategy takes over the listener and creates new worlds. *Transformation, not information.* The biblical proclamation of the gospel can generate new worlds in which to dwell, to which one can invite others. Biblical preaching and biblical listening unsettle the disencumbered self and propose the renunciation of the old world and the embrace of alternative worlds. In this fragile moment, preacher and hearer consider life anew. And the good news even reaches the ears of the poor. *All preaching is political. Keeping politics out of the church could mean keeping a revolutionary Christ out of the church.*

I have tried in this last section, against the grain of common expectations by believers and unbelievers alike, to suggest what an exciting life is at hand in the church's earthly pilgrimage—when people made ready experience the Bible reading them. Who knew? From such experiences come new social gospels, just in time for a reformation and redemption of American Christianity.

6

Earth Angels: Reconsidering the Human Prospect

A NEW CHRISTIAN HUMANISM

I have argued for the recalling of the God of the Bible. I have described a reliving of Christianity that returns the parade of religion to the streets, reminds the church that its essence is pilgrimage, and reminds everyone that "it takes an institution." Now, in these last three chapters of the book, I argue for the return of Christianity to the public stage and for the resolve to recontest public space if a worthy Christian humanism is to reappear in public and a new social gospel is proclaimed and enacted to succeed the age of Trump. Confident about something to be and something to say and something to do, the churches take up residence and speak their distinctive vernacular and occupy the public square alongside all competing world-views and courses of action. They offer a rival grand narrative among all the competing ones postmodernism makes room for. But they do claim that religion can insist on public space in a postmodern society. Arguments that religion should be barred from the public square in the name of the First Amendment's establishment clause are expressing a secular fundamental-ism to rival any fundamentalism that religion has produced.

The new social gospel after Trump that the church proposes in its pub-lic theology implies and assumes a new humanism, driven by a reconsidera-tion of the human prospect and the authorization of a theology of hope. That means a *new Christian humanism*. Early Christianity was bold to claim *theosis*, which is to say God became human that humans might become divine. To proclaim an elevated vision of the human today is to do so in a universe often construed as metaphysically meaningless and on an earth without a teleology and amidst an anthropology from which spirit has been subtracted, leaving only a materialist view of humanity.

A new humanism may find in humans "earth's angels," interdependent people rebuilding just communities on an earth reenchanted. Earth, as well as humans, deserves a convincing story, which it somehow lost with the rise of Enlightenment rationalism, science, and colonialism. This means that biology alone cannot define the limits of human nature, that rationalism does not equal the entire human enterprise or occupy all of public space, that modern science does not define all normative knowing.

Christians with imagination can see that in Jesus' ministry earth becomes capable of heaven. God's intention for the cosmos authorizes human hope as the correlate of God's own Becoming. The stage for God's Becoming must be erected by human hands.

The PTSD of modern America could be treated in the church as field hospital. But the remedies offered by Trumpian evangelicals will not create new worlds or bring wholeness to this one. The politics of fear and a nostalgic longing for an entitled American past are not the new social gospel we require. Nor are ironic detachment, metaphysical abstention, or abandoning the revolution to sloth. Between the human project on earth unbecoming or *becoming*, the latter is the better choice.

THEOSIS: ASPIRING TO GOD IN US, RETURNING TO OUR DESTINY

Most modern Christians, and certainly non-Christians other than New Age spiritual seekers, would be surprised, even aghast, at the idea prominent in the ancient church that God became human that humans might become divine. The early church fathers, in the Greek East more than the Latin West, affirmed this transaction with the Greek word *theosis*—deification. But the weight of Augustine's preoccupation with original sin, and Luther's stark distinction between the bound human will and the free grace of God, and the early American Protestantism propensity, led by Jonathan Edwards, to see "sinners in the hand of an angry God," not to mention a backing off from utopian views of human nature following the carnage of twentieth-century wars, make the divine capability of human nature, even when seen through the lens of Christ, a hard sell.

Consider the bold rhetoric of some of the early fathers of the Church. Whether rooted in the grace of God, or the power of the Holy Spirit sent over the earth, or the newly shared nature with Christ by virtue of the incarnation, Irenaeus, a second-century bishop-theologian, wrote that God has "become what we are, that He might bring us to be even what He is Himself." Within the Neoplatonist thought world of the church fathers, it was possible to imagine tracing an imperfect image back to a perfect original, returning from this imperfect world back to God's first idea in the garden of Eden.

Spirit in matter seems to have been God's big idea; the world and humans are God showing off. Irenaeus thought that original human nature had to be reexhibited, displaying God's original intentions, and after that what was mortal would be swallowed up in immortality. The Apostle Paul worked this out in his First Adam/Second Adam Christology. He wrote: "For this corruptible must put on incorruption, and this mortal must put on immortality" (1 Corinthians 15:53). Paul uses the phrase "in Christ" 165 times to suggest the immersion of human being in the incarnation of God in Christ.

Another second-century theologian, Clement of Alexandria, wrote that God in Christ became a man so we could learn from a man how to become a god. He added: "If one knows himself, he will know God, and knowing God will become like God." And it is always astonishing to read that a fourth-century Greek father, Athanasius, liked to say: "The Son of God became man so that we might become God." To an attentive ear, this may sound like the self-regard of the American Ralph Waldo Emerson or the optimism of Protestant liberals like the German Friedrich Schleiermacher, from whose legacy Karl Barth wanted a neo-orthodox Protestantism to escape. So what, then, are we to hope for? Only that Christians don't turn out to be even worse than everyone else.

Much of Christian theology has lost its nerve, given its determined realism about sin. John Wesley thought Luther's theology of justification as imputed righteousness stopped too soon and did not move on to the perfection of life. How are we doing with that ambition today? How strange that theologians of early Christianity, writing at a time when the order and reach of the Roman Empire had begun to decline and the classical world would be coming into disarray, should have such confident visions. Were they foretelling that Christianity's imagination would take root in human nature and culture?

Could we reopen this conversation at this beginning of the third millennium? Ontologically, talk of human transformation is aiming, with hopeful anticipation, at the incarnation. But the process was not just magical, something that happened suddenly at baptism. Both the Orthodox East and the Latin West paid considerable attention to how a prolonged spiritual practice—including meeting Christ in baptism and Eucharist, contemplative prayer, asceticism, mystical union, movements like monasticism, and yes simple people moving about practicing the "imitation of Christ"—could help to effect human transformation. But where is that today?

In early Christianity saints were seen as guarantors of continuing and persistent incarnation; they were deposits God was leaving to demonstrate God's abiding presence, Spirit on earth. We might say bread crumbs scattered about to lead us to our possibilities and our destination, to trigger the teleology built into us. While this vision has not mostly flourished on Protestant soil, the Quakers did imagine that the Presence of God on earth and the transformation that accompanies it could be accomplished by "standing still in the Light."

RECOVERING HUMAN AGENCY

The ongoing legacy of God's incarnation in Christ is to authorize ultimate hope for the earth and for our *life together* here. (Dietrich Bonhoeffer could imagine this in an underground seminary, only to achieve martyrdom a few years later.) That hope has been shaped by the primal story of the exodus, by the covenanted community envisioned by the Hebrew prophets, and by the God-human paradigm that is the ministry of Jesus. Together, these represent the future we could have, a new social gospel after Trump. (I understand how preposterous this may sound, coming from a Lutheran.) Don't Christians endlessly pray the Lord's Prayer, with this petition: "Thy will be done on earth as it is in heaven"? So earth is to become capable of heaven? To leverage this radical hope is to pull together until there is an overlay—Godspace and our space, to see human agency in a new way, to enter God's dreams for an open-ended future for earth, to find in each other intimations of God (Matthew 25)—even on the border, even sleeping on the streets, even amidst desperate workers trying to come together in unions for social justice.

If the universe is going to keep becoming, and if we are participating in the unfolding (if you like that term better) or completing of God, we will have to discover and create telling roles for humans laying claim to God's DNA. Anthropologists like Victor Turner saw that in primitive religious visions and rituals, God comes down to earth and "rides human horses." Ancient Israel experienced the power to move out of Egypt. *God's intention for the cosmos (Godspace) authorizes human hope (our space) as its correlate.* The prophets kept channeling Israel's exodus experience. The angels over Bethlehem announced that Jesus will be "good news for all the peoples." The Apostle Paul imagined a new creation and saw it as his task to begin gathering an eschatological harvest. The first fruit of the harvest is hope, and it creates the social capital for revolution. *Hope is the leverage required to expand human effort.* I say *leverage,* that Wall Street word, because we do not expect enough of ourselves and so must imagine our investment multiplied. We are always hunkering down, conceding, like those with Stockholm syndrome, our future prospects to historical determinism or to the ruling oligarchy. We are not to be taken in by the few who awaken to find themselves among the 1 percent and call it the end of history, certainly a premature ejaculation. The "woke" of cosmic consciousness is very different from the woke of Wall Street.

Of course it could be that human inertia is God's fault—which is to say, our view of God is seriously deficient, scaled down to our pessimism or relaxed ambitions and adjusted to a universe without good roles for us. (Bringing off a new social gospel in America would be quite a role.) Protestant Christianity is especially vulnerable to a *theology of grace that sucks the oxygen from the human stage.* Christians often bow to divine initiative and wait for God to take over. The highest many American evangelicals could hope for was the age of Trump. Pie in the sky will be served much later. So nothing happens; the revolution is indefinitely postponed. Sometimes the postponement of the revolution to heaven is funded by oligarchs to make sure nothing changes now.

When I was just out of graduate school and teaching my first courses in Christian thought and religious ethics, I was in a mood, fresh from Berkeley, to join the revolution. As I was reading Peter Brown's biography of Augustine, I came across a story that sucked the wind from my sails. The young contemporary of Augustine, Pelagius, rising fast in the Roman civil service, converts to Christianity. He hopes to use his fast-track abilities and his new religious commitment to change the world. In a still-famous series of arguments, in which Augustine distills the view of grace that is also Luther's (and my) inheritance, Augustine drowns Pelagius's enthusiastic ambitions with the line, "The church is never more than a hospital for sick sinners." In other words, Pelagius, don't get ahead of yourself.

But in the Hebrew Bible, God is "enthroned on the praises of Israel." If that is so, the divine zeppelin must be kept launched by human breath and effort. Perhaps God's dreams need a radical community like a black preacher needs the amens of the congregation. God plays the pipe organ, and we pump the bellows. The prophets understood that a platform for God's presence must be erected by human hands. In fact, God stories tend to have weak plots and no drama if there are no good lines for humans. God's DNA has to be sequenced, evidencing itself in a prophetic genome. And ours. To bring justice to all peoples, to reenchant the earth, to save the planet—these are worthy endeavors that require human imagination and action—empowered by God. To tantalize the believer and astonish the agnostic, consider this possibility: When we sign on to radical human endeavors, or decline them, *we become capable of contributing to, or diminishing, the Becoming of God—and the self-consciousness of the universe.*

Indeed, the Bible and subsequent religious history are brimming with fully engaged biographies, divine and human. I do not claim to have swallowed the Holy Ghost feathers and all (a pretension Luther once cautioned against), but I can imagine some of the themes through which humans reach new levels on their great ascent. But to start with God, consider the divine Becoming that God implies to Moses when God's name turns out to be: "I will be who I will be." Did God change as Israel moved out of Egypt? Did God agitate the prophets to keep the liberal DNA flowing? Moses spoke reckless truth to established power and cried, "Let my people go." Elijah mocked sycophantic priests and their gods, made himself an enemy of the state, and battered through the high wall enclosing the king's preserve with an audacious "Word of the Lord." God sowed the divine seed indiscriminately. Including in the king's face.

In the New Testament, the Virgin Mary "offers her consent" to energizing grace and becomes a model for humans who acquire (or recover) "agency" through interacting with God. (One can pause to reflect on the possibility that Mary should be ordained the patron saint of Christian agency. Oh, Catholics have already done that.) While it is true that Paul became the messenger of sovereign grace, he also converted the electrifying appearance of the risen Christ (a divine initiative) into a robust and frightening calling that speeds the Christian movement across the Roman world and risks all for the sake of a gospel that transgressed every social boundary and limitation (a human response). Yes, Augustine championed grace, but, in a startling effort of social and theological imagination, he filled the empty shell of a declining Roman empire with the burgeoning energy and new vision of the new Christianity. Yes, the "Benedict Option" consisted in a visionary saint establishing monastic communities (a new social gospel?) across a Europe in danger of losing its way. Yes, Luther argued that the way to God was a gift, but he also turned Christendom on its head and led a forced march back to the liberation of rediscovered sources. In all such cases, *watch how they act*, even as they're humbly giving God all the glory. God did not steal the oxygen from their revolutionary settings. Even contemporary Lutherans can surmount their quietism and think boldly. Carl Braaten went beyond the tidiness of Luther's two-kingdoms doctrine, in which the gospel prevails in the church and earthly powers prevail in the world. He imagined a revolutionary dynamic in which the gospel in the midst of the Christian community *sets off explosions in the secular world.*

The problem with much of the Lutheran (and Christian) past is that the eschatological dynamic of the gospel was shielded and not released into the power situations that decide for or against the inner historical transformation of society. So no new social gospel.

When Moses and Elijah and Mary and Paul and Augustine and Benedict and Aquinas and Hildegard of Bingen and Luther and Calvin and Martin Luther King Jr. saw and spoke and acted, the earth shook. They were great humans moving stridently across history and turning seized opportunities into new creations. Of course, they thought God's unexpected self-giving was what mattered. But they were not secretaries taking dictation. They were flesh and blood, fully vernacularized humans who turned the world upside down with inspired human energy and ambition and vision. They spoke new languages that held new ideas and sponsored new action. If our ultimate human calling is to write God's biography onto our age, as Augustine did, it is also "composing a life," living out an occupied Christianity in public space.

Secularists, too, have wanted to release human agency. Marx hoped to create the conditions for the emergence of "the new socialist man." Human nature can be altered, he was sure. Ironically, Marxist visionaries hoped to create an anti-religious religion, in which the faithful would be atheists and the religiously devout would be written off as blasphemers of human nature who doubt the human project of changing the world.

It is not going too far to speak of the "human ascent." In the religious imagination, human striving can be seen as following in the train of a daring God. The secular Tony Judt and others insist that the pursuit of material self-interest is not the summation of the human dream, but a wrong road taken only in the late twentieth century when capitalist thinkers made it the dominant human virtue.

Nancy MacLean's *Democracy in Chains: The Deep History of the Radical Right's Stealth Plan for America* elaborately documents the gradual destruction of any chances for social democracy. Or a new social gospel. (And this is why we got Trump.) American political economics is determined to drown the incipient Christian vision in the bathwater of late capitalism. Some assert that America's golden age of compassion was being eclipsed toward the end of the 1970s, coincidental with the rise of Reagan's presidency. The New Deal was ditched for good in 1980. Decades of social legislation and economic oversight for the common good were dismantled. The survival of the fittest, individual pursuit, and government (which FDR imagined thinking and acting together on behalf of the commons) came to be defined as the problem, thus drastically reducing collective purpose on behalf of the commons. What is remarkable is that a certain kind of

American evangelical (and Catholic) Christianity threw its weight behind this hopeless program—or was invaded and overtaken and converted by political operatives who bought Rightist Christianity off with promises of a restoration of their lost place in society. Intimations of a social gospel were surrendered in exchange for the abolition of homosexuality and abortion and the denial of equal status to women.

But for many progressive secular thinkers, and for progressive religion, a call for a new social gospel, a commitment to cultural and religious diversity not overruled by capitalism in the public square, and above all the possibility and virtue of collective action for the common good are essential to the human project. Such a revolutionary program includes such heresies as good government and institutions working for the good of the commons. Europe practices such social democracy, with well-developed habits of the heart, even if it has forgotten how to preach it.   *Elaborate!!*

These days the Gini coefficient documents the astonishing gap separating rich and poor everywhere, and among the Western democracies the United States leads the way in inequality. What an achievement! What a reversal of the human prospect. Religious establishments and moral zealots cannot even remember how to preach the good of the whole, though visions of covenant justice between God and the community are conspicuously evident in the Old and New Testament. They are still alive in the preoccupied house that is the Christian heritage. For good reason, "thinking the commons" today is as difficult as thinking about a liberal God in the public square, not to mention doing something about it, in a society of individualized identity politics and economics. Conservative religion has acquired the audacity to proclaim that democratic socialism is not only unachievable but would be a moral hazard and against God's providence. Without religious vision, people find it impossible to comprehend or acknowledge what we have in common with others. A loss of the prophetic genome means we can no longer project onto the social imaginary a state embracing and enacting the common good. Or see ourselves as collaborators with a liberating God on a grand project. If we could recover the communal memory of ancient Israel and historic Christianity, we could locate ourselves amidst God's intentions for a new earth.

Marx and others have decried human estrangement from our own agency and from the fruits of our own labors. Alienated humans have lost sight of themselves as creators of human culture and agents of their own destiny. Marx blamed religion for this, seeing it as an opium that clouds the human vision of its self-making destiny. Many modern theologians concede that Christians have often told their God-stories in ways that overwhelm, rather than complement and empower, the human story. Christianity has sometimes given the world a Christ in whom we can no longer find our own humanity, with only a projected distant God remaining, a gold nugget dropped from outer space. When contemporary critics *oppose humanism to religion*, they mean to decry a God who acts but leaves humans without a role—divine intervention and human passivity. But progressive religion with a high Christology imagines humans, in concert with God, remending the world they themselves have torn. They wager a new age of possibility by leveraging human responsible action in the present.

RECONSIDERING THE STILL-EVOLVING HUMAN PROJECT

The anthropologist Clifford Geertz argued that forms of human culture began to appear before physical evolution had run its course, so that *nature and culture* then must have proceeded together. Culture had become a part of human development before the evolution of the brain was complete, but eventually culture would outrun evolutionary biology. The *essentialist human nature assumed by many evolutionary biologists* stands in opposition to this view. In the social science view, "humanization," including religious propensities, continues to occur along cultural pathways. *We're not done yet.* There could lie on the horizon unimagined achievements of social justice and of interdependent life in community on an earth reenchanted.

Social capital is a cultural and religious product. Christian theologian Sallie McFague calls contemporary Christianity to move beyond a Son of God who does everything and leaves humans with nothing to do. The early Christian theologian Irenaeus famously postulated that *the glory of God is humanity fully alive.* It was radical in the second century and now as well to suggest that God is only fully God when men and women are fully human, so to many conservatives today this will not even sound like a Christian viewpoint. Progressive religion entertains the possibility that the biblical story invites humans to become estimable partners with God and that the fulfillment of this calling is the means through which the universe evolves.

In a Christmas liturgy the Church prays: "Father of our Lord Jesus Christ, our glory is to stand before the world as your own sons and daughters. May the simple beauty of Jesus' birth summon us always to love what is most deeply human, and to see your Word made flesh reflected in those whose lives we touch." In this prayer, divine incarnation beckons humanity to its ever fuller realization. Historic Catholic theology imagines God and humans as a dazzling entanglement of grace and nature. A long tradition in Judaism, resurrected today by progressive Jews often aligned with progressive Christians, sees the highest human calling as "repairing [or mending] the earth" (*tikkun*).

None of this is antithetical to science, the humanities, or the social sciences. This is not an irrational religious vision. Humans, who are the expansion of nature and the product of evolution, come to self-realization as *evolving co-creators in the universe*. In the freedom for which nature seems to have prepared us, in the evolution from biology to culture, in the self-consciousness of the universe, we *stretch the systems of nature so they can participate in cosmic purposes*. We do not allow our imagination of a just society to be hemmed by a late capitalism whose vision ends with the 1 percent.

A new humanity is both our evolutionary possibility and our evolutionary task. We are not finished evolving, but it's now in the realm of culture. Religious humanism more than evolutionary biology prevails.

ENLIGHTENMENT RATIONALISM SHOULD NOT SOLELY OCCUPY PUBLIC SPACE

For a long time faith and reason lived in balance, each making its unique contribution, each in tension with the other, each adding to the play of life. They were two ends of the teeter-totter. What happens when there is no dialectic?

The point of discussing reason and rationality now is to *see to it that human reason, under secular auspices, is not one-sidedly employed to rule out religion in public*. While "faith and reason" has a millennia-long discourse tradition, it has become common among public intellectuals and developers of public policy to argue that a secular-rational discourse should be the only lingua franca now allowed in the public squares—or specifically in governmental deliberations. At first glance, this is not a silly or intolerant argument, since presumably everyone speaks this language of reason, and the multiplicities of *religious* views are more likely to produce division than unity. The European Union manages to conduct itself in English as a purely utilitarian measure, without implying any denigration of the multiple vernaculars that flourish within its boundaries. But the appeal to reason as a univocal entity among all peoples is almost certainly suspect, and probably wrong. Feminists and anti-colonialists, for example, not to mention Marx or Freud or Kierkegaard, notice that reason all too easily dances to male Enlightenment tunes.

So a second look notices the questionable implications of the decree that in the public square of an exceedingly complex multiculture, only one network-standard, familiarly accented voice is permitted to speak. Imagine someone coming to testify before a city council hearing, or in a national debate, or in a letter to the editor, or at a hospital ethics committee, and be explicitly disallowed to draw arguments or insights from the religious worldview that encompasses everything that is most important and deeply felt—the fullest meaning of that person's life.

Of course, reason/religion is not the only binary. When Justice Sotomayor was being interviewed for a Supreme Court nomination, conservative senators took great exception to the suggestion that her womanhood and her Hispanic character might influence her legal voice. The voice of a white male was how a Justice was supposed to sound, the only voice that needed to be heard.

If varying worldviews produce vernaculars unique to themselves because they are specially honed carriers of meaning, they are on notice that, when in public, *only the voice of one worldview is permitted—and that is a (white) Enlightenment worldview. But precisely that viewpoint has come under radical postmodern questioning.* Let there be no denial that different cultures and genders and orientations and religions speak uniquely nuanced languages, which have grown out of them organically.

We have recently learned to acknowledge that there are *no disinterested voices*, no voice without a social location or point of view, including the voice of Enlightenment rationalism. Consider the points of view Thomas Jefferson's rationalism was easily able to overlook. Every voice comes encumbered with culture, economics, politics, and power. Every voice arrives trailing its own claims, its own stakeholders, its own preoccupation with and domestication in a particular worldview, its own *privilege*. Every voice, every mode of reasoning, is socially located in some discourse community, e.g. property owners.

The idea that the voice of (a sometimes militant) secular rationality is sufficient to speak for all kinds and conditions and times of human life and that it therefore can readily be enforced without harm to anyone else no longer bears close examination. Such an argument must go the way of the argument that the masculine pronoun actually includes all or that whiteness is a useful summary of all of humanity and we needn't worry about white skin privilege. The heart, too, may have reasons that lucid rationality cannot express. Champions of pure reason must consider a long line of detractors, beginning in the modern age with the Romantics, who challenge its unexamined triumphalism.

Two further clarifications are necessary. *Rationality* is a wider term than often admitted and it should not be reduced (or expanded) to *rationalism*. Religious assertions or ethical reflection cannot automatically be construed as irrational. Most theology, though perhaps not most mysticism, speaks in rational sentences and uses rational arguments when constructing a convincing worldview. Moral theologians and ethicists make their cases through rational argument. The issue here is *a particular kind of rationality that comes locked in the assumptions of an entire secular worldview*, which may imply the exclusion of religion or the *methodological individualism* of "rational choice theory" and its assumption of *homo economicus*. Many economists seem to believe that people who do not think and act with the mind of the market are not playing in the real world.

The other issue is that religious people, or others who speak in their most meaningful vernaculars, may still, from time to time, deliberately choose to confine themselves to the lingua franca of secular rationality. They may do this for strategic reasons, for example, to win over the largest possible sympathetic audiences. But they should not be required to dispense with being true to their own inner voices. Telling the religious to keep silent belongs in the same category as telling women, or blacks, or the southern hemisphere, or non property owners, to keep silent—or learn the accented sounds of landed, privileged, white males before speaking in public.

Speaking in two different languages or styles (*code switching*), for example, religious vs. secular, rational vs. romantic, standard English vs. dialect, once considered substandard or even ignorant, may occur for several reasons. A particular topic may suggest or require more than one language or symbol system. Quotations from another culture or even another point of view may evoke a different discourse style. A different symbol system may reflect a different group identity or discourse community. Nuances and values may require a vernacular other than one kind of rationalism to achieve proper expression. The insistence that everyone speak or make an argument in a single rationalist style may seriously discriminate or narrow the base of public argument.

A monoculture of purely rationalist discourse comes with its own dubious history. Postmodernism celebrates diversity and is suspicious of the totalizing unity of single, universally imposed grand narratives. The much vaunted lucid rationality of the Enlightenment is not without its downside. This was the language that prevailed in and was used to justify the world of colonialism and, eventually, late capitalism. When such a rationalism prevails as the law of the market and excludes religious or spiritual sensibilities, it eliminates, on principle, indigenous voices and compels all to speak in the network standard of Wall Street bankers—or of materialism or secularism. Was the "separation of church and state," still a persistent theme in Supreme Court cases and militant secularism, really meant to install one discourse style as the only allowed language in the public square? We need to make a distinction between an established church and the right to religious speech. We do not intend to be told to "go back to where you came from."

Some Christian philosophical traditions, and also Romanticism, have risen to argue that a full account of humanity must always include head and heart, matter and spirit. Thomas Aquinas famously envisioned a cosmos in which the *knower and the known* are joined in effective embrace. *Without religious language, will some things become unknowable, unclaimable?*

So it may be best to acknowledge that our postmodern age of diversity and multiplicity has also become, in some sense, a *post-secular* age, as well as a post-colonial age and a post-Enlightenment rationalism age. That is, we no longer can convincingly argue that once there was religion and now there is reason, once there was Christendom and now there is secularism. If the *establishment clause* of the First Amendment is taken to mean clearing religion from public settings, that would require the elimination of the *free exercise clause.* The American Constitution gave us a system of government without an establishment religion; it did not intend to grant us a public square free of religious discourse, argument, sentiment, values.

SCIENCE SHOULD NOT DEFINE ALL
NORMATIVE KNOWING

The famous evolutionary biologist, atheist, and critic of religion Richard Dawkins has seemed to claim that the universe scientists believe they have discovered has precisely the properties we should expect if there is, at bottom, no design, no purpose, no evil, no good, nothing but blind, pitiless indifference. We are riding a spaceship to nowhere, and with no point.

The greatest legacy of the modern world, certainly in the West, appears to be science—its methodologies and its results. To speak of *leveraging the human condition by appeal to eschatological hope*, a theme of this chapter, is also to involve the role of science in extending human knowledge and action and evolution. So successful has science become, however, and so indebted are we to its achievements, that humans are likely to make the mistake of creating or consenting to a monoculture in which *the only compelling variable when considering the course of the world or the universe is a certain kind of science and the only significant actors are scientists.* The point of discussing science here is to open the possibility of *religion and science fully embracing* each other on the way to leveraging human hope for a new earth with renewed people.

In the West, some (not limited to religious fundamentalists) worry that science may be elbowing every other way of knowing out of mind. Is there still room for meanings other than those defined and disclosed by science? Have many scientists deliberately intended to substitute science for religion or the humanities and social sciences, or has this happened by accident? Human eyes are blinded by the shock and awe of compounding *scienceandtechnology* and enticed by its benefits, but in some ways it went out of control in the second half of the twentieth century, portending environmental destruction or nuclear tragedy as it came into subservience to the national security state and international capitalism. Science, part of nature, seemed to deliver us from nature, offering the power to subdue and reify nature. And science, *a part of culture*, seemed to lord it over all other cultural pathways so only what can be counted counts.

But when humans or the cosmos lose their own grand stories and science alone is the default grand narrative, we are in trouble. Humans habitually ask for explanations, and many philosophers and theologians wonder what it is about us that makes us imagine that such questions and answers are possible. But some influential scientists profess no such interest and seem to aspire to displace all other forms of inquiry. Yet science is also a human culture, and a socially located and often economically subservient one at that, its ideological pretension of objectivity notwithstanding.

The biography of science and scientists is circuitous and not always more admirable than that of religion and the humanities, theologians, and artists. Problems that we acutely suffer from today began when the philosopher Descartes objectified the world and subordinated it wholly to man as the dominating human subject. Descartes split the universe into subject and object. Critical reason became the objectifying, distancing, controlling, outward gaze of the (male) thinker, scientist, explorer, colonist. Their questions became how to discover and acquire, how to reconstrue yet unclaimed space as the feminized other—how to discover, as Columbus wrote, the new world as a breast with paradise at its nipple. (Unfortunately, colonizing Christianity made similar assumptions.) Francis Bacon saw nature as female and the mandate of science to force it to yield, be penetrated, be subjugated. Deism, preferring a no-longer-involved distant God, freed science to investigate the world apart from any divine connection, apart from any hallowing story. *Deism is less a name for a God who withdrew than it is for a God who was exiled from human consideration.* It conspired with the Enlightenment to drive the gods (the sacred) out of matter, even to declare there is *no spirit, only matter,* while this book argues that *spirit in matter is God's great idea.*

Science, after all, and scientists, belong to earth, to the culture, to humanity; they are part of our mental ecology, they do not sit above it. Science, as well as all alternative quests, is a human construction. When science, having set itself free from religion and the humanities, fell into a *rival metaphysic, materialism,* it became a replacement religion and it was argued or assumed that *the matter that science masters is all there is.* If you cannot make meaning in scientific terms, then there is no meaning. Bound to such a philosophy, science often buried the lead—the story that the universe may be unfolding purposefully, evolving into self-consciousness and self-reflection, from an original radiance to our present radical amazement. Many scientists failed to see themselves as the leading edge of this self-reflection, and so they carried out their great work not in awe but with the mentality of the conqueror and the colonizer, learning to *replace enlarging wonder with arrogant reductionism.*

Recent science, especially theoretical physics, offers the means for science to get out of its quagmire of meaningless and reductionist materialism. Quantum theory suggests that the assumed reliable world of rationality is fitful and indeterminate at its subatomic roots. Counterintuitive quantum theory suggests the limited effectiveness of the world of "common sense" to which modernity was so committed and religion surrendered. It hints at a togetherness-in-separation, so that two entities that once interacted retain a power to affect each other, suggesting an unexpected holism in the universe. Theoretical physics seems able to posit an un-picturable electron because it positively relates to what else is known. Theology similarly conjures un-picturable spiritual realities. Global positioning devices that track every human move from distant satellites, even foretelling traffic jams ahead, can seem more astonishing than any Christian claims about God. And we are happy to trust in them, even finding them indispensable. (Meanwhile, Google Maps may have its own profit-making agendas.)

Consider this: If an atom were the size of the dome of St. Peter's in Rome, the largest dome in the world, then its nucleus would be the size of a grain of salt. Imagine all the world in between! Even that nucleus, thought to be the very matter that was the bedrock of an entire scientific enterprise, turns out to be a dance of energy. Matter, the foundation of the materialist worldview that cancelled every God hypothesis, turns out to be energy moving in patterns of relationship, unpredictably. We cannot observe it without changing it. The total set of conditions discoverable by science is insufficient to determine any precise outcome. There may be an ontological indeterminacy in nature. Nature is not closed, Newton was wrong, and William Blake called on poetry to awaken us "from single vision and Newton's sleep."

Still, religious fundamentalists go on decrying, mistrusting, and slandering science, and scientific fundamentalists go on celebrating freedom from religion as one of the "assured results" of the modern age. Consider the irony, as some see it at least, that modern science reached its great achievements in Christian Europe and this was no accident. The European

Christian legacy is a created universe with logical and consistent workings susceptible to reason and inquiry. In the Middle Ages, Thomas Aquinas, in some ways channeling Aristotle, insisted on the rationality of God. In Aquinas's view, the most promising way of *knowing is an encounter between the inquiring subject and the elusive object,* not a confrontation but a collaboration—each giving itself to the other. Finding its place between grace and nature, the mind actively participates in reality and by raising the inherent intelligibility of objects to light brings both them and its own powers to fruitful self-realization. The created world, as Aquinas saw it, becomes more real in the act of being understood, and the believing mind comes into its own in the process. In the act of knowing, not in the imperialistic act of objectifying, subject and object become one. *Religious and scientific knowledge are aspects of our collusion in reality.*

The alleged lifelong battle between science and religion is a false dead end rather than a comprehensive historical account. The face-off between science and religion has misguided enthusiasts on both sides. Many modern scientists have turned themselves into antireligious ideologues who make claims far beyond those that can justifiably be made by empirical science and who seem out to settle private scores or personal pique. Perhaps the real retreat from reason is the assertive claim that the universe came out of nowhere and that everyone is one meaningless accident, even while Einstein was saying that the real mystery is that the universe is intelligible to us. Meanwhile, Christianity has much to repent for, especially its persecution of some scientists in the premodern age. And today's passionate fundamentalists have turned their suspicions of Darwinism as the meaning of life into anti-intellectual, know-nothing political ideology.

Creationists seem caught in this impasse between science and religion, as conservative Christians cheer them on and scientists loathe them. But are creationists wrong to inquire whether the universe is driven by larger meaning and purpose, that religious thinkers and scientists and God and the earth may all be participants in the universe's unfolding consciousness? Or is their only mistake that they call what they are doing science, rather than religion? Or does that critique make the assumption that science and religion can never, ever join in asking similar questions?

There are more promising ways to think about the relationship between science and religion. Theologians and philosophers of science like John Polkinghorn, Ted Peters, and Ian Barbour suggest several common ways of thinking about it: conflict, mutual independence, dialogue, and integration. Could we move from conflict to integration?

The *conflict* model currently prevails. Scientific materialism provides all the knowledge that can be known, the natural world is the only reality, and religious knowledge is only pseudo-knowledge. Scientific imperialism seeks to conquer religion's territory and claim it as its own. Meanwhile, religious imperialism, as in the case of Pope Pius IX or contemporary fundamentalists, denounces science as an error of modernity.

Mutual independence sees science and religion as two quite different "discourse communities" who speak different languages and (perhaps) talk about different things. Science and religion are two different domains, two different languages, two different realities—the age of rocks and the rock of ages (Stephen Gould). Things go wrong when they enter each other's turf, when religion makes implicitly scientific claims and science proposes itself as a metaphysical worldview rather than a methodology of inquiry.

Dialogue proposes to cross the divide and begin an open-ended, nondefensive conversation, perhaps beginning with methodological parallels between the two.

The most daring approach is *integration,* in which science and religion share the questions. If the God question were postulated from within scientific reasoning, perhaps some consonances would emerge. What if the environmental crisis is also a spiritual issue? New Age spirituality wants to overcome dualism in a new age of holism.

Perhaps God moves over creation by actualizing various potentialities, improvising all the fugal derivations and combinations possible—like Bach's musical offering exploring the capacity of a fugue? Scientists, too, can be fanciful. Brian Swimme writes: "The universe is a green dragon. Green, because the whole universe is alive, an embryogenesis beginning with the cosmic egg of the primeval fireball and culminating in the present emergent reality. Dragons are mystical, powerful, emerging out of mystery, disappearing in mystery, fierce, benign, known to teach humans the deepest reaches of wisdom. We are dragon fire. We are the creating, scintillating, searing, healing flame of the awesome and enchanting universe."

THE PTSD AGE AND CHRISTIANITY AS FIELD HOSPITAL

It is intriguing to consider the claim that God friends us and sets us free, that this is convincingly witnessed to in the Hebrew Bible and the Christian New Testament, that we are the heirs of this legacy, that we have been moved by this discovered treasure to bet the farm, adopt the religious life that thrives in the community of the church, and wade into the reimagination of the human project and recover the language of hope.

Why then does our age seem stuck? Was the situation that gave us Trump and the trump cards he persistently played our irreversible destiny as a society? Was Pogo right: "We have met the enemy and he is us"? Why doesn't American Christianity look more redeemed? Why does a new social gospel seem like a dream? Are we the first-century invalids to whom Jesus said: "Get up and walk"? Americans suffer from a *post-traumatic stress syndrome*.

Here's what our chart says as we await release from the field hospital. The tight embrace of a national security state, the assured certainties of American exceptionalism, the extraordinary expenditures required by perpetual militarization and the far-flung outposts of empire, the redemptive violence of unending war on terror, an utterly unregulated free market in a world of banksters—these are what ails us, not our medicines. The current free market triumphalism requires the economic privileging of the fittest and takes a write-off on the pillaging of the earth, while the poor and working classes sink under the contagions of the market whose claims, like a god's, cannot be questioned. All of us are somehow estranged from the earth whose care we have abandoned, but we are unable to *name and mourn the lost mother*. Everywhere one observes a desperate escalation of individualism seeking personal salvation supplied by urban outfitters, an obscene accumulation of wealth on Wall Street, and a coincident trashing of the commons.

Most disheartening, some of those who suffer most from the current diagnosis have turned to evangelical Christianity as divine comfort for their lives and immunization against an anguished grief that could have turned into a radical prophetic critique—just as Marx predicted. False doctors, false cures. Many Christians seem immune to the good news available from the self-giving God of the Bible, unwilling to be connected to the biblical IV drip. They are addicted to a variety of opioids: everything is in God's hands; the American economic system is fair and requires no governmental intervention; anything is possible through hard work; healthy people do not deserve unemployment benefits or food stamps. Steadily tuned to Fox News above their beds, they do not see that it is time to get up and walk out of Egypt. When Moses makes rounds, they prefer the fleshpots they know to a counterintuitive new gospel in the wilderness. They are angry, but they cannot name the source of their condition. And they vote Republican. Almost as much as they believe in God, they believe government in the form of social democracy is not, cannot, be the answer. Social justice is fake news and fake medicine.

So is the entire country a field hospital owned and operated by the 1 percent? Wall Street demands its endowments while Main Street rages. The gap between the bonused and the foreclosed relentlessly widens. The field hospital seems staffed by volunteers from the Christian Right, who seem enthusiastic and confident. They're actually the self-confident chaplains. And by Catholic and Protestant volunteers who seem timid. Will the latter get the country off their opioids and come up with a new social gospel that will save the country? Social visionaries yearn for *public* selves who accept responsibility for constructing a good society beyond shelters. They lament the vast unbuilt spaces between atomized individuals and the national security state—wastelands in effect. In the face of cynicism about all institutions, from government to schools to churches to unions, we have lost the intuition that a fully engaged life requires social embodiment and social capital. The worst thing to say about public schools is to call them "guv'ment schools." Yet people used to know that good institutions make good societies. We have forgotten that the common good is the pursuit of the good in common. Instead, we have made on-your-own independence the stellar value in a skewed hierarchy where adolescent posturing crowds out adult virtues such as mutual care and generativity—Erik Erikson's word for a deep concern for future generations that comes over old age. Something entirely new is necessary. We are humans bereft of our true humanity, and another name for that diagnosis is the absence of God. We've been sent to long-term rehab and there may be no exit back to normal. The prevailing diagnosis is a sick social system occupied by disencumbered selves (the victims of a wildly free market) or unencumbered (libertarians and the wealthy) selves. The loss of consensus on the public good is far more prevalent in the United States than in Europe. The commitment to the whole, once at the top of a values hierarchy, may be called by its European name, social democracy— or even by that archaic term, Christian socialism. It assumes and invites collective action for the collective good, motivated by religious vision. In this view, for example, taxation, including progressive taxation, is a necessary contribution to culture and nation, not a government seizure, a positive good not a necessary evil. But we have *lost the language* for this exchange. In the hospital chapel stands an altar for the *worship of the private sector.*

MISPLACING SIN

It would be a mistake to assume that having a liberating and self-giving God would set us free from the concept of sin. Or that a post-religious age has no need of such a category. The human situation east of Eden has issues. In the midst of America's post-traumatic stress disorder, with a littered landscape and massive social capital pilfered from the commons, we need realistic categories of analysis. The secular intelligentsia has proclaimed liberation from the idea of sin because sin requires a concept of God or religion. Much of psychiatry has dispensed with sin because its correlate, guilt, has been deemed a maladaptive emotion. Some say that "original sin" has cast a pall over Christianity. Progressives give up sin because it seems anti-world, anti-sex, anti-female, anti-pleasure.

It may be time to reconceptualize sin. Women have found a flaw in the Promethean story of flying too close to the sun, overreaching. But patriarchal cultures force women into a different sin, underreaching. In a society where 1 percent profit and all the rest suffer, which sin needs to be called out and what is its name? Many moralists have determined that worrying over girls' virginity is the way to save our commonwealth. This takes our eyes off the ball.

If we misplace sin, we won't have the concept ready when we need it. Every Sunday morning, many Christians confess: "We are captive to sin and cannot free ourselves." Is this overdoing it? Is the issue being down on ourselves in a way that leads to low self-esteem, or finding and naming the really big sins when coming before God? What kinds of sins are useful to confess? How far should we go with self and societal examination? Looking around, we see a prevalence of greed and delusion, a powerful instinct to dominate and possess, the persistence of injustice, chronic anxieties that lead to hate and exploitation. Where do these sins fit in the human taxonomy? What about the unending disgrace of political practice in Washington? Reinhold Niebuhr thought original sin the most empirically confirmable of all Christian doctrines. Jim Wallis of Sojourners proposed that America does suffer from an original sin, and its name is white racism. Marx thought the original sin that drives capitalist systems is the systematic robbing and betrayal of workers. As "masters of suspicion," Freud and Marx taught us to doubt the self-serving stories we tell. What if there were public ceremonies where whites in particular confessed the long history of racism in the United States and in particular their own complicity? What if "Columbus Day" became a national repentance for genocide?

It seems that the Christian tradition, even with all its unfortunate detours, is the most realistic about the dark side of the human condition. Is there a root sin, from which all others grow? Consider self-centeredness or estrangement from our own better destiny or insisting on being disencumbered from all others. Is there a better word than sin, so everyone could think fresh thoughts and not get mired in resentments against religion or liberal/conservative contests? Depending on how we rename sin, *liberation rather than forgiveness* may be a better word for its solution. Above all, we must stop looking away and see that *sin is at least as embedded in social and political structures as it is gerrymandered in the evil hearts of nearly everyone.* Demonic sin is the perverse magnet to which all the filings of evil cling. Social and economic sin is the toxic accumulation of poisons in the pubic watersheds.

Sin seems to include thinking too much of ourselves—or too little. In this book the issues that count as sin are relapsing into nihilism or ironic detachment, giving up on a meaningful world, deciding God is too high maintenance for a good relationship. *Giving up on the revolution may be the greatest sin.* Sin is "settling"; sin is smugly or deplorably going around repeating "It is what it is"—the formula for resignation and self-knowing detachment.

The pervasive sin of the First World is to deny interdependency with all others and with the earth in order to favor the autonomy of the unencumbered, voracious, aggrandizing self—or nation or the 1 percent. A therapeutic culture gives no evidence of having cured us of this predilection, so jettisoning the concept of sin is proving to be a powerful delusion.

Progressive religion sees sin as a human propensity for *unbecoming*—the failure to evolve. The early women's movement often spoke of unreconstructed (evolutionary failures) male chauvinists whose long time is up. Hope wagers that society and we ourselves are on the way to justice and human fulfillment, and sin names the great refusal that is despair, apathy, or ironic detachment. *Unbecoming is the false consciousness that there are no meaningful choices and no possibilities and no obligations.*

The great mistake of conservative religion is to locate all the sin to worry about in personal moral behavior, or in the lives of others. So conservative religion specializes in homosexuality and is profoundly anxious about dangerous female sexuality, with abortion as the indispensable litmus test. When conservative obsessions have the monopoly on defining sin, progressive religion looks like no religion at all.

Progressive religion worries about sin, like heavy metals, accumulating in powerful institutions and in the market and among oligarchs—as well as in indifferent human hearts. Americans love to believe that terrorism is the organized violence of foreign individuals, not the massive apparatus of oppressive states, over there and over here. To name, unmask, and engage systemic sin (and our own complicity) is a profoundly empowering religious practice. It diagnoses the presence of sin inside the all-powerful political and economic structures of society. The Bible was not going too far after all when it imagined some sin as nothing less than *demonic*—so powerful it may take religious power and authority to call it out. Some moral theologians and ethicists now suggest that American capitalism may have a defective DNA that requires fundamental genetic modification, or new evolutionary mutations. Such powers are idolatrous forces that must be condemned in the name of God and of all the peoples of the earth. Conferring on these forces of worldwide domination a spiritual dimension that must religiously be contested means that demons are not located in an otherworldly devil nor projected conveniently onto our enemies. Life on earth is where they must be *named, engaged, and overcome,* as Walter Wink has argued in his trilogy on this topic. So economics and politics must be theologized—if we are to understand their demonic potential. This is why progressive politics needs progressive religion, with its capacity to symbolize in great cosmic stories what we are up against.

AUTHORIZING HOPE: HOW MANY ARE PREPARING A LANDING STRIP FOR A CIRCLING GOD?

During that utopian and now mostly forgotten time of candidate Obama's first yes-we-can, it seemed to some that they were signing up for the ultimate campaign, preparing the landing strip for God's arrival, for the rebirth of America, and the revival of the human project. Not much of that happened. Too much drama would have been required. When the second Obama campaign was successful and a new coalition born, it was still clear that God was not exactly circling overhead, waiting only for an all-clear from the Democratic tower. Our hope project was not radically ambitious, did not face its impediments, remained a hostage to economic forces that seemed more powerful than ever. (No one goes to jail for capitalist crimes.) And Obama's rhetoric never produced a come-to-Jesus moment for American society—the revolution was postponed or overpowered. Neither Obama nor Christians who adored him were speaking the language of a new social gospel, though various Catholic and neo-Anabaptist and some mainstream Protestants were releasing confessional statements that called the church to address and respond to the times—with something like a new social gospel.

America had not been hurrying to audition—or be auditioned by— the liberating God of the Bible. Although we are in political and economic crisis, its religious dimension until recently has been the *apparent unavailability of God for the road ahead.* (God doesn't do unregulated free market capitalism or governments that think small on purpose.) The churches are overdue projecting such a God on the social imaginary. Then we will be able to follow the signals and march out of Egypt.

Not everyone on the left is feeling *the absence of God,* and theological language is not the only medium for registering our present dilemma. Negotiating God's return from exile will not resonate with everyone who seeks the good of the land. The Democratic Party, with deep debts to secularism, does not seem determined to carry biblical visions of liberation. That we find ourselves homeless in the cosmos or living in society with a compromised conscience is not identified by everyone as a *theological* problem. Social justice for all and a protected and sustaining earth do not have to be experienced as religious callings. But the argument of this book is that the present crisis is best understood religiously and we should not continue to evade the call of God.

HOPE ANTICIPATES HEAVEN ON THE WAY

In *The Difference Heaven Makes,* Christopher Morse argued that heaven can be seen as the life that is now coming toward us from God, a life that overshadows our present age. The New Testament story of Jesus' ascension implies that the life he entered is the very life that is now coming toward us. God's unbounded love wants to break in to every situation. We don't go to heaven; heaven comes to us.

In chapters 1 and 2 we rehearsed the God-stories in the Hebrew Bible and the Christian New Testament. The accumulation of their power did not come to an end when the New Testament canon closed. Consider hope and heaven as intimations of God, scattered through human culture and still discoverable today when decoded by those who go looking for good news from God. There is also the possibility that God may be living among us under assumed names. Even in the Bible God is sometimes in disguise.

From early Christianity to the present, heaven has symbolized effervescent Christian hope, leaving untold metaphorical deposits in human language, without which our imaginations would be greatly impoverished. At times, heaven became the pie in the sky by and by, the sole hope for people, like American blacks, in devastating circumstances from which no earthly delivery could be imagined. But they did imagine it, and turned it into song. But even oftener, that view of heaven became an excuse, for oppressors, to postpone God's dreams and human responsibility for creating a new earth with good news for all the people. This may have been human pessimism, or the rejection of human agency in favor of God's grace, or lazy thinking, or human inertia and sloth, but in the interests of the powerful and the wealthy it became an excuse for not challenging the status quo. Billionaires helped fund the delay of heaven. In effect the rich said, *We have ours and you will get yours eventually. But it will take an eternity for the promised trickle down.* To this day, a very significant percentage of American Christians fully subscribe to this view, and they are waiting in line for theirs while morally cluck-clucking those who do fail to see wealth coming to them around the corner. It may be they cannot imagine a new earth now, or that their conservative politics tell them what we have is the best we can do, or that a new earth might imply governmental efforts on behalf of the common good, which they on principle oppose, or that social justice and a planetary ethic are written off as liberal projects (as indeed they are, rooted in a liberal God). More insidiously, *the Christian complicity in the postponement of heaven on earth is bought by the powerful and the wealthy in exchange for the pittances of family values support.* You postpone your grasp of heaven and we will help postpone abortion and homosexuality and the rise of women and the horrors of big government. This is painfully clear in what "the base" gets from Trump, or other recent presidents, and what the oligarchy whose money sponsors and controls elections gets.

But heaven has also fueled the dreams of radical utopians and millennial dreamers. They imagined the Godside coming down to join the earthside—as had already occurred, in the Christian view, in Christ's incarnation, and that defined the eschatological hope in Jesus' proclamation of the reign of God. Just as the exodus narrative can be seen as the inspired model and impulse for all subsequent revolutions, at least in the West, so heaven inspired human hope for second Adams and second Eves (in the Apostle Paul's theological imagination), the hope for a new creation—precisely on earth. The risen Christ, too, became the down payment on a resurrected earth—not God's dream indefinitely rerouted to the end of time. A new earth would become the eschatological verification of Christ's resurrection.

We do not have to reject heaven in order to favor earth. The best of heaven *above* as a transcendent value and heaven *coming down* as this-worldly hope can be conceptually and theologically united today—if we insist on seeing it that way. On this score, secular progressives might put aside their suspicions of all religion and heaven and make alliance with Christians looking to proclaim a new social gospel. True heaven is an eschatological absolute by which all dreams are measured, but also resonant with working towards a new earth. In God's dreams they come together, and *every religious ritual tries to pull together the world as experienced and the world as imagined,* as anthropologist Victor Turner saw. *Metaphors of heaven green an arid earth.* Any view of heaven should inspire Christians to open their eyes and hearts rather than wag their fingers at all the things that cannot be done. *Heaven as God's space unites blue sky heaven with green earth heaven.* Eternal life happens, even now in prototype, whenever God brings heaven and earth together.

How do hope and heaven come together? Hope is the *will to anticipate heaven on earth, to insist on seeing it on the road ahead.* It is easy for moderns to see in utopian hope (the stand-in for heaven) childish projection, wishful thinking, mystification, an unhealthy illusion. Marx and Freud were deeply suspicious. But earthly hope is a trope for what we long for. The (nonreligious) philosopher Ernst Bloch set out to rehabilitate hope and anchor it in the "infinity of the unfinished." There is so much of the universe still unfolding, and it is now the task of human culture far transcending biological evolution to imagine its way towards a more evolved earth. This is the call for the "earth angels" in the title of this chapter. The human propensity to project is a fine flower in the world, not a psychological habit to be outgrown. Bloch postulated the preconscious or the not-yet-conscious as stages in our cultural and religious evolution. We do not yet see all we shall attain—a truism in science, but we can anticipate it in religion and the humanities. That we aspire relentlessly to more than we can reach is a promising clue about the human project. Instead of pessimistic "realism" or defensive posturing against revolutions, we could learn to celebrate a human world chock full of dispositions and tendencies toward something beyond. A liberal God authorizes humans to leverage possibility, process, daydreams, utopias, and hope as the proper dispositions in a universe still unfolding. In the workshop of hope new earths are fashioned. Jews recognize this (or not) when they say "Next year in Jerusalem," when they imagine that final redemption comes when all of Israel keeps a single perfect Sabbath. The way Eucharistic celebrations are meant to sacramentalize food, and Christ as the bread of the world as a "foretaste of the feast to come."

The enemies of hope and heaven are sloth, on one hand, and irony, on the other. Sloth, one of the old "seven deadly sins," gives up the effort to change the world (or find God in a world of suffering) because it's just too hard. Irony is that cool detachment learned by college sophomores and perfected in life after graduation, in which individuals congratulate themselves on not being taken in by efforts that will probably fail, or that betray too much unsophisticated enthusiasm. In a 2008 commencement address to Duke graduates, novelist Barbara Kingsolver warned all those raised in an Age of Irony to get over it and join movements to change the world. Of course, she said, we all know that "we're a world at war, ravaged by disagreements, a bizarrely globalized people in which the extravagant excesses of one culture wash up as famine or flood on the shores of another." Nevertheless, Kingsolver called for *emancipatory hope in action:* "The arc of history is longer than human vision. It bends. We abolished slavery, we granted universal suffrage. We have done hard things before. And every time it took a terrible fight between people who could not imagine changing the rules, and those who said, 'We already did. We have made the world new.'" I once had a very bright student who kept writing imaginatively powerful papers in my social ethics class. When I commended him, he said he needed to get it all out of his system before graduation—as a business major.

If heaven, fully understood, drives hope, it is also true that hope treasures up the imaginal power of heaven and refuses to let go of it. But *the pull of heaven must be rescued from fundamentalists.* Lately, as in the "Left Behind" best sellers, heaven implies the destruction of the earth and designated enemies and all the stuff conservative Christians hate. No doubt theological ideas have consequences and these negative scripts lead to self-fulfilling prophecies (even President Reagan found them captivating and Trumpian evangelicals see him as God's apocalyptic appointee) about the fate of the earth. The "apocalyptic habit" can produce despair or revenge fantasies instead of hope for a new earth. The Christian Right regularly assigns the blame for hurricanes to homosexuals, though the hurricanes themselves do not reliably hit chosen targets. Why is destruction so much more head-turning than dreams of a new earth in which Godspace descends to effect our reenchantment? Why does Middle East cataclysm, rather than peacemaking, lead fundamentalists to tremble in ecstasy?

But if sophisticated Christians purged heaven from their vocabulary to rid themselves of fundamentalists, we would all *die for lack of metaphor.* Heaven has been called the mother of all metaphors. How impoverished our language and our mythology would be without heaven as the infinite horizon of our consciousness and of life on earth. We do not make ourselves better by starving our imaginal resources. With no transcendent pole star would we forget that we're heading somewhere, that our purposes can be drawn out in a very long arc? Who then would anticipate new social gospels? Images of heaven are visionary anticipations, engraved on the human psyche and embedded in our culture, rehearsals of the future. A new earth will not come to those who do not passionately desire it—above reason and even against reason. Once it recovers the baby accidentally thrown out with the bath water, progressive religion, with heaven as its driving metaphor and hope its mood, moves resolutely earthward. New social gospels are waiting to be born.

HOPE MOVES THE CHURCH

Progressive Christianity wants to write hope into its charter for the third millennium. When it reenters the public square, it wants Christian hope as its elevated platform. God brings release to the captives and good news for the poor in the Old Testament and in the New authorizes hope as the essential Christian praxis. As Ernst Bloch saw, hope lies within us and we express our full humanity when we activate it. The exodus story requires that we rise up and walk out of Egypt, which now encircles us. The ancient church saw that *lex orandi lex credendi*: if you get worship and its liturgical movements right, a proper theology will follow.

Weekly liturgies are meant to be performative. Following a God who called Israel out of Egypt, following Jesus who moved from death to life, Christian liturgy is meant to rehearse within the sanctuary the movement of God and then to *move out to the streets and into the public square*. But rituals often collapse into wordiness, as if that were all it takes. The disconnection from dynamic biblical versions of God goes unnoticed. *The Church forgets that sacred texts are to become scripts for a play.* Luther saw that the *Word is performative*; it makes new gospels happen. Will sermons provide the narrative setting for a God who takes on kings and landlords, transgresses the way things are, overcomes distances between people on earth, and moves unmistakably to the side of outcasts? Instead, sermons may dress God as an honorary American who takes lunch with the respectable and toasts a lot.

But liturgy is not the only dimension of Christianity that often fails to move. So does Christian theology fail to envision and drive the church's posture in the world. Americans, including the media, do not mostly witness or participate in a sustained debate with Wall Street and government (often the same) on the good of the commons, closely hemmed as they are by (unrecognized) captivating economic forces. Fundamentalists seem to quote the Bible loudly, but where is the examination of how and why their contemporary posture departs so radically from the strange God of the Bible? Do well-done sermons move mainstream Protestants to new iterations of a social gospel? Where is the conservative-progressive public debate over the meaning of biblical texts? Instead, each side simply writes the other off from their opposing silos. Liberals seem to have lost heart for such discussions and secularists disdain it and fundamentalists go on believing they have won the day and that they alone are faithful to God. When will there be *a national debate among Christians regarding a biblical vision for people in this country—and in the world—as Christianity reenters the public square?* It hardly happens. Each side talks only in its own ghetto. (I'm guilty too: I have 1,500 liberal Facebook "friends" who mostly sees things the way I do and one conservative relative who pesters them.) And progressive religion is far behind evangelicals in wielding the media, including social media, in outreach to their faithful audiences.

To engage the world, the Christian theological agenda must correlate with the intellectual, social, and economic issues of the day. In the New Testament, hope is a theological orientation without which the Christian community remains unformed and held back, and it is time to recover that hope and explore its modern forms and parade it through the public square. If this is not too farfetched, or literal, try to imagine this project through the somewhat fanciful language of science: *hope activates the human half of the double helix as it unites with God in upward movement.* Without radical hope, the churches will not consent to be pulled (dragged) forward by God's promised consummation in which this earth becomes new and the poor everywhere hear good news. God is political (hence Jesus' preaching of the reign of God and an oppositional ministry that aroused both empire and Temple) and Christian hope that tracks such a God must become political and historical—not isolating God in the sanctuary of one's own heart or, in the Lutheran quietist model, in two separate kingdoms. Christian hope is always hope for the world. After the devastations of the Second World War, Christian thinking began again the attempt, in the 1960s, to redraw hope in the face of threats to humanity and the earth itself. The World Council of Churches billed its 1954 meeting: "Jesus Christ the Hope of the World." Its 1968 theme became: "Behold, I am making all things new."

In this context the German Protestant theologian Jurgen Moltmann developed a theology of hope as a *revolutionary openness to the future.* He shared with left-wing Hegelians and Marxists the conviction that the proper theater of human thought and action is history itself, not some personal spirituality in the human heart. Moltmann's great insight was that the neglected *Christian concept of "the crucified God" (God fully present in Jesus on the cross) opens God to becoming, to change, to overcoming tragedy, to interaction with humans on earth.* The human enterprise, including also human failing, is taken up into the life of God.

Our project becomes God's project, and God's dreams become ours. Our steps toward achieving a new earth change God's (be)comings, as hope in God changes us and makes us new. Christians believe all this is rooted in Christ's cross and resurrection, with a new earth the ultimate *eschatological verification* of Christ's rising from the dead. In the Eastern Orthodox tradition Christ's descent to the world of the dead and his resurrection is a *corporate act*; he arises dragging along humanity with him, as some evocative Christian icons picture it. How astonishingly anemic is so much of Christian theology's hope today. Central to Moltmann's thought were the powerful lines from 1 Peter 1:3: "Praise be to the God and Father of our Lord Jesus Christ! In his great mercy he has given us new birth into a living hope through the resurrection of Jesus Christ from the dead." For Moltmann, the hope of Christian faith is hope that the resurrection of Christ crucified breaks ground for new life for earth and its peoples.

Because of the radical hope we hold, we can never merely exist harmoniously with the world as it is. We cannot thoughtlessly feast in the sight of the hungry. We cannot continue to fill our plates with food stolen from the tables of peasants, as the Hebrew prophets saw it. The virtue of hope drives the posture of discontent and the aspiration of reaching forward. *Eschatological reaching becomes, in modern theology, the beginning of the theological task, not the conclusion*—and certainly not a pious afterthought. Too often in systematic Christian thought eschatology comes only at the end of the semester, when students are already exhausted and anticipating summer break. When they return in the fall to start anew, they can't remember the unfinished business from the last semester. The believing community attempts to share with the world a passion for the possible. *Progressive Christianity is less interested in judgments than anticipations.* But clergy keep relegating hope to the quiet end of their sermons.

Reclaiming a theme from the Hebrew Bible, Moltmann envisions contemporary Christianity as an exodus church. This is the pilgrim people moving out of Egypt and journeying into the wilderness and being schooled by God in the ways of a new covenant, a new social contract. An exodus church focuses on the reality of Christianity as a pilgrim people of God whose walk, Luther also saw, was through the secular world, the world waiting for renewal, the world within which Christians hearken to their callings. If calling Christianity out to the streets constitutes the secularization of the church, a frequent charge against the Protestant Reformation, let it be so.

But what will be the markers of this exodus movement? Bonhoeffer in prison awaiting execution tried to imagine a religionless Christianity, a Christianity not reduced to customary trappings but imagining religious lives beyond them, or disconnected from the familiar on behalf of latching on to new things. Modernism has erased or paved over the natural paths blessed by Christendom, and so the church's self-understanding and mission were thrown off. The church's vision and ambition was reduced to trivial spiritual pursuits. To be sure, modern society is not conspicuously awaiting those who exercise an eschatological (subversive, nonconforming) obedience. But Passover and Easter liturgies can still convey that Egypt and sin and death surround us and it is possible to march out of bondage. An exodus church will have to figure out how to become good news for the poor, and evoke a planetary ethic. *Exodus and resurrection need to happen not in religious ghettoes (where the rehearsals happen) but on public land.*

Moltmann even believed that God's promise to appear in our futures is more important than what God has done in the past, and this understanding may free an exodus church to move forward without dragging along all the baggage of its customary adaptations. The church is called to active participation in the world becoming new, in joint ventures with the God who raised Jesus from the dead and established hope on the Christian compass.

Christians could try to be *hopers more than believers*. Just as we have learned to say believing is seeing, we could learn to say *hoping is enacting* the future.

If you have been following this argument, you must be exhausted by now. I am too. But this is not a solo project. As we saw in the previous chapter, all this is about *living together as a community of hope*—the church.

HOPE AND THE USES OF ENCHANTMENT

Who wants religion shorn of magic or mystery? The *uses of enchantment* (Bruno Bettelheim's reflections on the power of fairy tales) are many, and the earth is flat without them. It is said that the age of reason (and perhaps already the onset of Protestantism) and the bureaucratic way of the market have disenchanted the world and stripped culture of the metaphors that lend magic to human life on earth. Pre-Reformation Catholic theology and piety had stayed closer to mystery, the seasons, the earth, as Eamon Duffy argued in *The Stripping of the Altars: Traditional Religion in England, 1400–1580*. After sociologist Max Weber famously named *disenchantment* the dubious gift of the Protestant Reformation and capitalism, and after nineteenth- and twentieth-century theologians demythologized Christianity to accommodate it to the modern world and escape the three-storey universe of Bible times, a new age, recovering the Romantic impulse, saw that not everything was going well. There set in a *disenchantment with disenchantment*. So there came proposals to *remythologize* the biblical message as the prescription for an age dying for lack of metaphor. To do this requires a religious language that is concrete, poetic, imagistic and hence inevitably anthropomorphic, not one that is "enlightened," rationalistic, literal, or abstract. Progressive religion was slow to see that it needed poets more than analytic philosophers. A convincing social gospel may require these characteristics. Perhaps it must appear in the guise of magic realism.

The millions who know Tolkien's landscapes by heart are looking for a way back to the shire. Wicca celebrants dance at night in the woods, and goddesses appear in order to break the spell of hard masculine calculations. The physicist Niels Bohr said that the opposite of a profound truth is another profound truth, laying aside false dichotomies between science and religion. The Catholic theologian Karl Rahner thought that Christianity shorn of mystery is not Christianity. The Sierra Club needs nature poets as well as environmental scientists.

Myths are very old ways of seeing (and living) the unseen and holding close what otherwise would be lost. They deliver us from the overstimulation of facts and free us from the impositions of the everyday. Myths do not argue, they present and enchant. Culture has stored in myth the resources necessary for a rich human existence.

Rational choice economics and rapacious capitalism disenchant the world. Max Weber famously worried that the Protestant disenchantment of the world would become, in its worst possible permanent legacy, the iron cage of the modern bureaucratic, capitalist state. Commentators spoke of the "hurrying of the material" over a culture that formerly had room for spirit. Weber foresaw that the natural world would be stripped of its magical properties and its capacity for meaning. This has left the earth without a mythological story that protects it from grasping colonizers and bulldozers.

The anthropologist Clifford Geertz affirmed that humans are suspended in webs of symbolic meaning they themselves have spun. Culture is capable of being sublime, and should not be distilled as empirical explanation. Geertz wrote of his anthropology: "It has been the office of others to reassure; ours to unsettle; we hawk the anomalous, peddle the strange. We are merchants of astonishment." His goal of "thick description" can be seen as a way beyond the thinness of rational explanation. In fact, culture is a grand theater in which people tell stories to interpret themselves to themselves, playing out their meanings in public symbols. The then-new discourse of symbolic anthropology ran a middle way between the empirical and the imaginative. Enchantment named the relentless human propensity to search for larger connections. This is the world of religion. When Christians meet the world in the public square they should seem enchanting.

Myth was the last remnant of a world where reason had not yet completed the eradication of mystery. Myth-tellers still believe that *when cultures are fully awake, divinities make their appearance.* As one of the poetic protests against enlightened rationalism, Emily Dickinson suggested that awe occurs in the experience where an entire familiar world loses its normal significance and leaves one speechless in the presence of something one can no longer name. In literature, *magic realism* combines realistic representation with fantastic elements so that the marvelous seems to grow organically out of the ordinary. (Think of the Gospels.) Magic realism destabilizes prevailing definitions of reality and remystifies life through visionary power. Lost voices tuned out in the world of the everyday are heard again. Can't you hear redwoods screaming? This transaction occurs in the face of the culture of rationalism, engineering, and capitalism that claims to speak the one and only truth. An enchanted earth is one with space for diversity and *disruption* (that Silicon Valley mantra) of the way things are said to be. Its stories correct the prevailing conventions of causality, materiality, and motivation. If magic is real, then reality is magical. Like religious ritual, magic realism eschews a hard utilitarian individualism in favor of the performative practices that bind communities together. In the rituals of enchantment lies the liminal boundary where spiritual transformations and human metamorphosis can happen and we can move beyond the present exhaustion of our lives. The uses of enchantment are to recuperate the real, to surround ephemeral life with a fabulous aura, to grace our nature. The repertoire of human possibilities is wonderfully expanded. Enchantment is the best way back to religion, and progressive religion cannot live without it. If it limits itself to rational discourse and partnership with reductionist science, it will wither. And fundamentalist religion will no longer fear being left behind if the earth is again the place of enchantment, the place where God promises to touch down.

AUDITIONING HOPE: REIMAGINING WOMEN

How does hope change things? In her book *How to Read a Protest: The Art of Organizing and Resistance*, L. A. Kaufman argues that the women's marches of 2017 didn't just help shape and fuel a movement—they actually created one. In 1963 there occurred a now-legendary March on Washington. When millions of people took to the streets for the 2017 Women's Marches, there was an unmistakable air of uprising, of insurgency, a sense that these marches were launching a powerful new movement to resist a dangerous presidency. Marches are acts of hope and imagination. Kaufman shows the catalytic power of collective action and the decentralized, bottom-up, women-led model for organizing that has transformed what movements look like and what they can accomplish.

But Sarah Palin loved to taunt Obama's followers with, "How's that hopey changey thing working out for ya?" Eventually hope has to be tested. Indeed, we should always be alert for eschatological opportunities to move earth and humans forward. To demonstrate that a social gospel can move from page to stage.

It is a commonplace that Jewish and Christian Scriptures arose from within patriarchal societies. So the status of modern women becomes the place where the future of religion wrestles with its past. Among the options for Jewish and Christian (and Muslim) women are the following: leave the institutional church, whose male dominance distorts all religious experience and specifically oppresses women; "defect in place," meaning staying in but not buying in; stay in and commit to radical reform. Of course, the dilemma of women in patriarchal cultures is hardly limited to the world of religion, and women in all kinds of institutions face similar options as they struggle to "lean in" or, what is far more, pursue structural change. The women's movement that began in the 1960s had to face similar issues, conflicts, and opportunities as the civil rights movement. How would women function in a male-dominated social system? How would they accommodate, or not, patriarchal marriage? Could they open up space for gay marriage? How would they function in the religious traditions of their childhood, even as those traditions seemed unwelcoming to their new religious callings? *Do women have a right to the good news, and their roles in it, that come from a liberating God?* More recently and more concretely, the Me Too movement began to add up the thousands of ways in which women have suffered sexual harassment. Powerful men fell to women's hope and rage. At the time of the war over the nomination of Brett Kavanaugh to the Supreme Court and Dr. Blasey Ford's testimony against him, Rebecca Traister's book was appearing: *Good and Mad: The Revolutionary Power of Women's Anger.*

So women themselves can and must sow the seeds of radical transformation. Women themselves can and do hope. The Jewish feminist Judith Plaskow argued that when women steadfastly refuse to *sever* or *choose between* different aspects of their identity, they *create a new situation,* to which others are then forced to respond. When Jewish or Christian women remain in their traditions not in spite of but *as feminists,* then those traditions will be forced to change. Progressive theologians in general and feminist or womanist theologians in particular seek new understandings of the faith in new times and new places. If a liberal God is always *becoming* through interactions with humans who have discovered and claimed their agency, it cannot be a surprise that the church, too, must see that *its traditions are a dynamic, open-ended process, not an objective and unchanging treasury protected by the religious authorities. God is moving and women are becoming.*

What is the progressive agenda for women who work within religious institutions and for the secular women who align with them? In the recent past, perhaps above all in religion, patriarchy prevailed. God was evoked, induced, commandeered to bless the power and privilege of men. God became the authorizer and exemplar of patriarchy, as unreconstructed official Catholic theology, with the full force of the Vatican and most bishops in the world, still believes and practices. Much of Protestant fundamentalism and Jewish Orthodoxy and certainly conservative Islam follow the same path. Evangelical preachers and teachers devoutly proclaim the complementary view of marriage, meaning women and men each have a corresponding status with men on top. *New social mappings of lived religion suggest that conservatives across religious traditions have more in common with each other than, say, liberal and conservative Protestants and Catholics do with each other.* So a new social gospel of womanhood is likely to be ecumenical, bringing new experiences of sisterhood across denominations along with individual liberation in place.

The conservative argument is that Jesus (God) was a man and so were his leading first-century disciples, so all priests have to be men if they are to model Jesus' ministry and role in God's plan. Instead of God's incarnation deep into the entire human project, instead of lifting all of humanity up into the life of God, *Jesus' maleness became what most counts.* Not the full presence of God emptied out into the human condition is normative, but Jesus' gender. The incarnational theologies of early Christianity were far more radical than this, as they argued that the entire human condition, and its prospects, altered when the being of God took human form and engulfed humanity in its entirety.

Modern women are on the move, across the world, and they often epitomize the moral concerns and energy of progressive religion. In "Women's Creed," a document prepared for the United Nations Beijing conference on women (Hillary Clinton's highly visible attendance there was another of her unforgivable sins), they cried out: "We are female human beings poised on the edge of the new millennium. We are the majority of our species, yet we have dwelt in the shadows. We are the invisible, the illiterate, the laborers, the refugees, the poor. And we vow: *No more.*

> We are the women who hunger for rice, home, freedom, each other, ourselves. We are the women who thirst—for clean water and laughter, literacy, love.
>
> We have existed at all times, in every society. We have survived femicide. We have rebelled and left clues.
>
> We are continuity, weaving future from past, logic with lyric.
>
> We are the women who stand in our sense, and shout Yes.
>
> We are the women who wear broken bones, voices, minds, hearts—but we are the women who dare whisper No.
>
> We are the women whose souls no fundamentalist cage can contain.
>
> We are the women who refuse to permit the sowing of death in our gardens, air, rivers, seas.
>
> We are each precious, unique, necessary. We are strengthened and blessed and relieved at not having to be all the same. We are the daughters of longing. We are the mothers in labor to birth the politics of the 21st century.
>
> We are the women men warned us about.

All this we are. We are intensity, energy, the people speaking—who no longer will wait and who cannot be stopped.

We are poised on the edge of the millennium—ruin behind us, no map before us, the taste of fear sharp on our tongues.

Yet we will leap.

The exercise of imagining is an act of creation.

The act of creation is an exercise of will.

All this is political. And possible.

Bread. A clean sky. Active peace. A woman's voice singing somewhere, melody drifting like smoke from the cookfires. The army disbanded, the harvest abundant. The wound healed, the child wanted, the prisoner freed, the body's integrity honored, the lover returned. And everywhere laughter, care, celebration, dancing, contentment. A humble, early paradise, in the now.

Believe it.

We are the women who will transform the world.

HOPE CROSSES BOUNDARIES AND BINARIES: LGBTQ

The Christian Right, clinging to about six obscure and culturally conditioned verses in the entire Bible, and Catholic moral theology rooted in an antiquated natural law tradition and minded by celibate males—both of them in bondage to deep prejudices and profound boundary-tending fixations and anxieties—are determined to stand against homosexuality and queer paradigms and go down with that ship. And they will. In spite of rapidly spreading acceptance across the Western world, Catholicism and the Protestant Christian Right reduce homosexuals to being sick, for which they need a cure, or sinful, for which they need conversion, or threatening, from which our way of life requires legal protection—or, at best, a disorder in creation that must not be exorcised. There is little point in engaging this lobby, especially since the revolution on behalf of gay rights is very well advanced and has moved on without religious naysayers. In one more generation, modern knowledge and experience, or the present younger generation, will bury them. And progressive religion will light a far better path. But it is important for testing a theology of hope to see how far we have come in an astonishingly short time.

But today's conservatives are resolute, and they have learned to play the homosexual card as a source of cultural and religious anxiety—or as effective wedge strategies during national elections. Three things may be said about the use of the Bible to hammer homosexuality. First, the tiny number of Bible passages that appear to speak of gays are set in entirely different circumstances than that of gays in contemporary society, and their meanings are uncertain. Second, Bible times offer many sexual and other moral strictures that have been readily abandoned in the modern world (stoning adulterers, etc.), including by fundamentalists, because they clearly wear the cultural clothing of a particular time in ancient societies. Third, and most important, the central liberating message of the Bible, the canon within the canon, cannot be reduced to gender, or "orders of creation," patrol. *The Gospel at the center of the New Testament is not the good news of rigid and absolutist gender boundaries, but God graciously descending with open heart to friend all humankind.* Nevertheless, conservatives want anxious Americans to believe that the *essence of true religion is to save us through exclusions,* while *inclusions* are rejected as hopelessly liberal. In the claim that the practice of exclusion feeds religious authenticity and renewal, the Christian Right resembles Islamic jihadists, who believe that Islam can be revitalized if enough Muslims can be radicalized to fight the infidels.

We live in a time of freeze-dried biblical literalism in which many Christians confidently assert what they know God requires. But where does this certainty come from? The test case of morality and justice in the Hebrew Bible is how one treats the stranger within one's gates, widows and orphans, or the poor. God is a liberal and a liberator. In the New Testament, Jesus consciously set compassion (the social form of love) against purity in a contest over which system best achieves the kind of holiness God desires. Purity strictures were an all-encompassing sociopolitical paradigm; an attack on them by Jesus was fundamental and radical. So in the parable of the Good Samaritan, for example, the two religious professionals who pass by the man bleeding in the ditch did so because of an obligation to remain pure and free of contact with someone possibly dead or foreign, i.e. contaminated. Jesus demonstrates a new range of action required for being a good neighbor. Jesus himself drew people in rather than shut them out. His most memorable overtures are to women, to non-Jews, to unbelievers, to the socially outlawed like lepers or tax collectors. Jesus surrounded himself with victims of social exclusion, extending the circle of God's love beyond society's comfort zones. In prejudice-breaking action, Jesus reached out across all social and cultural divisions and made the new life in God available to all, while religious professionals meanwhile spent their time protesting his affiliations with sinners. *What would Jesus do* is a modern game. (Would Jesus pack heat? Whom would Jesus shoot? What kind of car would Jesus drive?) The answer is that if your interpretation of God's will contradicts the inclusive love evidenced in the ministry of Jesus, then you are not following Jesus. In the kingdom of God that Jesus proclaims, *love stretches law and custom towards new forms of social justice.* Arms full of antipathy to gays cannot carry the Gospel too. *What Jesus did* is normative for Christian ethics.

It is worth nothing that even though Christians did not lead the LG-BTQ movements, they are now catching up in important ways *and building acceptance into their own theologies.* A good example is the "Reconciling in Christ" movement among Lutherans and with equivalents among other progressive Protestants. The program moves forward through spiritual retreats and growth in faith, including these three steps: Building the Foundation, Living the Journey, and Setting Reconciling in Christ Milestones. This process is staged in Lutheran colleges and seminaries and of course in local parishes that have studied, voted for, and committed themselves to this movement and tend to place a prominent statement in every Sunday bulletin and every monthly parish newsletter: "The congregation of (X) Lutheran Church celebrates the amazing diversity of God's beloved children. We welcome all, regardless of age, ethnicity, abilities, faith background, race, family configuration, socioeconomic status, sexual orientation, gender identity or expression. We enthusiastically invite you into this worshipping congregation as we strive to share God's inclusive love with everyone in our community and in our world."

The real issue that drives the conservative preoccupation with gays is the cultural obsession with dangerous sexuality and the attending fear of blurred gender definitions that make us lose control of our certainties or God-given order in the world. In the case of the Catholic hierarchy, a deep distrust of embodied sexuality drives a male church into priestly celibacy, the rejection of women for priestly office, and above all to an obsession over abortion as a way of patrolling female sexuality. It cannot be a surprise, then, that such sexual obsession should also drift like a poisonous cloud onto gays as well—the test case of boundary diffusion and confusion. Against cultural uncertainty, the mission of conservative religion is to keep, or make, the world black and white, to compartmentalize life in the name of God's historic "orders of creation." For the Protestant Christian Right gays epitomize everything they fear—uncertainty, unbounded sexuality, multiculturalism, relativism, the failure of nuclear family values, the blurring of what were thought to be providential fixed orders and classifications in creation.

The astonishing triumph of gay liberation and now equality in marriage as well gives astonishing evidence that hope can triumph, the future can arrive, new creation can be accomplished. Gays above all are amazed at the extremely short time in which their liberation has occurred. What else then? What revolutions will occur that actually cost Wall Street something?

If sexual mores were set free, can economics be? How radical can theological hope become? What new species of social gospel will emerge from its gospel-driven hopes?

HOPE OVERREACHES: MILLENNIAL GOALS

Sometimes governments, more than or alongside churches, take the lead. The United Nations Millennial goals were an invitation to religious communities to become allies in changing the world. One can argue that a year with three zeroes is an irrelevant artifact of the Western calendar, and time games can indeed be trivial pursuits. But calendars, in fact, are stories humans tell themselves about time and history and culture. We keep watch, we pay attention with them.

The year 2000 was a chance to begin. *Millennial dreams are always about the pressure of what could be, the pull of the not-yet, living beyond the means of present assumptions and prevailing truths.* Progressive religion is afflicted, or graced, with an unslakable thirst for more, impatience for new heavens and new earths, a longing for justice for all people and sustainability for every natural thing. The time "after Trump" may come to carry equal significance to that of the new millennium. Or not.

It is true that progressives never call themselves millennialists, because fundamentalist Christianity has taken over that word. Or because it lately refers to the teenagers and twenty-year-olds that older people love to pillory. Modern religious millennialism arose in the nineteenth century and was aided by the divvying up of God's ways of dealing with the world into several different *dispensations*. These were meticulously outlined in the marginal notes of the Scofield Reference Bible, and continue to hold great power today among certain fundamentalist Protestants. The wildly successful *Left Behind* books and movies demonstrate the staying power of the millennial vision. Based mostly on obscure passages in biblical books like Revelation or Ezekiel, millennialism depicts, in several competing versions, an end-of-times story in which Christ returns and rules mightily for a thousand years, but not without the near triumph of cataclysmic evil just before or just after. (Lately, President Trump has achieved a starring role in millennial hopes.) The "rapture" refers to true Christians being spirited off the earth (as in the bumper sticker: "If I'm raptured, take the wheel") just before the world's descent into hellishness. Most significantly for the aspirations of progressive religion, Christian millennialism almost never harnesses its visions to efforts to create an earthly utopia drawn by the power of God (that was an earlier liberal vision). Meanwhile, Catholics and mainstream Protestantism pay little or no attention to millennial thought and are commonly referred to as amillennial.

But "millennial" and its close cousin "apocalyptic" are resonant in ways beyond fundamentalist Protestantism. Marxism and Nazism and Maoism are sometimes thought of as millennialist movements, with their fervid expectations of redemption about to break in upon a corrupt world. In his book, *Heaven on Earth: The Varieties of the Millennial Experience*, Richard Landes finds millennial or apocalyptic fascination in every season's new crop of "post-apocalyptic" horror movies. Pop culture uses our preoccupation with alien invasions as a metaphor for our fear of immigrants, pandemics, and "the other."

Hopeful millennial dreams fueled liberal Protestant and early New Age communitarian movements on the nineteenth-century American frontier. It seemed to some that the age of Obama might presage new millennial dreams, if he did not lose his nerve, if the secular left and progressive religion would light up his way with their dreams and passion. Consider the "Millennium Development Goals" that had already emerged from the United Nations Millennium Summit in September 2000 and that constitute a powerful agenda for progressive religion and its allies. To take them seriously and imagine them into reality is to participate in a radical eschatological hope. To hold out for radical eschatological hope in the face of the corruptions of late capitalism is to be a progressive millennialist, a dreamer, a utopian. Will the times after Trump bring a new social gospel, a new millennial hope?

In chapter 2, we saw the never-realized ideal of the Old Testament Jubilee Year that entranced ancient Israel's radical thinkers and hovered over the ministry of Jesus. The modern movement that called itself "Jubilee 2000" took up this ancient theme and proposed Third World debt relief. It was a grassroots campaign by religious and secular activists on behalf of world poverty, and it spread from Europe to the United States (note the direction). It is an inspiring example of the idea of a "tipping point." When a relatively small number of people, sometimes originating in the churches, takes hold of an idea and works zealously on its behalf, it can become contagious and produce nothing less than radical cultural change—in this case, economic miracles. Who could imagine that in the ruthless capitalism of the West, a redistribution scheme might take hold? It was this activism that engaged Bono, of the band U2, and also President Bill Clinton and Prime Minister Tony Blair. What happens in the streets can influence the suites. Can Jubilee again be thought out loud? There was however little echo of this in the 2016 election, except perhaps from Bernie Sanders. Here are the Millennial Goals:

1. Eradicate extreme poverty and hunger. Target for 2015: Cut in half the proportion of people living on less than a dollar a day and those who suffer from hunger.

2. Achieve universal primary education. Target for 2015: Ensure that all boys and girls complete primary school.

3. Promote gender equality and empower women. Targets for 2005 and 2015: Eliminate gender disparities in primary and secondary education by 2005 and at all levels by 2015.

4. Reduce child mortality. Target for 2015: Reduce by two thirds the mortality rate among children under five.

5. Improve maternal health. Target for 2015: Reduce by three quarters the ratio of women dying in childbirth.

6. Combat HIV/AIDS, malaria, and other diseases. Target for 2015: Halt and begin to reverse the spread of HIV/AIDS and the incidence of malaria and other major diseases.

7. Ensure environmental sustainability. Target for 2015 and 2020: Reduce by half the proportion of people without access to safe drinking water; achieve significant improvement in the lives of at least 100 million slum dwellers.

8. Develop a global partnership for development. Targets: Develop further an open trading and financial system that includes a commitment to good governance, development and poverty reduction; Address the least developed countries' special needs; Deal comprehensively with developing countries' debt problems; Develop decent and productive work for youth; In cooperation with pharmaceutical companies, provide access to affordable essential drugs in developing countries; In cooperation with the private sector, make available the benefits of new technologies, especially information and communications technologies.

In 2016 the Millennium Development Goals were succeeded by the Sustainable Development Goals. But who has heard of them? Is the UN more messianic than the Christian churches? These represent a more integrated and comprehensive global agenda centered around seventeen goals and 169 targets that now apply to every country in the world, not only to developing countries. They combine a commitment to end extreme poverty by the year 2030 with commitments to protect the environment, address climate change, combat inequality, promote peace, and improve governance.

They aspire to a worldwide social justice that "leaves no one behind." Do they reflect Christ's "option for the poor"? Do they reach towards the prophetic mandate to prioritize the welfare of the widow, orphan, stranger, and all those living in poverty? Faith-based organizations like World Vision, Lutheran World Relief, Islamic Relief Worldwide, Caritas International, American Jewish World Service, the World Council of Churches, and the World Evangelical Alliance helped ensure and shape these Sustainable Development Goals. Are these evidence of a *divine economy*, which is the subject of chapter 8? Are they secular anticipations of a new social gospel in America? Do they suggest the substance of a theology of hope?

7

Imagining the Divine Economy

WHAT A CONCEPT

In early Christian theology, the "divine economy" referred to everything characteristic of God's dealings with the creation and redemption of the world. Congruent with God's inward turning in the Being of the Trinity, it was God's outward-turning action toward "managing the household," which is a literal translation of the root word for economy. It is provocative to imagine that God's impulse to self-manifestation and God's economy of earth care would become the exodus and the social-justice covenant and the prophets speaking truth to power and the fullness of humanity displayed in Jesus Christ. When the divine Becoming touches earth it points toward liberation and justice.

The Christian ethicist Sallie McFague proposes that the *context in which contemporary Christian discipleship is tested is economic.* Think of all the sermons that never touch economics. Think of all the God-bless-America cheers that take no notice of our history of slavery and genocide and rapacious capitalism. Christian hope and Christian resistance must take place in the face of powerful economic forces. Social compassion (love) that reaches beyond the village to the world without confronting economics is merely sentimental. It may be that the pressing religious question that contextualized Luther's soul-searching was, "How can I find a gracious God?" But in an age that requires a planetary ethic to which Christians and all religious people must contribute, the question now is: How can we who have found a gracious God all survive and prosper together in God's world? The evangelical propensity for seeing the *gospel and salvation in individual terms* has its

147

own integrity but misses the vital connection between *individual* disorders and underlying *social* disorders. The horizon on which it imagines God acting is much too small and perhaps mirrors a conservative vision that knows liberty but not equality or fraternity. The ministry to individual sinners cannot neglect the diagnosis of social and structural sin and the necessity of a social justice that fulfills the biblical vision and allows everyone to prosper under a reign of God that heals all the earth. A passion for social justice by no means precludes God's coming to us in individual moments of grace and turning us around, but even that is likely to occur in social settings.

Every relevant theology must be a liberation theology, McFague believes, and her theme is living sustainably and justly. *Liberation theology must be a common interest theology.* Where is the pain greatest? Could American Christians learn to look for the answer to that question or might they mindlessly be causing the pain? *Unregulated free market capitalism constitutes the illiberal world in which a liberal God must be imitated.* We are not talking about a socialist dream derived from secular sources, but the covenant dream of the God of the exodus and acted out in the paradigmatic ministry of Jesus. And so a social gospel must be nonconformist, dissenting, even insurrectionist.

Yet free markets and Anglo-Saxon capitalism seem like settled—almost eternal—arrangements, not test cases for discipleship and prophetic denunciation. The American economic system is accustomed to a free pass from Christianity. If we have gone to the confessional, we are not typically seeking absolution for our participation in a ruthless market. Like President Trump, we would be glad to confess if we needed to, but we cannot think of any sins we've committed. On Sunday morning when Lutheran Christians confess that they are "in captivity to sin and cannot free themselves," they are not typically thinking about capitalist markets, although as they leave worship every Sunday they do hear the Assisting Minister say, as did the early church, "Remember the poor."

But McFague, a contemporary Protestant theologian and ethicist, is not a sentimentalist, not a utopian, not an otherworldly mystic, not a biblical literalist, and not naïve. Borrowing a phrasing from the early church fathers, she takes as her starting point: "The glory of God is every creature fully alive" and concludes that we live to *give God glory by loving the world and everything in it.* She situates the visionary imitation of Christ on the largest possible stage and does not confine it to the believer's heart—or make it exclusive to Christianity.

It should not then be a surprise, as we saw in chapter 1, that not so long after God introduced post-exodus ancient Israel to a covenant theology for the common good, prophets began to stretch their imaginations and draw startling conclusions. First, there came the implications of the fourth (third) commandment: Remember the Sabbath to keep it holy. Instead of relentless striving and greed and economic anxiety, the Sabbath requires *work stoppage*, and also worship, and also the enhancement of the neighborhood. The Sabbath provides *time to mend the world*. The Sabbath tempers economic productivity with acts of communal imagination and renewal. In effect, the Sabbath becomes the great equalizer, the sacrament of God's reordering of life, the one day when economic exploitation cannot happen, cannot drive human life, cannot determine the meaning of everything else. Especially on this day, God-the-liberator is worshiped and God's designs for the commons are exemplified and economic systems are relativized. Judaism turned *Sabbath into an art form*, a sacred aesthetic of common life.

Then in Deuteronomy's covenantal code, we see the first social safety net in the history of the world. God and Israel guard the good of every neighbor and hem in every propensity of the rich and the powerful to render the neighbor a means to their own ends. Imagine—it comes to be that debts owed by the poor must be canceled after seven years so that no permanent underclass develops. (Ask somebody in a presidential primary to embrace this.) Interest is forbidden, no collateral is required on loans to the poor, permanent hospitality is to be a communal norm, justice is extended to aliens, leftover abundance is reserved for widows and orphans. As we have seen, the Jubilee Year is even more radical as a redistribution system of social justice. Never is the economy meant to be a freestanding autonomous system—that would break the first commandment, devoted to God's priorities. Don't ever reduce the biblical witness, in Old Testament or New, to a personal piety that never touches the ground of earthly and, yes, economic life.

God's economy! What could that possibly mean? A movement calling itself the New Left has begun regular postings on Facebook. In answer to the expected criticism that anytime religion enters the public square it must be seeking to impose theocracy, the Religious Left responds: "If Christians wanted to create a real theocracy they'd find more ways to feed the hungry and house the homeless and tend to the sick and speak for the oppressed." Medicare for all, for example, would as in Europe be an abundant blessing on the commons offered by government. No social democracy in Europe is a theocracy.

Today there has almost disappeared from public discourse any interest in the economic implications of biblical religion, lest it taint true spirituality—or set an impossible standard for the real world. Or question the American way. Hence the argument of this book to think the biblical God out loud again and write such a God into the social contract. Jews and

Christians lately are calling the national budget a "moral document," but few in Congress are listening. But the Hebrew Bible decries the exploitation of the poor or the needy for economic gain. In the New Testament, Jesus talks about money, possessions, and wealth second only to his proclamation of the reign of God. Half of Jesus' parables are situated in the marketplace—where most contemporary sermons don't go. The entire Bible is full of admonitions regarding poverty, wealth, production, distribution, and labor practices. Economic justice is always posed as fundamental to life in community. The Old Testament is preoccupied with the *trinity of widows, orphans, and strangers.* Imagine regularly talking about this "trinity" as the foundation of social ethics or social justice! A potentially individualistic "love commandment" must be rerouted towards social compassion, an idea even President Bush tried out before losing enthusiasm. Some today are learning the mantra, "The social form of love is justice."

Modern economic theory tends to move between the poles of Adam Smith and Marxism and does not have a religious oar in the water. The Adam Smith side of the argument presumed that unvarnished capitalism would inevitably increase human well-being. Marxists claimed that unregulated capitalism, built on exploitation, would alienate workers from their own labor, cheat them out of their just deserts, destroy community, and dehumanize common life until proletarian movements would arise to replace it with communitarian visions. *But where is the rival discussion of a new social gospel?*

In between Adam Smith and Karl Max, modern Christian moral theology arose to make such claims as the following: religion is not simply an artifact of material society but can in fact significantly and independently influence economics; religion can be an upstream force and not just a downstream derivative; the early twentieth-century Protestant "social gospel" and in Europe various forms of Christian socialism and Roman Catholic moral theology of the last hundred years can mitigate the devastations of modern economic life in the name of a reasserted biblical social ethic; liberation theology can bring together the biblical ethos of social justice and a Marxian structural analysis of the forces that lead to injustice; Catholic social teaching wants to safeguard the poor and labor, perhaps by finding a third way beyond capitalism and Marxism; the World Council of Churches adopted a steadily suspicious view of free market capitalism as a force for good in the world; evangelical groups, especially in America, tried to adapt free market capitalism to its individualistic view of personal salvation and making God the visible providential hand of the market, but the Sojourners movement, originating in American neo-evangelicalism or neo-Anabaptism, has been one of the most vigorous Christian champions of social justice. Imagine the world after Trump! Are we ready to proclaim and embody a new social gospel? This needs to be a persistent topic in sermons and faith formation studies.

In the view of many, however, 1989 marked not only the beginning of the end of the Soviet empire but an end to the relevance of the Marxian critique of economic life. Capitalist and other conservative thinkers were pleased to believe that not only Communism as a state-run economic system had died, but so too had any Marxian approach to economic analysis. With Marxism moribund and the prophetic Christian voice having muted itself into irrelevance, with the apparent triumph of Western economics and the establishment of free market capitalism as an objective science, *capitalism in effect was given a free pass* and readily escaped religious and moral scrutiny. Few noticed that *capitalist consumerism itself had become the chief rival to biblical religion* as an all-encompassing worldview. We had reached, in a self-congratulatory phrase, the "end of history."

While radical Christianity welcomes the astute analysis of a totally unbalanced economy from secular economists, there is also the Catholic tradition itself to return to. An occupying Christianity, a radical religion, a Christian Left would do well to immerse itself in the deep wells of Roman Catholic social teaching. In mid-2018 Pope Francis appointed fourteen new cardinals and said in selecting those who will one day choose his successor, he was looking for leaders who represented a church of the poor and for the poor, humble pastors "with the smell of the sheep." But radical Catholic social doctrine goes back to the end of the nineteenth century, when a special encyclical analyzed the *condition of the working class*. That encyclical was honored by Pius XI forty years later, and followed by Paul VI's *Populorum Progressio*, John Paul II's *Sollicitudo Rei Socialis*, and Benedict XVI's *Caritas in Veritate*. Following up on this tradition Pope Francis has been particularly outspoken.

UNMASKING (LATE) CAPITALISM

Circulating on Facebook in early 2019—fake news?—was the following data on CEO pay vs that of the average worker, in major countries: Japan 11:1, Germany 12:1, France 15:1, Italy 20:1, Canada 20:1, South Africa 21:1, Britain 22:1, Mexico 47:1, Venezuela 50:1, US 475:1. In 1965, fifteen years before the Reagan reverse revolution, the average CEO made twenty times a median employee's salary.

President Thomas Jefferson said: "I hope we shall crush . . . in its birth the aristocracy of our moneyed corporations, which dare already to challenge our government to a trial of strength and bid defiance to the laws of our country." President Franklin Roosevelt warned Congress in 1938 that the growth of private power could lead to fascism: "The liberty of a democracy is not safe if the people tolerate the growth of private power to a point where it becomes stronger than their democratic state itself." President Dwight Eisenhower, in his famous 1961 Farewell Address to the Nation, denounced the conjoining of an immense military establishment with a large arms industry and stressed "the need to maintain balance in and among national programs—balance between the private and the public economy, balance between cost and hoped for advantage."

But a new vision for the economy championed by President Reagan could and did negate these earlier strictures; a new Pharaoh could emerge who "did not know Joseph," as the book of Exodus describes the discontinuity with the past that led to new bondage in Egypt. How did things change so rapidly in the late twentieth century? Joan Didion, in "In the Realm of the Fisher King," suggests that the character and legacy of the Reagan White House was to enact a politically effective, if hollow, pageantry in which a new economic vision, birthed in the Chicago school, could emerge at the edges and move resolutely towards the center. Reagan was the Trojan horse from which a *ruthless and deregulated capitalism* could emerge to take over the city on the hill. A total overhaul in the relationship between the people, the state, and capital was underway. *The new covenant was neoliberal economic theory.* The state would get out of the way of the market when it was booming and pitch in at the expense of the public sector when it was busting. (Obama's handling of the market and mortgage loan crash carefully resembled this approach.) The public emerged from the trance of the Reagan years to find that its government had undergone a total theoretical and practical renovation. It rationalized the change as a natural evolution in political-economic dynamics when really it had been a *neo-capitalist coup.* The Reagan era had accomplished the most massive upward transfer of wealth ever seen in American history. The opposite of the social gospel would be good news for the wealthy and very bad news for the poor. The tax rates on the wealthy prevailing in Eisenhower's time were drastically reduced and the brakes on billionaires removed—to the devastation of the 99 percent.

The situation is getting worse not better in the twenty-first century. Thomas Piketty's *Capitalism in the Twenty-first Century* not only documents the growing concentration of income in the hands of a small economic elite but argues that we are on the way back to "patrimonial capitalism," in which the commanding heights of the economy are dominated not just by wealth, but also by inherited wealth, in which birth matters more than effort and talent. Eventually we could see the reemergence of a world familiar to nineteenth-century Europeans. In this "patrimonial society," a small group of wealthy rentiers lives lavishly on the fruits of its inherited wealth, and the rest struggle to keep up. This is the reversal of the Jubilee Year vision. The Republican Party has determined to clothe what used to be called the "estate tax" in what is now called the "death tax"—in order to make everyone ashamed of multiple robberies of the wealthy.

The long list of critiques of American corporate capitalism, the least regulated and most rapacious in the Western world, includes social inequality, unfair distribution of wealth and power, corporate-governmental interchanging oligarchies, economic imperialism, counter-revolutionary wars fought to maintain corporate prerogatives, exploitation of Third World countries and of the earth, repression of workers and unions, social alienation stemming from economic individualism, planned unemployment, overweening individual property rights that threaten the commons, an ever widening gap between the rich and the poor, and the utter decline of the middle class. Are there regular Sunday sermons or denominational pronouncements to address the socioeconomic structures in which Christians and all citizens find themselves imprisoned? Could a new social gospel even breath in such an atmosphere? Who will launch it, preach it, march it into the public square?

Those who suffer are tricked into siding with their oppressors. Consider how the following "self-evident truths" lard the public pronouncements of Senate Majority Leader Mitch McConnell and chief libertarian Rand Paul: A safety net for the masses is denounced for its moral hazards, and a social Darwinism is installed to provide cover for the 1 percent. *The "positive rights" to public services and the chance for a good life, in a libertarian slight of hand, are cynically turned into the "negative right" to be free of government interference.* The benefits of a social democracy are relabeled government *entitlements* and then relabeled again as government encroachments from which citizens are to be protected. This slight of hand can happen when liberty prevails as the only value and equality/fraternity drop out of the equation. Noam Chomsky has remarked: "The idea of a free contract between the potentate and his starving subjects is a sick joke."

The first time a humorist said we have the best Congress money can buy it was sly. Now it is a given, especially after the Supreme Court voted 5–4 in "Citizens United" to allow an unlimited flow of "dark money" into the political process, in the name of individual (i.e. corporate) free speech. (Norway, by comparison, does not allow any private or corporate funds to enter the political process during elections.) Congressional and presidential campaigns are utterly beholden to massive injections of private, "self-interested" money. Regulatory agencies are largely controlled by policies written by those who are to be regulated. Congress and corporations are interlocking oligarchies, a point Jimmy Carter has recently been making. Could a new social gospel get a hearing? Fire from heaven?

Daniel Bell, and long before him Wesleyan Methodism, famously worried over the "contradictions of capitalism." The culture it reliably creates turns out to be a hedonistic consumerism that nullifies the very Protestant values that helped make it flourish. There is no godly good of the whole, just an endlessly fueled personal gratification. Traditional cultural values rooted in the community are eroded by egoism and nihilism.

Some conservative critics avoid recognizing the *structural deficits* of capitalism and attribute the failure of the American underclass and working class to their inadequate cultural values. Earlier this was blamed on the black family, but now Charles Murray's *Coming Apart* finds a severe erosion of middle-class values in white culture as well. Curiously, conservative Christians, wanting to prioritize freedom and individual conversion as the essence of Christian salvation, find common cause in this analysis. They are determined not to see economic devastation and the dregs that a ruthless capitalism leaves behind. The easier meme for leaving the status quo untouched is "if only their values were better." This becomes the predominant lament for the poor and the newly permanent underclass.

Can Christianity and others seeking the wealth of the commons gum the capitalist system up by depriving it of willing subjects? Could churches become communities of alternative development for the common good? For this to happen, theologians must take the lead in encouraging Christians and others to step back and see clearly how the wider economic culture forms people for agendas that run counter to vocations that take seriously the moral meaning of work, and the care of the community, and of the earth. Instead, as Marx predicted, we see widespread immiseration. When the spirit of capitalism and the spirit of American Christianity have blurred together, it is the calling of theological ethics to open up space between them, to make public space where a social gospel could be heard and grasped. Christianity must accept its own calling in the world as the most important rival to the all-demanding values of the market. Preachers must become "wilderness prophets," not status quo lackeys.

Judaism and Christianity will have to make the connections, and in their liturgies and theology perform alternative visions. Baptismal renunciations, in the ears of the congregation, could lead to new spiritual formation. Christian education could become the boot camp for a life of resistance that fights on behalf of God's justice. Turning ourselves into disciples rather than consumers could be identified with the life of the church. Let the Eucharist be a banquet for the world laid out by a servant church. Of course the church must first repent for its economic complicity, as when St. Paul's Cathedral in London and the Episcopal landlord in lower Manhattan evicted, in collusion with corporate interests, the Occupy movement. In "Charity in Truth" Pope Benedict XVI spoke against the "grave imbalances that are produced when economic action, conceived merely as an engine for wealth creation, is detached from political action, conceived as a means for *pursuing justice through redistribution.*"

Of course, it is argued that one commits a "category mistake" to subject capitalism to moral critique. Like seeing gravity as a moral shortcoming. It is claimed that "neoliberal" economics is an objective science not subject to moral review. Its requirements and beliefs are not to be questioned: the right to make as much money as possible, anywhere and everywhere; the valorization of greed as the solution for fair distribution; the eradication of unions and worker benefits (where are the Christians when "right to work" legislation gets passed—celebrating individual liberties?); freedom from environmental or governmental regulation; a pass from religion and ethics. If capitalism thinks about religion at all, it wants to divide the world up between God and itself, and an amazing percentage of American Christians are glad to go along: *God gets the privacy of your home and Jesus in your heart and private religious liberty; capitalism gets everything else.* As the authorities said to Jesus: Leave things alone. Do not make trouble in the community.

In the New Testament, Jesus' proclamation of the reign of God and Paul's theological elaboration of it name the demonic "principalities and powers" and give them an ontological significance as the opposite of God's intentions for the earth and its peoples. But since the Enlightenment and, more so, the triumph of free market ideology, these ideas are called quaint and become the unmentionables of our culture. No need to worry about Satan or absolute evil in a demythologized world. But the materialism that triumphed and the world it produced may be the presence of the demonic in modern life.

And so a trilogy of works by the New Testament scholar Walter Wink have become groundbreaking and indispensable in Christian theology and ethics. First came *Naming the Powers: The Language of Power in the New Testament.* Not sufficient to call them out, it becomes necessary to analyze their pretentions, and so volume 2 came: *Unmasking the Powers.* Still, the analytical task is insufficient, and religious resistance is required. So the third volume came: *Engaging the Powers: Discernment and Resistance in a World of Domination.*

Let there be no doubt that capitalism is a far more effective economic mechanism than socialism. Its strengths are everywhere evident: it is a marvelous machine of production; it creates economies of scale; it is highly successful at raising capital from large numbers of investors which then invested flows to ever new ventures; it offers a global perspective that transcends local prejudices and idiosyncrasies.

But the weaknesses of capitalism are as well-concealed, to most onlookers, as a ravaged face covered with expensive make-up. The downstairs help are not supposed to see what the upstairs is really like. But the servants know, because they have up close experience with the faces of capitalism before the morning disguises are put on and the suits go to work. We cannot hide our eyes as environmental degradation is relegated to the status of "externalities" that are not part of its balance sheet; from the obsession with short-term goals that produce long-term disasters; from the privileging of the individual entrepreneur over the good of the community; from the deification of the market as the measure of all values; from the sheer misery produced alongside immense wealth. For example, sweatshops are not an unfortunate accident of capitalism, but the maximizing of its systematic approaches. Is it too much to say that an underlying function of a capitalist economy is to sacrifice human beings and suck their blood for financial gain? In 2009, just after the Wall Street crash, the *Rolling Stone* reporter Matt Taibbi saw Goldman Sachs as "a great vampire squid wrapped around the face of humanity, relentlessly jamming its blood funnel into anything that smells like money."

If capitalism is to be freed from its pretensions, not utterly renounced, religion must remain one of the *players left on the board*, the one worldview that could relativize capitalism's claim to be the only treasure in the field, the one thing to bet the farm on, the ultimate wager. While an extraordinarily successful system of wealth creation, capitalism must be *relieved of its pretensions to be an ultimate system of meaning that displaces all others.* How tragic, then, when conservative Protestantism offers itself as capitalism's champion rather than its critic. Liberty University, founded by Jerry Falwell, names free enterprise capitalism one of its core Christian values and its current president, Falwell's son, is certain that Donald Trump is God's anointed, with Falwell holding a key position at court.

Will progressive religion rise to the occasion? Will new prophets called by a God of the exodus speak up for the victims? Didn't the aftermath of the 2008 collapse open space for the revival of insurgent, nonconforming religion? The Occupy movement rejected the claim that concern for the poor and the disenfranchised was un-American, but it had little success convincing the working class that voting for billionaires was not in its best interest. In the moral space opened by the Occupiers, though not too successfully, progressive religion could have led a vigorous public debate about the meaning of our lives. People of good will could join United Nations agencies, and NGOs, and leftist intellectuals, and progressive religion in learning to temper enthusiasm for capitalism's accomplishments with a clear-eyed examination of its devastations, from the poor thrown up as the necessary and calculated detritus to the damaged goods of the commons. It is religion's task in every age to give voice to the losers that capitalist strategies keep turning out, while the winners are singing their songs. Will people come forth with the prophetic imagination to see how social cohesion and our vast interconnectedness as a human family have been sacrificed to profits for the few? As nuns who work in soup kitchens sometimes say, "Nobody gets to heaven without a letter of recommendation from the poor."

In view of all this, *Oeconomicae et pecuniariae questions* was a statement from the Vatican, released in May 2018, that sounds like an unimaginable Christian utopia when compared to the economic system that prevails in "Christian America." But it *was* imagined. Its vision reached toward the ultimate horizon of the common good that the church, understanding itself as the universal sacrament of salvation, seeks to advance. It purports to be an anticipation of the reign of God. In Christ we see the redemption not merely of individual persons but of all social relations and the human commons itself. It comes out on the side of the excluded and marginalized, but without naively rejecting all effective economic systems.

Perhaps audaciously this moral statement calls on universities and business schools to supplement their curricula in a way that forms students with such a vision. "The social doctrine of the church would be a considerable help in this connection." It clearly sees that entrenched unregulated economic forces are supernational agents that undermine and overrule government and religious efforts to create a just society. This document closes by acknowledging that no one can resolve these problems alone. In the church today, "We are all called, as sentinels, to watch over genuine life and to make ourselves catalysts of a new social behavior, shaping our actions to the search for the common good, and establishing it on the sound principles of solidarity and subsidiarity" (two profound words essential to Catholic moral theology).

CAN YOU SEE THE POOR FROM WHERE YOU ARE?

American capitalism, and indeed the policies of both political parties, have increased the gap between rich and poor at home and abroad. But free market ideologues cannot abide the idea that global capitalism has a fatally flawed DNA. Trickle-down economics resembles capitalist heaven as the sweet by and by that takes our eye off the present. Mainstream America, including many people of good will, disputes as one-sided progressive religion's concern for *the least, the last, the lost.* Liberation theology taught Catholicism God's "preferential option for the poor," and this has lately led the bishops to look up from the culture wars and challenge Congressional budget proposals. But a remarkable number of American Christians, not to mention all the nones and dones, just do not get this. It seems bleeding heart to them, perhaps nice but not required and certainly not structural. And possibly a moral hazard that excuses individuals from doing their hard working part or from redeeming themselves from their sorry economic state by turning their individual lives around through Christ.

In the prophetic traditions of the Hebrew Bible, in the New Testament teachings and actions of Jesus and the letters of St. Paul and others, and in the practice of early Christianity, one sees an *obsession with the plight of the poor.* In the Old Testament, the plight of the poor and the stranger and the marginalized was second only to idolatry as a pebble in God's shoe. Though grounded in Israel's view of God, it can be expressed in admonitions as simple as that in Leviticus 23:22: "When you reap the harvest of your land, you shall not reap to the very edges of your field, or gather the gleanings of your harvest; you shall leave them for the poor and for the alien: I am the LORD your God."

Middle-class Christianity may suffer from a lack of proximity to the poor. If the kind of worshiping community idealized in early Christianity prevailed today, Walmart and Bloomingdale's customers would regularly greet each other in church, join hands at the Lord's Prayer, and meet at the Communion rail, while singing "One Bread, One Body, One Lord of All." People out of work would be singing and praying beside people whose policies had put them out of work, and this would produce useful conversations during the "passing of the peace."

But the real issue is a failure of moral imagination, sometimes a deliberate blindness (there are none so blind as those who will not see) and sometimes a sin of omission. Consider Esther Duflo's eye-opening commentary in *Poor Economics:* "We tend to be patronizing about the poor ...Why don't they take more responsibility for their lives? And what we are forgetting is that the richer you are the less responsibility you need to take for your own life because everything is taken care of for you. And the poorer you are the more you have to be responsible for everything about your life. Stop berating people for not being responsible and start to think of ways of providing the poor with the luxury that we all have, which is that a lot of decisions are taken for us. If we do nothing, we are on the right track. For most of the poor, if they do nothing, they are on the wrong track."

As the Apostle Paul's adventurous missionary journeys were beginning and his audacious theological justifications for them were being worked out, there was only one criterion stipulated by the home church in Jerusalem, before it would grant its blessing: "Take up offerings for the poor." Make the gospel available to everyone, but *remember the poor.* All early Christians coming from the Jewish tradition knew the verse from Psalm 22, "The poor shall eat and be satisfied." The collections Paul gathered for the poor in Jerusalem while on his travels were later embedded in the liturgical practice of the second century, when every liturgy ended with "Remember the poor," an admonition again recovered in recent decades. Ideally, remembering is not a quick mental image but performative action, as in "Do this in remembrance of me." Out of this New Testament witness, Gordon Lathrop, in his book *The Pastor: A Spirituality,* makes *diakonia* (service) one of the essential tasks of the clergy and concretizes that service in the on-the-ground acts of remembering the poor. The pastor is, in effect, to wait on tables. Indeed, Christian theology is partly formed around the emotional experience of all those hearers who come to know themselves in need of God, the God who became poor for their sake (2 Corinthians 8:9).

It seems that a counterintuitive biblical admonition is "Learn dependency," which is to say, "Learn to trust the God whose gifts come to the entire community." American Christians tend not to see that central New Testament word, *grace,* as having social implications. How unnatural it would be for the American Horatio Alger, self-made, to think himself born of grace, or to have a clue about Luther's last words as he lay dying, "We are all beggars." In every Christian worship service what Luther called "the amazing exchange" happens: worshipers trade in their neediness for God's abundance. The poor in the world are as concrete as the bread and the wine of the Eucharist, and God appears in both of them.

But no one in Washington pays attention. Oxfam International claims: "The top 100 billionaires added $240 billion to their wealth in 2012—enough to end world poverty four times over." A sociopath may be defined as someone whose conscience owes nothing to anyone, a person who is completely devoid of moral imagination. Look around. They are easy to spot. Then repent. A meme currently making the rounds of social media goes: *Poverty exists not because we cannot feed the poor, but because we cannot satisfy the rich.*

IS CHARITY THE RELIGIOUS SOLUTION?

In March 2019, Bread for the World, a Christian lobbying group, reported that every religious congregation would need to raise an additional $400K each year for the next ten years to make up for proposed cuts to antihunger and antipoverty programs in the 2020 federal budget. Federal programs provide ten times more in food assistance than congregations and charities. A single bad vote in Congress can undo an entire year of Christian charity.

It seems to be true that Republicans give more to charity than Democrats do. What does this mean? The New Testament word for love comes out as charity in the King James Version of the Bible. Today charity is an IRS category, for which one gets a deduction. It suggests well-meaning and generous help for the disadvantaged, given, in the realm of the private sector, by the more advantaged. Charity is a good thing that all people, and certainly Christians, should practice in response to a great variety of opportunities.

But the insidious side of charity is that it can become a substitute for justice. Conservatives, including the Christian Right, love charity for several reasons: it puts the emphasis on how generous Americans are, who give more to charity than other countries; it limits itself to the private sector and gives churches something to stand out on; it hints that it is a much more worthy approach to human need than government programs; it relieves government of its obligations to the human wreck created by unregulated capitalism; above all, it distracts moral scrutiny from the economic system that creates the need for charity and gives capitalism and free enterprise a free pass. Charity devotes itself to individual, private generosity and nicely avoids systemic critique. Charity lovingly bandages wounds, and does not inquire about who is inflicting them. Charity organizes teams to pull bodies out of fast-flowing water downstream, and does not occupy itself with discovering who is throwing them in upstream. An AARP Bulletin in May 2019 warned about charity done in the interest of corporate profits. So the Healthwell Foundation, a nonprofit, helps pay prescription medicine bills for people who can't afford it. It is funded by Big Pharma and is intended to reduce public pressure on drug-makers to lower their drug costs.

New York Times columnist David Brooks has drawn criticism for implying that religion's role in a just society is as a palliative resource easing the burdens of those being crushed by a ruthless economy, rather than as a prophetic denouncing of an unjust socioeconomic system. Brooks, a conservative centrist, seems to put religion on the side of accommodation and adjustment, almost never on the side of critique and revolution. The Hebrew Bible is far more aggressive in what it calls God's voice-through-the-prophets to say and do. It is willing to press the urgency of release from debt and redistribution of resources, and singles out those who are "grinding the faces of the poor." Jesus does not separate his message from that tradition, but reinforces it.

Charity's highest calling should be to turn to *advocacy* on behalf of those who need it and, ultimately, to demand a just system that is fair to all. Grounded in love, charity when it becomes wise and prudent moves towards justice, even while aiming its intentions toward something that exceeds laws and regulations. Charity should be leading the parade towards social justice, which must be seen as the social and structural form of love.

RECOVERING THE DISCARDED VALUES OF EQUALITY AND COMMUNITY

Three great ideals of early modern Europe were liberty, equality, and fraternity (the latter better rendered as community or kinship). They were brought together in the great slogan of the French Revolution, but these three musketeers (all for one and one for all) never made it together into the founding documents of the United States. In Martin Buber's analysis, *liberty went west to America, but flying solo it changed its character and became freedom without responsibility for the commons.* Equality went east into Marxism, but all alone it became the equality of the government-controlled masses. Fraternity, or kinship or community, went into hiding, disparaged by secular elites because it was the most religious of these three ideals. It hid in the religious lives of those suffering oppression, but emerged again in the civil rights movement or, alternately, in the women's movement— "Sisterhood is powerful."

Equality and community are strong impulses of progressive religion, but they are deeply distrusted by American conservatives. Equality bespeaks class warfare or Marxism with its hints of redistribution or the current interest in black reparations, and it is rendered as the great threat against which libertarianism mobilizes its appeal. *Kinship or community will not grow up in America as long as society is deeply divided between red and blue, between Christian and everyone else, between whites and people of color, between men and women, between individualism and the commons, between the 1 percent and the 99 percent, between the makers and the takers.* (Candidate Mitt Romney inadvertently named this dilemma in the 2012 presidential election when he ridiculed the 47 percent who are takers.) As in the Bible, a covenanted community requires an act of social imagination that manages to discover a human family within the masses of people, but the far more prized American virtue, individualism, is unwilling to risk its free-standing autonomy and its prerogatives on behalf of the suspicious ideal of an interdependent human family. Community is the way God sees humans (and earth), and we are called to see with God's eyes, as in Christ.

REIMAGINING THE COMMONS

The commons was the name for the public space shared by all in New England towns. It is the root of *commonwealth*, a nice term for an entire civic entity, like a state, in which every citizen is viewed as a stakeholder. Its values are the opposite of those decried in John Kenneth Galbraith's lament about "private wealth and public squalor" in a completely unbalanced commons.

Economic conservatives seem indifferent to the commons, even deliberately starving the commons because it may imply big government or because it offends the freedom of the rich from excessive taxation. *The commons is just an abstraction,* people seem to think. This means the demise of "social capital" (the sum total of all social networks and human investments in a community or polity) and civic values shared by all, and their surrender to utilitarian individualism and the dominance of the market. The commons has regressed to a figment of the (moral) imagination. Social democrats lament people's inability or refusal to think of an entire interdependent community. There are continuing attempts by conservatives to abolish Social Security or Medicare (again in 2018), or privatize them, but more far-reaching is the conviction that nothing good should be expected from government, or even from social institutions, and that the commons are no one's responsibility. Indeed, Europeans, living in their social democracies so much feared or decried by American conservatives, are far more likely to talk enthusiastically about the benefits of government than Americans are. Because they see themselves as the government. Here, holding culture or wealth or the good in common has given way to a privatizing individualism or to a political economics that starves the public sector and privileges the private. (Even Wall Street bailouts imply private gain but socialized risk.) It is hard even to imagine and care for a community enterprise, like healthcare or social security, for the good of all. Indeed it is anathema to convinced conservatives. We have learned to recognize the ontological reality of the individual, but we have forgotten the meaning of collective nouns like the *commons* or the *state* or the *village*. Positing that "it takes a village" is treasonous to the libertarian spirit, as Hillary Clinton found out years ago.

EARTH ACTION

It's not just the commons that requires attention and reimagination. Modern American society has mostly lost the capacity to imagine the earth as our mother. Few see one of Christianity's missions as the reenchantment of the earth—in the face of modernity's disenchantment. But there is hope, and abundant resources in the Christian tradition.

The Catholic sacramental tradition, at its best, sacralizes matter and the earth as instruments of a religious vision. The Bible's eschatological hope never leaves earth behind and cannot be rerouted to some immaterial future awaiting the arrival of raptured Christians. Most religious ethicists writing today, for example Sallie McFague, aspire to a *planetary ethic* as what is required of a biblical ethic in the modern age. Coinciding, as it must, with social justice for all peoples, it is the indispensable direction Jewish and Christian ethics must take.

Leaders of the Christian Right have called global warming a myth, a fiction created to destroy America's free enterprise system, and a plot for a bigger, regulatory government. Rush Limbaugh pronounced: "If you believe in God then intellectually you cannot believe in man-made global warming." But many evangelical Christians, even while remaining socially conservative, are rallying around *creation care*. Contemporary Christian ethicists like Cynthia Moe-Lobeda are shifting the gaze of ethics towards structural evil and making *resistance* the necessary Christian calling. Love, or compassion for earth and its peoples, is the new ecological-economic vocation. An acute focus is required, including "naming and engaging the powers," which is to say the collective ecological and economic damage done by the rich through an indulgent and wasteful way of life and especially the *structural evil* driven by the unaccountable and unlimited power of global capitalism, an evil largely hidden, and one that hides from itself its accompanying global degradation. The contemporary moral crisis is not homosexuality or the dangerous sexuality of women, but the extent to which we live off the suffering and deprivations of others—and of the earth. All this requires not just a new imperative to care for the earth as God's garden entrusted to us, but a rethinking of the way we do religious ethics. The earth crisis cannot be understood apart from the larger human crisis—economic equity, social values, and human purpose are bound up with the planet's survival. Now, the whole earth is the moral community that requires our critical analysis and our radical hope. Meanwhile, Republicans in general and the Christian Right as well enthusiastically denounce climate science, discernment of global warming, and most of the environmental movement. President Trump has conspicuously withdrawn the United States from worldwide efforts on behalf of the environment and instructed his cabinet to renounce or undermine such stewardship.

In fact, there is indeed a presence of religion in the environmental movement. Stephen Ellingson documents it in *To Care for Creation: The Emergence of the Religious Environmental Movement*, based on extensive interviews in 2006 and 2007. There are enough "religious environmental movement organizations" to merit the acronym REMOs in social science literature. Church-based movements have wanted to maintain their religious identities while also interacting with secular movements who are prone to disacknowledge the role of religion. Nevertheless, there are attempts at bridging between REMOs and SEMOs (secular environmental movement organizations). Religious movements have felt most comfortable in preparing an explicitly Christian admonition with phrases emphasizing *creation care*. That term allowed environmental concerns to be adopted by evangelicals as well as mainstream Protestants and Catholics, though conservative political impulses wary of the role of government were always a problem for the former.

On the environmental left, activist-scholars like Bron Taylor have pioneered the concept of "dark green religion," in the hope that it might precipitate a global, civil religion of the earth. Taylor subtitles his book *Nature Spirituality and the Planetary Future*. This view perceives nature as sacred and alluring, with its own intrinsic value, sees humans and the environment are interconnected and mutually dependent, imagines all life sharing a common ancestor, and posits a kinship ethic with responsibilities to all living things. Such perceptions lead people to see more continuities than differences between their own and other species and generally leads to humility about one's place in the grand scheme of things.

Who remembers the Earth First! movement, which emerged in 1980 and drifted into political (and institutional) anarchy in the 1990s? I mention it here to notice its successors among green religion, even if the somewhat apocalyptic Earth First! failed to last. Environmental recovery requires not dreary apocalyptic breast-beating, but celebration and consciousness-raising. A newly focused attention to planet earth led to the first Earth Day in 1970. It gave birth to the insight that we are not living daily on present income, the continuous energy from the sun, but on accumulated capital, for example ice age water, oil, and minerals. A look to the future requires a reappraisal of the past. We began to see that we have mortgaged our grandchildren's future. The concerns of environmentalism are energy, global warming, ozone depletion, pollution, available and safe water, sustainable agriculture, and population control. These bracing new insights were answered with counter-delusions: that over-consumption is an interesting moral issue but not a biological one (Dick Cheney); that nature can best be addressed in aesthetic terms; that if there were real environmental problems, signals from the prices of commodities would alert us; that the past sheds sufficient light on the future; that rapid economic growth is actually good for the environment; and that the "big government" necessary to address environmental disaster would do more harm than good, especially of course to free markets.

To the free market mentality, natural resources seem infinite and therefore economically valueless: ecological considerations are "externalities" beyond the scope of economic calculations and are no-shows on corporate balance sheets. Meanwhile, interest and profits escalate the pace of exploitation. A society that extols unlimited acquisition cannot be expected to honor the integrity of life on earth. Capitalism's great myth is the self-regulating, self-healing mechanism of market growth, and it has degraded and debased cultures everywhere—and the earth as well. An ecological economy must be a *moral economy*, in which economic relations are expressions of care and interdependence, not aggression and exploitation.

While contemporary biology and earth science are now leading the way in the environmentalist movement, it has been recognized that modern science had also contributed to the earth's denigration by imagining nature as a place of human conquest and by a secular philosophy that "disenchanted" the earth, stripped it of the presence of God, and stole or eroded its mythological story. Women especially noticed that the earth long ago—but no longer—had often been identified as a cosmic mother and that deities connected to nature were typically feminine. It did not escape their observation that both women and earth had then become subject to ruthless male domination, that alienation from the body and its wisdom is the inner aspect of the ecological crisis. They noticed that what happens to bodies, to women's bodies, and to nature are all connected. Until women led the way, no one, including no one representing biblical religion, was mourning the lost mother.

The religious concern for the environment is not limited to the West. A fascinating example of spiritual sensibilities brought in defense of the earth is the tree-hugging movement initiated by indigenous women in northern India in the 1970s. It combined Hindu devotion to the integrity of the forests with Gandhian nonviolence. The women fasted, embraced ancient trees, lay down in front of logging trucks, and uprooted eucalyptus plantation seedlings. They simply defied Western dualisms of public/private, morality/self-interest, biocentrism/anthropocentrism, and militancy/pragmatism. The Third World, they saw, was being turned into an international debtors' prison, and a vast plantation run for the benefit of masters far away. They believed that the earth cannot and should not be owned, but respected and cared for. Their intuitions are remarkably similar to those of the Hebrew prophets speaking on behalf of a liberal God.

Progressive religion, finding God in all things and all things in God, wants to remythologize earth and nature—something scientists should not reject. It recovers the imagination of the earth as God's body. The mono-theistic terror of pantheism, so characteristic of Western religion and so convenient for the plundering of the earth as safely "not-God," can give way to a new cosmogenesis. The archaic sacrilization of earth is reasserted against the tendency of Western religions to privilege history over nature as the locus where God is to be encountered. Everything is holy to those who open their eyes and take off their shoes.

CHRISTIANITY IS A SOCIAL JUSTICE MOVEMENT IN THE ECONOMY OF GOD

Justice was Merriam-Webster's 2018 Word of the Year. *Justice* appeared 74 percent more often than in 2017. Is this good news? Is a fundamental con-cept in biblical ethics achieving a comeback? Is a new social gospel on the way? Have we all come to see that justice is the social form of that prized word—*love*? Maybe. Trumpian Christians, and perhaps many other con-servatives, have mobilized to argue that social justice is a left-wing value, a political agenda, and has nothing to do with Biblical Christianity.

All the more important, then, is Stanley Hauerwas's contention that the New Testament sees the church as a colony of heaven and that "being the church" will always constitute a divine intrusion into the world's settled arrangements. The church is called to speak its own language, tell its own story, offer the world a new way of seeing and something new to see.

The church that is returning to a full presence in the public square (next chapter) comes true to its calling by continuously moving back and forth between contemplation and action, having something to say, some-thing to be, a way to behave. In *believing, teaching, confessing*, and acting, the church performs itself as the body of Christ on earth. Christians are resident aliens who speak with an accent that offends the ear of capitalist ideology. To be the church is to engage in moral resistance, insurgency, nonconfor-mity, protest, movement. Every so often, to keep itself seeing clearly and acting conspicuously, the church must assemble, study the times, see what is particularly incompatible with the gospel, and confess anew to the world around. "Reclaiming Jesus: A Confession of Faith in a Time of Crisis" is a recent example of the church practicing being the church and acting out itself in public. It is not medieval or individualistic to aspire once again to the "imitation of Christ."

At various times in the church's history, Christians have seen themselves as a company of pilgrims, which often included dissent and nonconformity. Some contemporary best sellers, for example by Brian McLaren, call contemporary Christians to get up once again and move out of Egypt, which also means renouncing the self-privileging accommodations made with earthly powers.

The church cannot accept being relegated to private homes and bedside stands. It must act out being the church in public, it must be prophetic. What if radical Christianity were today the only place where the values of the market, the "principalities and powers" of late capitalism, are consistently named, unmasked, and challenged?

Christianity has often helped keep the world safe from godly utopianism, from the church's vision of Christ, from joining heaven and earth, by relegating heaven to a safe distance, where it will not infect earth. *Utopia,* the eschatological inbreaking of heaven, is always the stepchild disinherited in the last will and testament that makes realism the only legitimate human legacy. The powers that be remain safe from radical Christian vision, from the "infinity of the unfinished." But Christian hope looks for the day when heaven crosses the threshold of earth, as when God became incarnate in Christ and earth became capable of heaven.

Many evangelicals have precisely resisted the meme of social justice, insisting it is merely a liberal political value and in many ways objectionable at that. In 2019 the conservative evangelical/fundamentalist John MacArthur released a public statement opposing the new (progressive) Christian emphasis on social justice. Soon 7,000 pastors signed on to it. They denied that social justice was an essential dimension of the Christian proclamation of the gospel, because it short circuits what is more fundamental to Christianity—the individual believer's conversion to Christ, and implies the religious orbit is fundamentally social when conservatives see it as individual freedom. Perhaps even more importantly, MacArthur strongly rejected any social justice that included an affirmation of homosexuality and equal rights for women. He seemed comfortable with a gospel without reference to God's heart for the poor.

GODLY UTOPIANISM, THE WEDDING
OF HEAVEN, AND EARTHLY HOPE

When at the beginning of the sixteenth century Thomas More wrote a humanist utopia, the word *utopia* actually meant *nowhere,* and many then and now took it to mean idealistic reforms that were not practicable. Indeed, some believe that More himself was actually writing a satire on contemporary England rather than a genuine proposal for the future. But perhaps More hoped that a humanist idealism could seriously improve the social and political structures of his age, that justice, equity, and the public good would replace the feudalism of the past and the present rule of kings and lords. Utopian idealism soon found itself amidst the new currents of the Protestant Reformation, and sometimes was conjoined with the radical millennial hopes of the Anabaptists or the visions of the medieval visionary Joachim of Fiore.

Eventually, utopianism joined with the Enlightenment belief in inevitable historical progress. Americans have a long tradition of utopian thought, and it especially blossomed during the nineteenth century. Marxism dreamed of a socialist utopia as an inevitable outcome of its philosophy of history. But confident philosophies of history and the optimism that accompanied them crashed in the first half of the twentieth century. Social critics like Huxley and Orwell worried that utopian thought inevitably looked to a totalitarian state as its enforcer, as it indeed did in the Soviet Union and China.

So the second half of the twentieth century trended toward a political and social realism that saw utopianism as a sheer romanticism that refused to deal with the world as it was and/or a vision that too readily gave itself to fanaticism, a vision of excessive certainty determined to do whatever was necessary to bring about the world it imagined. The excesses of Stalin's and Mao's Communist vision are now well known, and the tens of millions sacrificed on their altar are acknowledged. So the Y2K movement at the end of the second millennium scaled hope down and wanted nothing so much as an unchanging world, not a third millennium utopia. Hope was redefined as assurance that everything in the New Year would work just like everything in the old year.

Realists and others with heavy investments in a status quo that has served them well are disdainful of utopianism, and often actively oppose such thinking. Utopianism, by definition, wants to dis-establish and transcend the way things are. The radical thinker Joachim of Fiore disturbed church and society in the twelfth century by dreaming of a "third age of the Spirit," one that would displace or succeed the present order of Christendom, including, of course, that of the established church. In the fourth century, as Rome was failing, Augustine proposed a civil order anchored in Christianity and its vision of the City of God. In the process, he relocated the powerful apocalyptic energies of parts of the New Testament to eternity. Such visions would hold no power or illumination for the road just ahead. Seven hundred years later, when the Augustinian vision still held sway in Europe, Joachim was looking for a time of new testaments, new institutions, new authorities, a time to give voice to long repressed yearnings and dangerous dreams, a new age with its own (dangerous) "eternal gospel." (Has that time ever come?) In his train there came later heretics and prophets and singers and artists and wanderers chanting the form-breaking narratives of writings like the last book of the New Testament, Revelation. Was Julia Ward Howe utopian when she sent the grapes of wrath through the divine winepress in "The Battle Hymn of the Republic"? Were American slaves utopian when they decoded the story of exodus as God's secret message to them? Were the French revolutionaries utopian, right up to when they turned to redemptive violence as necessary societal cleansing? Did the sixteenth-century German Anabaptists quickly chasten their utopianism after they succumbed to violent temptations in Muenster?

When society lacks or suppresses a utopian hope that could be politically and culturally powerful, the pressure of the repressed yearning produces surprising eruptions. Widespread body piercing as the millennium turned became the transgressive actions by which an urban underground imaged its unwillingness to queue for mainstream assimilation. Their bodies were turned to the art of resistance against the commodification of a one-dimensional age. But eventually they regressed to a new form of bodily imaging, a non-threatening personal style statement. Everyone has a tattoo today, and they're not changing anything but the aesthetics of fashion and public display of self. All the revolutionary resistance was co-opted and redone as urban fashion. Tattoos are plentiful at the local YMCA. Utopian imagery can readily be commodified.

Utopian thought also occurs on the right, as fundamentalists see God imminently arriving to right wrongs. In Israel there began to appear in the 1980s a "Jerusalem syndrome." In an atmosphere charged with religious expectancy, international visitors began to believe they were the incarnations of biblical personages, *Elijah redivivus*. The Holy Land was their field of dreams. They were treated in Israeli clinics with anti-psychotic medications and recovered in a week. Something about dopamine uptake. But they were urged to avoid in the future the hot spots of apocalyptic stimuli.

Utopianism, delightful in literary form, is so easy to dismiss or disparage when it appears in real life. *Utopia is always the stepchild disinherited in the will and testament that makes realism the only legitimate human legacy.*

As this book closes, I want to argue that utopianism can be revisioned as the promising wedding of hope and heaven, God and humans.

We have seen that Ernst Bloch rehabilitated hope from the sophisticated doubts of Marx and Freud and gave it an ontological parentage in "the infinity of the unfinished." He turned possibility, process, and utopia into the most telling characteristics of the human project. He saw us always pointing toward something more. We are unfinished, and what we will become awaits the utopian imagination. We are flowers leaning towards God's light, as the Gospel of John intimated. Hope imitates God's risky venture. When conservatives tie utopia only to a distant heaven, they are *keeping this world safe from infection with God's liberalism.* This must be called a failure of religious imagination.

Ultimately, hope looks for the day when heaven crosses the threshold of earth, as Christians believe happened in what the New Testament proclaims as the incarnation of God in Jesus Christ. But if heaven is the mother of all metaphors, we must attend to the carrying capacity of contemporary language to keep it on our horizon. Utopian hope makes the connection, and we die for the lack of it. We must resist all those who want to free us from religion, from poetry, from words of mystery and transcendence—and resist fundamentalists who want to save us through literalism. Against those who want to set us free by reason, we go with poets in search of the missing words.

What did we gain by denying the existence of larger stories? How are we better for failing to write a liberating God into the social contract? Indefinitely postponing God's arrival, protecting capitalist DNA from divine mutations, tethering God to small ambitions and familiar prejudices—all these strategies squander the liberations the God of the Bible offers. Mind-blowing revelations are boiled down to the comfortable road ahead. But no good comes from uprooting the human project from its rich imaginal ground. We only become disconnected from the life of the spirit and alienated from our own deepest longings. When so much of the world suffers, it is no time for the iconoclasm that disallows the imaging of God amidst the human project. Believing is seeing. *Isn't utopianism the fraught attempt to imitate a liberal God on an unliberal earth?* At the beginning of the reception of the Eucharist, some celebrants say, "Behold what you are; Become what you receive."

8

Proclaiming and Becoming a New Social Gospel

Recontesting the Public Square

NAMING SECULARISM AS THE PREOCCUPIED PUBLIC SQUARE

Secularists often project an aura of self-congratulation. They devoutly believe that the triumph over religion is one of the "assured results" of Enlightenment rationalism, science, and modernity. Like religious fundamentalists in other settings, they bring an uncritical confidence into the public square and demand exclusive rights. Religious discourse, they are certain, should stay at home or be confined to churches, or, better yet, be retired. To force their point they confidently assert that the establishment clause of the First Amendment requires the exclusion of religion from almost all public space, and mid-twentieth century Supreme Court decisions often agreed. But the Court did then begin a trend in which the freedom of religion clause and, better yet, the right of free speech, were seen as maintaining the rights of religion alongside all other communities of discourse.

Trump supporters fully expect that new Court appointments may begin to reverse the depriviliging of religion and reassert its rights in the public square. The June 2019 decision allowing a large cross, commemorating veterans, to stand on public property seemed early confirmation of that hope. Among the noteworthy statements of support in this 5–2 decision were the following: "The Religion Clauses of the Constitution aim to foster a society in which people of all beliefs can live together harmoniously, and the presence of the Bladensburg Cross on the land where it has stood for so many years is fully consistent with that aim." Perhaps more importantly: "A government that roams the land, tearing down monuments with religious symbolism and scrubbing away any reference to the divine will strike many as aggressively hostile to religion."

In this chapter *I am calling for a vigorous Christian presence in the public square*. I do not mean the takeover of the public square, as in a militant theocracy, or Christianity as the established religion, but an unashamed Christian presence, with something significant to offer and to be, in the life of society. I am calling for Christianity's (and religion's) right to be present in the commons, to recontest public space. In chapter 6 I have already argued that religious or spiritual people must contest the assumption that Enlightenment rationalism is the only discourse style, the only community of discourse, allowed in the commons.

A way into reflection on the rights of religion is to consider the concept of *aural landscape*. There is a provocative study of the role that church bells have played in the aural imagination of France. For much of French history, bell-ringing had marked both religious and secular time, calling citizens to prayer or civic assembly. But the French Revolution came to see that to control the bells was to control symbolic order, the loyalties of life. Municipalizing church bells, it was seen, could bend them to the new national interest, could secularize them. So the revolutionaries melted down one hundred thousand bells, intending to disenchant the landscape, to free civic life from the aural dominance of religion, to subvert ancient makers of the holy. The historic culture of town bells had mixed sacred and profane together. Villages prided themselves on being a "ringing town." Bell castings were great occasions, featuring expert advisers, drinking bouts, and finally the baptism of the bells, with mayor and priest competing to control the town's biorhythms. But after the revolution, mayors insisted the bells belonged to the town on every Bastille Day—and perhaps every day. On occasions of religious dissent, insolent clerics could ring their bells at will, perhaps ringing a funeral peal at an inappropriate time. As France grew more secular, the bells could still be summoned to sound a religious voice, to sound a vertical or transcendent frame amidst a horizontal or immanent frame. In contemporary America, cities sometimes pass urban ordinances that consider bells an interference with sleep or the right to silence, a religious torture from which secular relief is demanded. Aural space, too, is contested.

Secularism as the modern default worldview of science, status elites, higher education, and a very significant number of Americans and

Europeans refers to the decline or elimination of the God hypothesis as a convincing way to make sense of human origins and destiny. It is an ideology that insists that faith and religion have no place in shaping public conversation and public policy. Many see a post-Christian world as a significant legacy of the Enlightenment, and there are important theories about how it has gone hand in hand with modernism. It has meant the gradual withdrawal of more and more dimensions of human life from under the interpretive umbrella of religious symbols. To some, secularism is the best antidote for troublesome religion; but to others, including me, *good religion* may be a better cure for what ails us.

In his influential book *A Secular Age,* Charles Taylor argued that we live now in a postmodern world in which both secularism and religion are more fluid concepts than formerly. Some now see postmodernism as both post-religious and post-secular (secular being a modernist concept). And some theorists even call secularism one new form religiosity (concern for absolute meaning) takes. Secularism is not the great and conclusive philosophy of no absolute meaning that lays all rivals to rest, the absolute assertion of *nothing,* but another competing *something.*

In the social sciences the "secularization thesis" was based on a single global idea of religion, a definition of secularity as the absence of religion, and a supposed inevitable evolution in which economic growth, urbanization, social mobility, the rise of science and technology, and the triumph of instrumental reason would lead inevitably to the *marginalization of religion,* and then the *subtraction of religion* from the public sphere.

For the purposes of my argument, religion that approaches and seeks a return to the public square may come upon and be challenged by a *total secular occupation.* And of course secularism as an ideology but not typically thought of as a religion had the advantage in escaping the strictures of the First Amendment's prohibition of an established religion. In the face of this I am calling for Christians to co-occupy the public square as well. And to *enter the public sphere with something to say, a persuasive platform, something to do, something to be.* Of course saying/doing/being already precisely constitute many discussions of the church as the body of Christ, the church as a colony of heaven. Especially in Anabaptist discussions of the church, any activist attempts to transform culture (a typical Calvinist impulse) must be preceded by a thoughtful determination to *be the church, to talk the church's unique language, to tell the church's stories.* Notice how contrary this is to the attempt of many Christian liberals to sound as much as possible like the secular culture in order to gain a hearing. *So the church, under the freedom of religion as well as on free speech grounds, has the right to proclaim and seek to speak its own language and proclaim a new social gospel.*

A focus on the religious becomes *one* of the stories jostling for acceptance in a postmodern age, one of the master narratives. Some *believe* that amidst competing stories, God-stories are better because they are, in David Tracy's phrase, "more adequate to the human condition." The religious story occurs amidst radical changes in the way we experience the world and asks what it takes to go on believing in God—but in the absence of the intellectual, cultural, and imaginative supports characteristic of premodern Christianity. The contemporary social imaginary includes all those ways in which we attempt to understand, picture, and dramatize the world around us, including both what we have called secular and what we have called religious. So instead of bringing displacement and substitution, secularism can now be understood as one process of recovery and adaptation.

There is no doubt that a secular culture, at least since the eighteenth century, has seriously weakened religion as a worldview and source of meaning. But that secular culture itself did not turn into an adequate substitute for discarded religious symbols. This has produced a civilizational crisis, as the plausibility structures within which religious systems of meaning should thrive become eroded, and images of God and humanity destabilized.

A world disenchanted soon becomes disenchanting. We have landed in a world of social practices in which transcendence or the sacred seemed, initially, no longer to make sense. In such circumstances, we experimented with no longer posing deep questions. (For example, if facing death head-on requires religious resources, we will choose to avoid thinking deeply about human mortality, a historical process I describe in my book *The Last Passage: Recovering a Death of Our Own*.) But even in severely altered social and cultural conditions, transcendence went underground, or turned into magic realism, to reappear in literature and the arts and new religious movements that intimated new forms of awareness of the sacred. All these eruptions occur in the face of an alleged meaningless universe, evolving without purpose. Many could not reconcile themselves to the earth as a ship to nowhere.

Consider the context in which these changes occur, above all global capitalism often with specific intent recently called *late capitalism*. A social order bent on producing wealth as the only meaning of life cannot avoid producing people whose souls are superficial and whose daily lives are captured by mere sentimentalities—not to mention all those who do not profit from a capitalist economy and become detritus thrown aside. Amidst capitalist splendor, there is much loss of light. We need a solstice ceremony no less than our European ancestors did, in order to drag back the sun as darkness threatens. Metaphysical and metaphorical loss characterize the bleak midwinter, and everywhere there is anxiety for the receding light of meaningful human life and our place in the cosmos. The answer may lie in postmodern religion as a competing story about life and meaning, or a modified and chastened secularism as a kind of religion. The public square cannot on principle be denied a new social gospel. In whose interest is it to ward off religious critiques of late capitalism?

A particularly useful way of conceptualizing secularism and its basic ways of knowing and seeing is that of Charles Taylor's term, the *immanent frame*. Imagine that all the windows on life in the public sphere permit only one way of seeing, and permit only one set of realities to be seen. A consequence of the disenchantment of the world, this frame constitutes a *natural* order, to be contrasted to a *supernatural* one, an *immanent* world over against a possible *transcendent* one. It is easy and common to fall into this mind-set that closes off much of possible reality and reduces spirit to matter. The immanent frame is by no means ethically neutral. It renders "vertical" or "transcendent" worlds inaccessible or unthinkable. It operates as a philosophically reductionistic stance, a moral position that Taylor calls *exclusive humanism*. (In chapter 6 I called for a Christian humanism.)

The house in which the mind, including the captured mind, lives is often referred to as the *social imaginary*, the totality of images and metaphors and stories that define our world. An important dimension of this is the marginalization of religion and transcendence in Western culture and the triumphant *subtraction story* in the Western Master Narrative, where science replaces religion after Christendom. In this perspective, the growth of science entails the death of God or the recession of religion. Taylor does not accept the hermeneutic of meaning in which science becomes equivalent to secularism. The resistance to this and an alternative hermeneutic of the human prospect in the world gave the title "earth angel" to chapter 6.

We have proceeded too easily from science to atheism, from modernization to secularization. Angry atheists want no backsliding from what they consider an obvious conclusion, no religious return to public space. But such a view, such a process, is not in fact based in or necessary to science. Materialism is a human construction not arising from science, but a story we tell ourselves about the cosmos and our place within it, our value, identity, trajectory, and purpose. This naturalistic metaphysic is the one that wants to be the faith that prevails in the public sphere. Everything is based on *matter*, and there is no obvious *spirit*.

The claim is that religious belief is a childish temptation and a Peter Pan world. The religious lack the courage to acknowledge (or protest and lament) the social imaginary we see out the window of the immanent frame. Growing up and taking up residence in the public square (or going to college) means leaving faith in God behind. But Taylor does not concede that loss of faith in adulthood is an obvious fact of observable reality. Instead it is but a particular construction of human identity and our place in the world, a particular way of seeing and being the world. When religion returns to the public square it questions this hermeneutic and wants to expose its inadequacy to the human prospect.

NAMING AMERICAN EXCEPTIONALISM AS THE IDOLATRY OF NATIONALIST CAPITALISM

The applicants for place in the American public square are by no means reduced to the either/or of secularism disguised as America's established ideology or historic religions like Christianity, Judaism, or Islam. What is often called American exceptionalism, a kind of official civil religion of America, is another candidate, differing from both secularism and Biblical Christianity.

Scholars like Robert Bellah, drawing in part on the nineteenth-century observations of Alexis de Tocqueville's *Democracy in America,* proposed the term American *civil religion* to describe a nonsectarian quasi-religious faith that exists in the United States, with sacred symbols drawn from national history. This civil religion, not unlike historic religions, is a cohesive force and a common set of values that foster social and cultural integration.

Bellah saw a common civil religion with certain fundamental beliefs, holidays, and rituals parallel to but independent of historic religions like Christianity. Among its characteristics are filial piety, sacred texts and symbols like the Constitution and the flag, sanctified American institutions, belief in God, rights divinely given, freedom as a gift of God through government, God as sovereign judge, American prosperity as a product of God's providence, America as a city on a hill and a beacon of hope and righteousness and serving higher purposes than mere self-interest. It seemed like an American Shinto, grounding us in the past—minus genocide or slavery, minus critical self-examination.

In Bellah's view, and hope, civil religion began as a dialectic between utilitarian individualism and concern for the common good. But as American history progressed, that vigorous dialectic relaxed, and civil religion came to look more and more like a mostly uncritical celebration of American exceptionalism. Civil religion is especially tolerated in the public sphere if religious specificity is subtracted. The American way, unleavened by a distinctive Christian social gospel.

This can be seen in the evolution of the term "city on a hill" to describe the American experience. The phrase comes from Jesus' Sermon on the

Mount in Matthew 5:14, where he says: "You are the light of the world. A city set on a hill cannot be hidden." In his seventeenth-century shipboard sermon on Massachusetts Bay, Governor John Winthrop admonished the Puritans about to disembark with a very high standard of aspiration. Some have seen this allusion as a boast, casting America as the envy of the world, a beacon of liberty in a sea of oppressive regimes. President Reagan liked to add *shining* to our status as city on a hill. Others have invoked it more as an aspiration—an ideal that inspires us even as we fall woefully short of achieving it.

In *As a City on a Hill: The Story of America's Most Famous Lay Sermon*, historian Daniel Rodgers argues that the "we" in Winthrop's "we shall be as a city upon a hill" was never the future United States, or any other human kingdom. The Puritans who joined Winthrop in a pilgrimage to a new world came in order to purify and enlarge the church, not to found a new nation or extend an existing empire. If anything, Winthrop's metaphor cautioned the Christian not to be at home in the world. It testified to an inescapable tension between Christ-followers and the surrounding culture, and it reminded them that even the most devout were prone to stumble.

Winthrop meant not to puff the Puritans up but to chill them with the judgment of God. But we have subsequently preferred to tell ourselves that even a century and a half prior to independence, one of the earliest of our "founders" prophesied that God had chosen the future United States for a special mission to the world. Yet Rodgers claims that this great metaphor was a call to humility and faithfulness, not to destiny and greatness.

So American exceptionalism became a kind of national self-congratulation whose invocations appear in nearly every political speech ("God bless you and God bless America" has become obligatory, almost like the John 3:16 banner at a football game). American exceptionalism idolizes American nationalism, including often a deregulated capitalism whose invisible hand is the very providence of God.

Civil religion as self-congratulation lacks the prophetic voice and covenantal justice of the Old Testament, and the unsettling proclamation of the reign of God in the ministry of Jesus Christ in the New Testament. It specifically wants to live without obligation to the concept of social justice. While the American civil religion may claim Lincoln as its most famous theologian and martyr, a pervasive racism continues to prevail. White nationalism is again under President Trump making explicit and unavoidable claims. Earlier analyses of civil religion did not typically mention unregulated and hallowed capitalism as essential to its self-understanding and a mark of God's providence, though conservatives in general and the Christian Right make it foundational to their self-understanding. It has become the case, however, that American exceptionalism as a national religion specifically rejected nonconformist or religiously radical ideas and movements. The idea of the American president as the leader of the civil religion has become preposterous under Trump. Or not. The run-up to the 2020 election will again see "socialism" defined as blasphemy to the civil religion. In the rejection of social justice Trump plays high priest.

The *Saturday Night Live* "church lady" liked to say, "Aren't we special!" If victors write history, why shouldn't Christianity be an American tale? If the sign of divine election were dying with the most goods, America would be the capital of heaven. If true religion elevates self-regard, no other nation comes close to being as pious as we are. A recent survey of American young people finds that what they really believe, faithfully inherited from their parents, is "moralistic therapeutic deism," a Christianity in which God fixes things, roots for your team, and rewards good behavior with a happy afterlife. (On the other hand, American young people show an increasing toleration for socialist approaches.) The Spanish American philosopher George Santayana wrote that "American life is a powerful solvent. It seems to neutralize every intellectual element, however tough and alien it may be, and to fuse it in the native good-will, complacency, thoughtlessness, and optimism." Stephen Prothero subtitled his book *American Jesus: How the Son of God Became a National Icon.*

American exceptionalism is the confidence that Americans, under God, can try and succeed at social and political experiments the rest of the world could not even dream of. (This astonishes northern European social democracies.) The constraints that apply to all historical projects do not apply to us. Imagine Bush and Cheney screening *The Lord of the Rings* in the White House situation room. They leave to get popcorn during the revelation that the ring represents a bedazzlement with power that must be renounced and the ring thrown into the cracks of doom. When they return, it is just in time to join the fellowship of the ring, which they conclude commissions them to use military power to eradicate foreign evil and bring American good to the world. So it becomes our destiny to be handed the power of the ring, and the Republican religious base is self-constituted as the fellowship of the ring. The great advantage of *making God the subject of your own predicates* is absolute certainty and freedom from the doubt that characterizes the foolishly humble.

To take a very particular example, an egregious form of American exceptionalism is our gun culture. Lamenting one of the many outbursts of gun violence, public intellectual Gary Wills wrote that it is "theologically inconceivable" to implement real gun control in the United States. He argued that Americans believe that God gave us guns to show us who we are. Giving up guns would surrender to evil. The gun is patriotic. The gun is America. The gun is God.

In her recent book, *Loaded: A Disarming History of the Second Amendment,* Roxanne Dunbar-Ortiz traces the historical and religious roots attaching to the sanctity of the Second Amendment. The NRA borrows from a larger ideology that preceded them. The apparent irrationality of open-carry laws and widespread resistance to gun safety measures become comprehensible when viewed within the overall trajectory of a religiously infused American exceptionalism. Dunbar-Ortiz's earlier book, *Indigenous Peoples' History of the United States,* points to white Europeans' genocidal treatment of Native Americans. Following that came the overwhelming need to control black bodies in building a slave-based economy. She argues that we were the first nation-state founded on the principles of raw capitalism, with land viewed as a commodity and with human beings viewed as chattel. This model required a great deal of lethal force. We *needed guns* to facilitate westward expansion. We *needed guns* to remove or exterminate Native Americans. We *needed guns* to control blacks and defend our way of life, the Jim Crow South. Colonists both North and South were required to be armed and available for marauding duty in irregular militias, before there was a Second Amendment. Once slaves began arriving, Southern white men were required to arm themselves for slave patrol duty. President Andrew Jackson schooled us in defending civilization against savagery. Historians with a keen eye for concepts not taught in public education see the religious underpinning of the gun culture: divine election, covenant, and blood sacrifice. God's elect are authorized to take the land and its inhabitants in fulfillment of the divine purpose. Such special election is rooted in Puritan-Calvinist theology, none more so, as the American experiment went on, than the Scotch-Irish. John Fea's book on religion under Trump argued that fear of the other is central to the American evangelical mind-set.

There are competing discourse communities, competing messages, in the American public square. And perhaps in every public square. Following the example of the Barmen Declaration by the "Confessing Church" in Nazi Germany, Sojourners's Jim Wallis and other theologians made "A New Confession of Christ" for our own times. In this book's terms, consider it to be laying the groundwork for the proclamation of a new social gospel.

> 1. Jesus Christ knows no national boundaries. We reject the false teaching that the attributes of Christ can be applied to a nation. 2. Christ commits Christians to a strong presumption against war. We reject the false teaching that a war on terrorism supersedes ethical discriminations. 3. Christ commands us to

deal with the evil in our own hearts, and not only that in our adversaries. We reject the false teaching that America is a Christian nation representing only virtue, that America has nothing to repent of. 4. Christ shows us that enemy-love is the heart of the gospel. We reject the demonization of our enemies. 5. Christ teaches us that humility is the virtue befitting forgiven sinners. We reject the false teaching that those who are not for the United States politically are against it or that those who question American policies are to be considered evil-doers.

RECONSIDERING THE CHURCH/STATE STAND-OFF

It is easy to call for a high wall separating church and state when one scorns organized religion, as Thomas Jefferson did. In Jefferson's view, "priestcraft" was always in league with despotism, and the church would always ruin the pure teachings of Jesus. But what if one has earthly and material hopes for religion? What if progressive religion is the best defense against the encroachments of an unregulated capitalism that despoils the poor and the earth? *What if the dissenting church is the only community with moral standing that tells a counter-story to that of all-powerful late capitalism?* The American constitution makes a distinction between religious establishment (no) and religious freedom (yes). Secular liberals, who might become potential allies of any religious movement that imitates a liberating God, are prone to watch closely for religious encroachments in the public square. But this book argues for the imitation, including the *political and economic imitation*, of a liberating God—in the public square, not merely in the quiet of our hearts. This book calls for *Christianity recontesting public space.*

Perhaps many are wary of church-state transgressions because they fear the triumph of the Christian Right or the Catholic bishops or the (now moribund) Puritan establishment. One regularly sees on Facebook dark allusions to the "American Taliban," almost always referring to the Christian Right. Would this objection be used against a social justice Christianity as well? Religious entanglement with government worries people—at least it worries liberals or devoted secularists. The American Constitution does not use the phrase "separation of church and state," but Thomas Jefferson did, and in the second half of the twentieth century the "wall of separation" first grew higher but then slightly lower. The Supreme Court swung back and forth between condemning too much religious encroachment and then too much religious restriction. For awhile, a "legal secularism" prevailed, in which public discourse and public space and public policy had to be free of religion, and this looked to many Christians like the *establishment of a quasi-religious secularism* as the only acceptable worldview—not counted as a religion. But then the court began to shift towards the free speech clause, and this challenged attempts to single out religious speech and silence only it in the public square. This seems to be the currently prevailing presupposition of a majority of the Supreme Court. Evangelicals devoutly hope that foreseeable Trump appointees, after Justice Gorsuch and Brett Kavanaugh, may *swing the Court radically away from establishment clause obsession to free exercise enthusiasm.* So provisionally, evangelicals will cheer. *But isn't it conceivable that also progressive Christianity might cheer a Supreme Court that legitimizes its return to the public square and its right to live out its story there, including contending for values that challenge the prevailing social and economic order?*

Following the *1965 Declaration on Religious Freedom* emanating from Vatican II, some American Catholics have very importantly argued that the courts should acknowledge religious symbols, monuments, events in public places; should allow religious cooperation in secular projects; should recognize that for millennia humans have been seen to be *homo religiosus;* should acknowledge that a religious life in public precedes the Constitution and is not a state-granted concession; should acknowledge that the "free exercise" clause of the First Amendment should apply not just to individuals but also to individuals acting in community; and should affirm that government owes not merely neutrality or keeping distance but proactive and positive care of the conditions of social life under which people seek fulfillment and transcendence. Government should be *not merely neutral towards religious freedom but nurturing and enabling.*

Formerly, liberal Protestantism was somewhat likely to join forces with the strict separationists, especially the ACLU and Protestants United for the separation of church and state. But lately, an increasing postmodern mentality, an emphasis on multiculturalism in the public square, an unwillingness to rule out all faith-based public discourse, the fairness issue that gives all forms of free speech including religion equal entitlement, and the Religious Left running to catch up to the Religious Right in its political and moral presence in the country—all these are shifting progressive religion towards a more assertive stance on the issue of religion and religious discourse in the public life of Americans.

Radical Christianity would like to be the yeast that leavens the commons, that imagines alternative public lives and worlds, that proclaims and becomes a social gospel in the public sphere. Radical Christianity, and the Jewish Tikkun movement for example, want to proclaim the God of the exodus and Jubilee. *Radical religion is not willing to concede the point that politics, but not religion, is the realm of cultural power.* Already Max Weber began a tradition in the sociology of religion that could see religion as an independent variable in society and culture, and not always merely an epiphenomenon. *Culture and economics and politics can be downstream of insurgent religion.*

The real religious problem with the American Constitution, which half a century of Supreme Court opinions tried to work through, or around, is its intellectual setting in the world of the eighteenth century Enlightenment. The "originalists" who seem always to be conservatives somehow do not see this. The founders, with fresh and painful memories of European religious wars and with sublime confidence in their own Enlightenment rationalism, believed they could divide the world up. What started out as the separation of church and state became, as Enlightenment and then secular thought gained ever greater dominating power, the separation of religion and culture, and of private (the sphere to which religion came to be relegated) and public, the world of the heart versus that of politics, economics, real power, and, in the current economics jargon, rational choice. But no world religion, and certainly not Christianity, was ever merely a matter of private belief. No religion ever willingly consents to being ousted from the public sphere.

Didn't God lead Israel out of Egypt? Wasn't Jesus despised by the Jerusalem establishment and crucified by the Romans? Didn't early Christianity insist on making its foremost confession *Jesus is Lord*—when *Lord* was also the term for the Roman Emperor? Whether establishing, or transcending, or resisting, religion has always been a public player whose influence governments and scholars (and the CIA) underestimate at their peril. To some extent, we now live in a post-Enlightenment, postmodern age, in which all diversities are to be recognized and weighed and accommodated, or even celebrated. Proponents of this insight always mention race, class, and gender. It is past time to mention religion when discussing "intersectionalities."

Could all Christians ever come together to represent the presence of a liberating God in the life of the commons? Is a new social gospel proclaimed and lobbied and embodied by Christians too far a dream?

THE CHURCH AS SOCIAL MOVEMENT INTO THE PUBLIC SPHERE

Contemplation and action are commonly named dimensions in spiritual formation—from seeing Christ meditatively to imitating Christ on earth. In 2013 the new Pope Francis began modeling the saint whose mark on the twelfth century was the profoundly significant Franciscan movement. Like Francis of Assisi, the current pope understands that you have to *see something and be something and do something*, if you are to be a disciple of Jesus Christ. He is living simply and developing that aspiration for the whole world. And he may be choosing to open the Catholic Church as a home for all, a place where people can encounter and come close to Christ—not a private chapel for orthodox purity or self-regarding clericalism or self-serving sexism.

In a contemporary world where civic virtue, not to mention civic engagement, have gone missing, movements of moral resistance, insurgency, nonconformity, and protest are needed. To call the church to community organizing and political action is to say the church invites the world to consider its social vision. But is the vision of Christ in short supply?

The Christian faith the times require is one that decodes the exodus, embraces the prophets, and follows Jesus as the earthly paradigm of a liberating God. A Christian gospel discounted for sale in an American setting cannot provide robust motivation and clear vision for the road ahead. The bite of the Hebrew prophets is not now breaking through the oppressive economic forces that constrain public life. Conservative Bible believers somehow miss the Messianic program Jesus proclaims, detouring it to gender wars and American nationalism. A Congress reeking with religious hypocrisy pretends the national budget is not a moral document so much as an Ayn Rand postscript. Best-selling evangelical heroes inspire many acts of Christian charity and urge a purpose-driven life, but they mostly do not attempt a structural analysis of injustice. Their enthusiastic Christian lives are carefully *restricted to paths predetermined by their conservative political convictions.* In recent decades, American religion as an heir of historic Christianity has gone into a long descent. America as a city on the hill has drifted from a Puritan ideal of public righteousness beckoning to all the world toward a self-satisfied American exceptionalism that locates evil elsewhere and privileges American interests. If it weren't already clear, this is now the official doctrine of "Make America Great Again." And it is a profound embarrassment to, indeed a reversal of, any social gospel.

In the last quarter of the twentieth century, Roman Catholicism in America began a cautious retreat from the fresh winds of the Second Vatican Council of the 1960s and from its historically rich social teachings—in the direction of institutional retrenchment and an ever-narrowing reduction of Christianity to an obsession with abortion and contraception and homosexuality and the hemming of women. A political party that supported this agenda would be supported, often enthusiastically, by the bishops. Most American bishops in effect turned themselves into conservative Republicans for the sake of the anti-abortion agenda. Recent literature has argued that American Catholicism (e.g. the Knights of Columbus) has undergone a conservative captivity similar to that of the evangelical Christian Right.

In fact, many papal decrees, not just those of the new pope, trace moral theology back to the Hebrew Bible (see chapter 1). In 2011 the Pontifical Council on Justice and Peace spoke out decisively against *free market fundamentalism* and identified with the Occupy Wall Street movement as "in line with Catholic social teaching." This produced howls of outrage from Catholic conservatives, as Catholic moral theologian Daniel Maguire described them: "like panicked devils shrinking from God's face in a medieval tapestry." But Pope Benedict XVI had already declared in his 2009 encyclical, *Charity in Truth*: "The conviction that the economy must be autonomous, that it must be shielded from 'influences' of a moral character, has led man to abuse the economic process in a thoroughly destructive way. In the long term, these convictions have led to economic, social and political systems that trample upon personal and social freedom, and are therefore unable to deliver the justice that they promise." A Jesuit theologian called this document closer to the Occupy movement than anyone in Congress is. Some Catholic parishes identify themselves as "peace and justice" communities.

Meanwhile, progressive Protestants were working to regain the nerve they had displayed in the heady social gospel days of the early twentieth century. Some, especially the neo-Anabaptists and neo-evangelicals, began calling themselves Matthew 25 Christians, choosing to imitate the radical message of one of Jesus' last parables—in which people who have recognized Jesus in the most unlikely earthly faces and places are now heading in the direction of eternal life. But the Democratic Party, fully compromised by Wall Street money and sensing religion as a dangerous third rail for its secularist constituencies, remained clueless about progressive religion. In *The Party Faithful*, Amy Sullivan described the God gap among Democrats. In the aftermath of the cultural wars, Republicans learned to play the religion card and Democrats abandoned any attention to religion except among blacks. The mainstream media and much of the public concluded that Democrats aren't and can't be religious, and if they say they are, they are hypocrites and dissemblers. Meanwhile, Catholics went on the "wafer watch" to ban liberal politicians from Communion. And yet the election of Trump was such a profound shock that some Protestants began presenting themselves, haltingly, as the new Religious Left. God works in mysterious ways. But this was not yet the rediscovery of the prophetic genome hidden in the backroom of the Temple, as in ancient Israel, as we saw in chapter 1. We are still waiting for rediscovery and reform. Will new prophets arise in 2020? Will national voices emerge from progressive Christianity? Are we due our next Martin Luther King Jr.? Will James Cones's legacy of powerful writings on black liberation find a much wider voice? Can whites build on the black social gospel?

A few years ago the Occupy Wall Street movement went viral and spread around the world in no time. *Occupy* can mean take back, or take over, or fully encompass. Among best-selling books urging American Christianity to reoccupy its own historic traditions and also contemporary culture, some are addressed to conservative evangelicals, urging them to free themselves from the triumphalist nationalism and Trump-bound bondage they presently evidence. Others are addressed to mainstream Protestantism, urging it to get with the historic Christian program and move self-confidently beyond its current lethargy. Inspired by Pope Francis, other books from Catholic presses are urging theologians to recover historic Catholic moral theology and reclaim liberationist traditions and for Catholic parishes to identify as peace and justice movements.

Brian McLaren has written more than a dozen books attempting to waken mainstream Protestantism (and evangelicalism) to a vigorous, renewing, adventurous Christian spirituality. Among them were books with the provocative titles *A Generous Orthodoxy* and *A New Kind of Christian*. His latest is *The Great Spiritual Migration: How the World's Largest Religion Is Seeking a Better Way to be Christian*.

Put simply, he urges churches to stop worrying, fretting, and apologizing, to change course, to get up and move. He pictures Christianity, like ancient Israel, standing at the Red Sea, the water ahead and Pharaoh's army behind, and he is calling: "Move, Let go, Let be, Get going, Migrate." He calls not for more doctrines but for stories about God on the move that can become the church's own stories. An interesting proposal is a *love curriculum*, centered on teaching and ritualizing the practice of love in the life of the church, instantiated in every dimension of worship and teaching and in the celebration of Advent, Christmas, Lent, and Easter. He does not shrink from calling for Christian "branding" and strategic plans. Of course many theologians, such as Cornel West, are emphasizing that justice is the social form of love.

McClaren shrewdly emphasizes that accepting the call to follow Jesus may require changing your mind about God, which will mean renouncing and repenting. He suggests that most (white) Christians carry trusty credit cards in their wallets that they are going to have to take out and throw away. These historical artifacts and present encumbrances weigh Christianity down and keep it from migrating from a violent God of domination to a nonviolent God of liberation. He identifies Christian "Doctrines of Discovery and Dominion" that suggest that whatever the West discovers it can take and use, from foreign peoples to the natural world. This means a genocide card in every wallet, played when needed. It means white Christian privilege, racism, sexism, empire. He wants to recover the New Testament concept of kenosis (Christ's self-emptying), or what Luther called a theology of the cross, which rejects dominating supremacies so common to religion. To follow Jesus is to let go of our triumphalist understandings of God. Given the authoritarianism that readily clings to American evangelicalism, McLaren argues: "For the world to migrate away from violence, our God must migrate away from violence."

Borrowing from information technology, McLaren traces the stages of our working images of God from God 1.0 (I'll be there for you), to God 2.0 (Be nice to your sister), to God 3.0 (Play by the rules), to God 4.0 (God and country), to God 5.0 (the inclusive we). Christians will not follow Jesus, will not get where they need to be, until they let go of their working-God-images that are dominant but untrue to the biblical witness to the gospel. An example is Latin American liberation theology's letting go of the law-and-order God who upheld dictators to the inclusive God 5.0 who "loved the landless, the farmworkers, the slum dwellers, the illiterate, and the indigenous people living in the jungles." In view of Christian conservatives' rejection of liberation theology, it is well to name what has been dominant—oppression theology? Supremacist spirituality?

Sometimes we have to get over ourselves, including our hallowing of the status quo, and get on to something bigger. McLaren wonders if the Spirit of God is calling the church to stop saving itself and instead to join God in saving the world. He discusses a document that arose among American Christians, a *Charter for a Just and Generous Christianity*. This is to respond to an ecological, economic, sociopolitical, and spiritual-religious crisis, as we face the century ahead. This is a summary (McLaren, 155–62):

1. We call upon just and generous Christian communities who have embarked on this great spiritual migration to identify themselves. Where no such communities exist, we call upon Christians to start creative new ones.

2. We call upon Christian leaders and parents to begin afresh with children, youth, and college-aged adults.

3. We call upon Christian communities, movements, and institutions to recruit different leaders and train them differently.

Were such a charter to be adopted, the radical migration at the dawn of the third millennium would be from *organized religion* (self-preservation) to *organizing religion* (for mission and the common good). To such possibilities Pope Francis has spoken:

Along this path, popular movements play an essential role, not only by making demands and lodging protests, but even more basically by being creative. You are social poets: creators of work, builders of housing, producers of food, above all for people left behind by the world market. The future of humanity does not lie solely in the hands of great leaders, the great powers and the elites. It is fundamentally in the hands of peoples and in their ability to organize. It is in their hands, which can guide with humility and conviction this process of change. I am with you.

What are the chances that a progressive Christianity could come forward out of its many historic traditions as the fitting response to the call of the liberating God of the Bible? Could a revitalized Protestant and Catholic Christian left reenter this scene with new energy and new ideas that would bring together social democracy and postmodern religious vision? (I am persisting in using the term *left* because I think there is no escaping its radical critiques of neoliberal "late capitalism," with its idolatry of the unregulated free market, and its relegation of the commons and the environment to mere externalities.) It is easy to assemble an entire bookshelf with new works on progressive religion or the Christian Left, all written since 2000. Some of these books champion a genuine biblical theology supplanting conservative economic ideology, as this book does.

Other books find the way forward by escaping the crustiness and institutional self-absorption of many churches, with the mantra, "Follow Jesus instead of the church," though this books places the church in the center of mediation between God and the world. Diana Butler Bass has written several books that describe and applaud a thriving Christianity that somehow escapes the notice of the media and that suggest a spiritual awakening not registered in Pew data: *A People's History of Christianity: The Other Side of the Story; Christianity After Religion: The End of Church and the Birth of a New Spiritual Awakening; Christianity for the Rest of Us: How the Neighborhood Church is Transforming the Faith.* Her latest is *Grounded: Finding God in the World, a Spiritual Revolution.* Bass is unusually adept in the study of contemporary American Christianity. Unlike many critics, she is hopeful. She finds religion not dying but transforming, not declining but changing—and perhaps not where many critics are looking. She brings Christian theology back to earth (as the incarnation first did). She is able to ground new movements of God and Christianity, in spite of the failing church attendance and growth of the "nones" that disheartens many Christians and makes secularists smile. Distancing herself from those who routinely answer the "Where is God" question with the answer "Up in heaven, I guess," Bass is determined to find, evoke, and demonstrate a changed conception of

God, a rebirthing of faith from the ground up, a suffering God identifying with the human condition, in a reenchanted earth. Neither otherworldliness nor secularism is the answer. She purports to be reporting on a revolution of the sacred.

In the eulogy for Martin Luther King Jr., mourners were reminded that he had said that "if death had to come, I am sure there was no greater cause to die for than fighting to get a just wage for garbage collectors." In his last sermon, anticipating his death, King said: "I'd like someone to mention that day that MLK tried to give his life serving others. I want you to be able to say that day that I did try to feed the hungry. And I want you to say that I tried to love and serve humanity."

BELIEVE, TEACH, CONFESS—A CHRISTIAN PLATFORM

Remember "take back the night" demonstrations in which women and men march against rape and sexual oppression and for safe public space for women? To occupy public space, which is Christianity's calling, requires public statements and public action. In Christian history a decisive public statement is often called a confession or declaration. Sometimes such declarations occur amidst a *status confessionis*, a situation that demands the church speak out and act out. Consider the following example, led by Sojourners and signed by evangelicals, mainstream Protestants, and Catholics:

> "Reclaiming Jesus: A Confession of Faith in a Time of Crisis" (2018)
>
> We are living through perilous and polarizing times as a nation, with a dangerous crisis of moral and political leadership at the highest levels of our government and in our churches. We believe the soul of the nation and the integrity of faith are now at stake.
>
> It is time to be followers of Jesus before anything else—nationality, political party, race, ethnicity, gender, geography—our identity in Christ precedes every other identity. We pray that our nation will see Jesus' words in us. "By this everyone will know that you are my disciples, if you have love for one another" (John 13:35).
>
> When politics undermines our theology, we must examine that politics. The church's role is to change the world through the life

and love of Jesus Christ. The government's role is to serve the common good by protecting justice and peace, rewarding good behavior while restraining bad behavior (Romans 13). When that role is undermined by political leadership, faith leaders must stand up and speak out. Rev. Dr. Martin Luther King Jr. said, "The church must be reminded that it is not the master or the servant of the state, but rather the conscience of the state."

It is often the duty of Christian leaders, especially elders, to speak the truth in love to our churches and to name and warn against temptations, racial and cultural captivities, false doctrines, and political idolatries—and even our complicity in them. We do so here with humility, prayer, and a deep dependency on the grace and Holy Spirit of God.

This letter comes from a retreat on Ash Wednesday, 2018. In this season of Lent, we feel deep lamentations for the state of our nation, and our own hearts are filled with confession for the sins we feel called to address. The true meaning of the word repentance is to turn around. It is time to lament, confess, repent, and turn. In times of crisis, the church has historically learned to return to Jesus Christ.

Jesus is Lord. That is our foundational confession. It was central for the early church and needs to again become central to us. If Jesus is Lord, then Caesar was not—nor any other political ruler since. If Jesus is Lord, no other authority is absolute. Jesus Christ, and the kingdom of God he announced, is the Christian's first loyalty, above all others. We pray, "Thy kingdom come, thy will be done, on earth as it is in heaven" (Matthew 6:10). Our faith is personal but never private, meant not only for heaven but for this earth.

The question we face is this: *Who is Jesus Christ for us today?* What does our loyalty to Christ, as disciples, require at this moment in our history? We believe it is time to renew our theology of public discipleship and witness. Applying what "Jesus is Lord" means today is the message we commend as elders to our churches.

What we believe leads us to what we must reject. Our "Yes" is the foundation for our "No." What we confess as our faith leads to what we confront. Therefore, we offer the following six affirmations of what we believe, and the resulting rejections of practices and policies by political leaders which dangerously corrode the soul of the nation and deeply threaten the public integrity of our faith. We pray that we, as followers of Jesus, will find the depth of faith to match the danger of our political crisis.

I. WE BELIEVE each human being is made in God's image and likeness (Genesis 1:26). That image and likeness confers a divinely decreed dignity, worth, and God-given equality to all of us as children of the one God who is the Creator of all things. Racial bigotry is a brutal denial of the image of God (the *imago dei*) in some of the children of God. Our participation in the global community of Christ absolutely prevents any toleration of racial bigotry. Racial justice and healing are biblical and theological issues for us, and are central to the mission of the body of Christ in the world. We give thanks for the prophetic role of the historic black churches in America when they have called for a more faithful gospel.

THEREFORE, WE REJECT the resurgence of white nationalism and racism in our nation on many fronts, including the highest levels of political leadership. We, as followers of Jesus, must clearly reject the use of racial bigotry for political gain that we have seen. In the face of such bigotry, silence is complicity. In particular, we reject white supremacy and commit ourselves to help dismantle the systems and structures that perpetuate white preference and advantage. Further, any doctrines or political strategies that use racist resentments, fears, or language must be named as public sin—one that goes back to the foundation of our nation and lingers on. Racial bigotry must be antithetical for those belonging to the body of Christ, because it denies the truth of the gospel we profess.

II. WE BELIEVE we are one body. In Christ, there is to be no oppression based on race, gender, identity, or class (Galatians 3:28). The body of Christ, where those great human divisions are to be overcome, is meant to be an example for the rest of society. When we fail to overcome these oppressive obstacles, and even perpetuate them, we have failed in our vocation to the world—to proclaim and live the reconciling gospel of Christ.

THEREFORE, WE REJECT misogyny, the mistreatment, violent abuse, sexual harassment, and assault of women that has been further revealed in our culture and politics, including our churches, and the oppression of any other child of God. We lament when such practices seem publicly ignored, and thus privately condoned, by those in high positions of leadership. We stand for the respect, protection, and affirmation of women in our families, communities, workplaces, politics, and churches. We support the courageous truth-telling voices of women, who have helped the nation recognize these abuses. We confess sexism as a sin, requiring our repentance and resistance.

III. WE BELIEVE how we treat the hungry, the thirsty, the naked, the stranger, the sick, and the prisoner is how we treat Christ himself. (Matthew 25: 31–46:) "Truly I tell you, just as you did it to one of the least of these who are members of my family, you did it to me." God calls us to protect and seek justice for those who are poor and vulnerable, and our treatment of people who are "oppressed," "strangers," "outsiders," or otherwise considered "marginal" is a test of our relationship to God, who made us all equal in divine dignity and love. Our proclamation of the lordship of Jesus Christ is at stake in our solidarity with the most vulnerable. If our gospel is not "good news to the poor," it is not the gospel of Jesus Christ (Luke 4:18).

THEREFORE, WE REJECT the language and policies of political leaders who would debase and abandon the most vulnerable children of God. We strongly deplore the growing attacks on immigrants and refugees, who are being made into cultural and political targets, and we need to remind our churches that God makes the treatment of the "strangers" among us a test of faith (Leviticus 19:33–34). We won't accept the neglect of the well-being of low-income families and children, and we will resist repeated attempts to deny health care to those who most need it. We confess our growing national sin of putting the rich over the poor. We reject the immoral logic of cutting services and programs for the poor while cutting taxes for the rich. Budgets are moral documents. We commit ourselves to opposing and reversing those policies and finding solutions that reflect the wisdom of people from different political parties and philosophies to seek the common good. Protecting the poor is a central commitment of Christian discipleship, to which 2,000 verses in the Bible attest.

IV. WE BELIEVE that truth is morally central to our personal and public lives. Truth-telling is central to the prophetic biblical tradition, whose vocation includes speaking the Word of God into their societies and speaking the truth to power. A commitment to speaking truth, the ninth commandment of the Decalogue, "You shall not bear false witness" (Exodus 20:16), is foundational to shared trust in society. Falsehood can enslave us, but Jesus promises, "You will know the truth, and the truth will set you free." (John 8:32). The search and respect for truth is crucial to anyone who follows Christ.

THEREFORE, WE REJECT the practice and pattern of lying that is invading our political and civil life. Politicians, like the rest of us, are human, fallible, sinful, and mortal. But when public lying becomes so persistent that it deliberately tries to change facts for ideological, political, or personal gain, the public accountability to truth is undermined. The regular purveying of falsehoods and consistent lying by the nation's highest leaders can change the moral expectations within a culture, the accountability for a civil society, and even the behavior of families and children. The normalization of lying presents a profound moral danger to the fabric of society. In the face of lies that bring darkness, Jesus is our truth and our light.

V. WE BELIEVE that Christ's way of leadership is servanthood, not domination. Jesus said, "You know that the rulers of the Gentiles (the world) lord it over them, and their great ones are tyrants over them. It will not be so among you; but whoever wishes to be great among you must be your servant" (Matthew 20:25–26). We believe our elected officials are called to public service, not public tyranny, so we must protect the limits, checks, and balances of democracy and encourage humility and civility on the part of elected officials. We support democracy, not because we believe in human perfection, but because we do not. The authority of government is instituted by God to order an unredeemed society for the sake of justice and peace, but ultimate authority belongs only to God.

THEREFORE, WE REJECT any moves toward autocratic political leadership and authoritarian rule. We believe authoritarian political leadership is a theological danger that threatens democracy and the common good—and we will resist it. Disrespect for the rule of law, not recognizing the equal importance of our three branches of government, and replacing civility with dehumanizing hostility toward opponents are of great concern to us. Neglecting the ethic of public service and accountability, in favor of personal recognition and gain often characterized by offensive arrogance, are not just political issues for us. They raise deeper concerns about political idolatry, accompanied by false and unconstitutional notions of authority.

VI. WE BELIEVE Jesus when he tells us to go into all nations making disciples (Matthew 28:18). Our churches and our nations are part of an international community whose interests always surpass national boundaries. The most well-known verse in the New Testament starts with "For God so loved the world" (John 3:16). We, in turn, should love and serve the world and all its inhabitants, rather than seek first narrow, nationalistic prerogatives.

THEREFORE, WE REJECT "America first" as a theological heresy for followers of Christ. While we share a patriotic love for our country, we reject xenophobic or ethnic nationalism that places one nation over others as a political goal. We reject domination rather than stewardship of the earth's resources, toward genuine global development that brings human flourishing for all of God's children. Serving our own communities is essential, but the global connections between us are undeniable. Global poverty, environmental damage, violent conflict, weapons of mass destruction, and deadly diseases in some places ultimately affect all places, and we need wise political leadership to deal with each of these.

WE ARE DEEPLY CONCERNED for the soul of our nation, but also for our churches and the integrity of our faith. The present crisis calls us to go deeper—deeper into our relationship to God; deeper into our relationships with each other, especially across racial, ethnic, and national lines; deeper into our relationships with the most vulnerable, who are at greatest risk.

The church is always subject to temptations to power, to cultural conformity, and to racial, class, and gender divides, as Galatians 3:28 teaches us. But our answer is to be "in Christ," and to "not be conformed to this world, but be transformed by the renewing of your minds, so that you may discern what is the will of God— what is good and acceptable, and perfect" (Romans 12:1–2).

The best response to our political, material, cultural, racial, or national idolatries is the First Commandment: "You shall have no other gods before me" (Exodus 20:3). Jesus summarizes the Greatest Commandment: "You shall love the Lord your God with all your heart, your soul, and your mind. This is the first commandment. And the second is like unto it. You shall love your neighbor as yourself. On these commandments hang all the law and the prophets" (Matthew 22:38). As to loving our neighbors, we would add "no exceptions."

We commend this letter to pastors, local churches, and young people who are watching and waiting to see what the churches will say and do at such a time as this.

Our urgent need, in a time of moral and political crisis, is to recover the power of confessing our faith. Lament, repent, and then repair. If Jesus is Lord, there is always space for grace. We believe it is time to speak and to act in faith and conscience, not because of politics, but because we are disciples of Jesus Christ—to whom be all authority, honor, and glory. It is time for a fresh confession of faith. Jesus is Lord. He is the light in our darkness. "I am the light of the world. Whoever follows me will not walk in darkness, but will have the light of life" (John 8:12).

But wait! It may seem that all we need to do is summon together social justice Catholics, progressive Protestants, and then invite neo-Anabaptists or neo-evangelicals coming with their own strengths and differences—and then move on together. But so far that is not to be. Some evangelicals who identify as the Christian Right and Trump's court would say, "Over our dead bodies." But another evangelical impulse, not necessarily in the name of the Christian Right though possibly so, is mounting a full frontal attack on the very concept of social justice.

In 2019, pastor and author John MacArthur released a blog called "Social Injustice Threat to the Gospel," in which he claims that the social justice manta claimed by liberal Christians and many secularists is "the most subtle and dangerous threat so far" to the Christian gospel. Some 4,400 fundamentalist pastors have joined MacArthur in a document "For the Sake of Christ and His Church: The Statement on Social Justice and the Gospel." This is their argument: Even if social justice means to live justly in the world, that emphasis is not a definitional component of Christianity's understanding of the gospel. In fact, they make two strong objections to social justice. One is that social justice manifestly includes accepting homosexuality, the elevation of women to equal status with men, and the labeling of white racism on the one hand and blacks as its victims on the other hand. Regarding women their statement stipulates: "In marriage the husband is to lead, love, and safeguard his wife and the wife is to respect and be submissive to her husband in all things lawful. In the church, qualified men alone are to lead as pastors/elders/bishops and preach to and teach the whole congregation." The second reason is that social laws and regulations possess no inherent power to change sinful hearts; only individual salvation through Christ can save.

It could be that some of these signers are conservative Lutherans who worry that social justice belongs in the "kingdom of God's left hand" (the world of government and the realm of the *law*) but the church and the gospel function in the "kingdom of God's right hand." And they may also worry that social justice is a kind of "works righteousness" that claims to save us, rather than God's atonement in Christ. But progressive Lutherans would appeal to Luther's mantra "faith active in love" and claim that social justice (the social form of love) is an outcome of a gospel life, not a means of achieving salvation. That said, there is a historic Lutheran "quietism" regarding revolution or transformation of government and society—even if the Reformation itself would seem to belie that.

Regarding the fundamentalists or evangelicals who signed the statement against an emphasis on social justice, I say again that two things are determinative. One is that social justice as widely understood contradicts their view on women and gays, and that those views are more non-negotiable to them than social justice. And perhaps even more importantly, these evangelical traditions are individualist rather than social or structural, and inviting Jesus into one's heart or being personally saved by Christ as an individual far trumps anything happening in the social imaginary. Finally, freedom and not social justice is the preeminent value for conservative Protestantism.

THE IMITATION OF CHRIST IS THE MODE
FOR RADICAL CHRISTIANITY

Is the "imitation of Christ" too fussy a term, too privately spiritual, too exclusive, too medieval, too anachronistic to be embraced by radical Christianity in a post-Christendom age? Or is the resonance of Jesus in a postmodern age sufficient to ground religious resistance, insurgency, vision, and action? And by the imitation of Christ can we also imply the exodus liberation movement and the prophetic imagination of a covenanted people?

And does imitating Christ imply our own commitment to a collaborative eschatology implicit in Jesus' proclamation of a new reign of God? Can you imitate Christ in the public sphere? Can it become a new social gospel just when the times require it?

During the fifteenth century a German monk named Thomas à Kempis wrote a little book called *The Imitation of Christ*. A meditation on the life and teachings of Jesus, it advocated that Christian believers practice a daily internalization of the kind of life Jesus lived. This produces what Catholicism calls spiritual formation, as the grace of Christ gradually infuses the character and actions of the believer. (Dorothy Day's life in the Catholic Worker movement is a good twentieth-century example.) The goal is to acquire the disposition to think and act like Jesus in all things. This style of piety prizes discipleship more than a learned or cognitive belief system, though it does not surrender historic orthodoxy. Thomas wrote: "At the Day of Judgment we shall not be asked what we have read, but what we have done." And again: "All men desire peace, but very few desire those things that make for peace." Above all, Thomas advocated the way of the cross, which requires self-examination, humility, and love. In current spiritual language, the imitation of Christ suggests a practiced "mindfulness" through which we stay tuned to the larger stage on which God acts and to which we are called. It is not enough to sit back and observe from a back seat in the audience; we are invited to leave our seats and join the action on the stage.

In contemporary ethics, three approaches are often discussed: a utilitarian ethic that is formed around projected or desired outcomes; a Kantian or principled ethic that judges the absolute rightness or wrongness of actions; and a virtue ethic (going back to Thomas Aquinas or Aristotle) that concentrates on the development of moral habits of the heart that then eventuate in proper behavior and direction. While there is a tendency to reduce the imitation of Christ to an inner mysticism, it can also produce the kinds of virtues in Christian individuals and community that would become a Christian humanism and a social gospel. A virtue ethic would not be able to put little children in cages even before an overall strategy for dealing with immigrants is worked out.

Already in the New Testament, the letters of the Apostle Paul evoke being "in Christ," sometimes called Paul's "Christ mysticism." Paul radicalizes the Christian ethic into a life of *subversive obedience* to the love command. Another way of saying that is *revolutionary disobedience*, the refusal to go along, *blend into the system, be the system*, a way of life Vaclav Havel analyzed in his native Czechoslovakia under Soviet Communism. The idea is that men and women are to be set free from self-aggrandizement (or system-aggrandizement) to live lives of love as social compassion. This is the imitation of Christ in the world.

How would the imitation of Christ proceed today? Thomas placed his spiritual practice within late medieval monastic life. Paul's horizontal ethic of love to the neighbor grounded in the vertical grace of God must find its way in ever changing situations. The Protestant Reformation "secularized" the Christian calling to new life as it sent Christians out of the monastery and onto the streets. There in the life of the world Christians would attend to the voice of God and seek their calling. Christians cannot willingly accept that their calling has no place in the world.

But today is not the world of Paul, or the monastery, or the new epoch envisioned by the Reformation. What is the nature of the situation in which contemporary Christians must heed the call of God? To test, just for the moment, the power and authority of the liberating God of the Bible to speak into the American situation, consider from hundreds and hundreds of Bible verses just the following two, one evoking the Old Testament covenant and the other the New Testament church. Can one hear any echoes at all of these verses among the shouted exhortations from many American Christians who claim to be literal Bible believers? Do these admonitions fill religious radio?

"If there is among you anyone in need, a member of your community in any of your towns within the land that the Lord your God is giving you, do not be hard-hearted or tight-fisted toward your needy neighbor. You should rather open your hand, willingly lending enough to meet the need, whatever it may be." (Deuteronomy 15:7–8)

"With great power the apostles gave their testimony to the resurrection of the Lord Jesus, and great grace was upon them all. There was not a needy person among them, for as many as owned lands or houses sold them and brought the proceeds of what was sold. They laid it at the apostles' feet, and it was distributed to each as any had need." (Acts 4:33–35)

The most prized American values, the kind that show up in party platform statements and salt political posturing, demonstrate a glaring indifference to these intentions of a liberating God. Middle-class language is considered acceptable and praiseworthy; that's as far as politicians are willing to go. The poor are voiceless. How did this come to be? Can true Christianity only exist in some other environment, outside the American system? Is this what we have learned from reflecting on Trump evangelicals? Are we to assume a massive and deliberate misreading of the strange God of the Bible, in favor of American conservative ideology or the expediency of electoral politics? Are we seeing the end of a very long process in which a radical Christian gospel was slowly accommodated to the needs of the American Way or, more simply, Wall Street? But then why is northern Europe so different, where people don't go to church on Sunday but seem to imbed biblical values in the social democracy their countries practice on Monday? Even candidate Obama's telling Joe the Plumber in 2008 that it would be good to "spread the wealth around" provoked an outrage and remained a Republican talking point. The good of the commons as a predicate for moral action was unimaginable. Obama's sentiment was clearly perceived as un-American. In 2019, Howard Schultz, who founded and built up Starbucks, based his short run for the presidency on a single-minded sense of his own accomplishments that showed no connection to the commons and insisted, for example, that Medicare for all would be a betrayal of the American way and an assault on millionaires. But even the very wealthy can "get it." In mid-2019 a small group of wealthy Americans began arguing that the situation that had produced their inherited wealth was a disgrace and one solution for American social justice is the heavy taxing of people like them.

Of course, the imitation of Christ will have to take place in a rough neighborhood. And it will have to occupy Wall Street. And replant itself in the church. And may it be said of self-identified Christians in Congress, whose percentage is above that of Christians in the general population, "Still, they persisted." In the neoliberal economic model that is the law of the streets now, the name of the game is dividing up scarce resources in ways that maximize the success of the most successfully greedy, while tricking the working classes and lately the middle class into believing the surplus will eventually trickle down to them. The local rules for playing that game have been written by the economic mafia, and they posit that objective economic policy is immune from ethical scrutiny and will be enforced through an unquestioned and unregulated system. And in this system untouched by the needs of the commons, the one certainty, continually demonstrated by national data, is that the rich get richer and the non-rich get poorer. When economic success is held up by politicians, it is the astonishing success of the wealthy.

A "preferential option for the poor" (a phrase typical of Catholic liberation theology) is a no-go in politics. Highly objectionable, in fact. The poor-be-damned is the more common sentiment among politicians. So Catholic moral theologians spoke directly to the previous Speaker of the House: "Our problem with Representative Ryan is that he claims his budget is based on Catholic social teaching. This is nonsense. As scholars, we want to join the Catholic bishops in pointing out that his budget has a devastating impact on programs for the poor." In a public letter to Ryan, the Georgetown faculty wrote: "*Your budget appears to reflect the values of your favorite philosopher, Ayn Rand, rather than the Gospel of Jesus Christ. Her call to selfishness and her antagonism toward religion are antithetical to the Gospel values of compassion and love.*"

IMITATING A LIBERATING GOD REQUIRES RELIGIOUS INSURGENCY

The book of Genesis pronounces that human beings are *made in the image of God*. At least for Jews and Christians this means that we are to carry out our earthly mandate in ways that model or imitate God's character in the biblical stories. If God rested at creation, God's people should observe the Sabbath—as work stoppage, rest for the earth, attending to communal life, honoring God. If God liberated Israel from the oppression of Egypt and led them into the wilderness to learn a new kind of community, then God's people would have to return periodically to the wilderness where they can be tutored in the values of covenant community. If God created a garden of earthly delight, then God makes humans stewards of the earth, gardeners, vintners, shepherds, who are held responsible for God's land as a gift of creation and for sharing its bounty with each other.

God's exodus project did not always go well. Beginning with the Ten Commandments and carried forward by prophets who prosecuted covenant lawsuits, human greed and rapaciousness (capitalist virtues) are continuously brought to court as destructive to the community, the land, and the reign of God. Old Testament religious leaders, envisioned as shepherds of Israel, are again and again denounced as careless plunderers who care little for their flocks and much for themselves, who remodel God into something God is not. In the New Testament Jesus again and again evokes this theme by telling parables in which God is the landowner, and religious leaders are the upstarts who disobey God and ruin the land and take no thought of the "commons" that is God's vineyard. Always the implicit question, in the Old Testament and the New, is: *Why are the people in charge not imitating God?* Why are they not in tune with God's covenant dreams? Why are they not carrying out God's purposes? Why do they not lead the resistance against those forces that despoil the earth and its peoples? And the implied solution is: perhaps God will raise up a new people to reenchant the creation, do good for the commons, tend to the neighborhood, take special care with widows and orphans and the poor and strangers and aliens. Latin American liberation theology always saw that elites, whether patriarchal or capitalist, do not willingly surrender power; the poor, the oppressed, women—or the church on their behalf—will have to rise up and change things.

This is not a call for theocracy, but for individuals and communities of Christians to become political actors—as we saw in the black social gospel, anti-war, civil rights, women's, and gay rights movements. Religious insurgency did not turn out well for the prophets, always in conflict with the king and the wealthy as they practiced in-your-face religious radicalism and were killed for it, as was Martin Luther King Jr. Nor for Jesus, whose audience tried to run him off a cliff after his inaugural Jubilee sermon and who was finally driven to the cross by those who rejected his mission because it threatened their interests. The *cost of discipleship* comes with biblical religion. Progressive religion is supposed to run the risks Jesus and the prophets did.

The imitation of God in our time is not reducible to a preoccupation with dangerous women and homosexuals. Given the economic context that constrains the modern moral imagination, progressive religion is called to unmask and engage the power and greed of deregulated free market capitalism, the ruination of the poor and the environment, the marginalization of the other. Because the God of the Bible speaks in multiple vernaculars and in many communities of discourse beyond the precincts of religious institutions, religious insurgents will have to speak multiple vernaculars and learn to play on many stages too, always resisting the moral nihilism of national security and international capitalism and also the defend-the-fort exclusivity of those who want to own God as a scarce commodity. We will have to relearn and reclaim and reproduce the liberating stories of the exodus, of the prophets, and of Jesus, and turn them into contemporary stories that set people free, and the planet, too.

In an age where moral space is greatly narrowed, where politicians wear blinders so they cannot see the effects of their policies, the first task of insurgent religion is an ambitious moral imagination that can project alternative visions onto the social imaginary—that *occupies public space. Progressive religion must reclaim public life and public policy as a venue, not just the interior of the church*, as the locus of religious and societal transformation. In the face of the anti-government mantra reigning since the Reagan years, we will have to *make public policy and the public square the place where religious insurgency carries forth.* Because we understand covenant, we can see through how strictures against big government favor the wealthy and the powerful and keep the 99 percent from hoping for structural and nationwide solutions to their plight. To what end has the Christian Right cheered on an *individualism for which the Bible has no word*, and why have secular progressives (and most of the Democratic Party) too easily forgotten that the good of the commonwealth has been a persistent and, yes, godly pursuit in Jewish and Christian traditions? The imitation of God can surely occur in the mystical ecstasy of the soul, but if we watch it progress in the Bible, from the exodus to Jesus' proclamation of the reign of God, we see that it also provokes religiously legitimated social engagement.

REIMAGINING SMALL COMMUNITIES AS BASES FOR A NEW SOCIAL GOSPEL

The general council of Roman Catholic bishops meeting at Medellin in 1968 declared: "The grass-roots community is the primary, fundamental core of the church. On its own level it must take responsibility for the riches of faith and for its propagation, as well as for worship, which brings faith to expression. It is consequently the initial cell of the church's structure, the focus of evangelization, and at present the main point of departure for man's improvement and development." The chief characteristics of these communities are voluntary association of members, Christian fellowship of manageable size whose life is mutual friendship and whose intentional devotion makes specific tasks possible, the awakening of creative powers in every individual and the surrender of natural privileges, local autonomy in the formation of the spiritual life, and a deliberate return to a simple Christ-centeredness in devotion and action. These communities have outlived the rejection of popes. Another kind of reputable community is that of Catholic nuns whose vision modeled a Christian communal formation in ways undreamt and unregulated by supervising bishops. Jesus was a community organizer. So was the pre-presidential Obama.

In the Middle Ages, wandering flagellants formed themselves as communities, as they moved from place to place, in bands of fifty to five hundred, practicing chastisements of the body, hoping to achieve forgiveness for their times, imagining themselves on a redemptive quest to save humanity. Beginning in Italy, then spreading to Germany, they became *a collective imitation of Christ*, hoping to repent for their whole age on behalf of the abuses of the wealthy and the indifferent—and a corrupted church. Their uniform was a white robe with a red cross front and back. Each community was organized similarly, with a lay leader, and they were celibate. What kinds of communities does the dawn of the third millennium require? Could the readers of this book become collective imitators of Christ, advance guards of a new age?

The idea of community suffered a failure of moral imagination towards the end of the second millennium. Utopian social thought had given way to a utilitarian calculus that lionized individual freedom, autonomy, and self-actualization, but lost the cultural knowledge that a good society, not to mention a new earth, would only come as the product of new communities pooling social capital for the good of all. It takes villages, to begin with.

Can the readers of this book become a community? I've wondered if they could even get along, be on speaking terms, much less unite. My wife once gave me a book, *Dictionary of the Khazars*, that was published in two versions, one for men and one for women. We were teaching in two different places at the time. We each read our version. Then when we came together we placed the books snugly together on our shelf, to nuzzle next to each other and live happily ever after. I thought about writing a version of this book for lapsed Christians, another for fervent leftists and hardcore movement types seeking a whiff of spirituality or alliances with the religious, another for earnest "peace and justice" Catholics, another for reforming, awakening, recovering Protestants who believe the church should look more like Christ, and of course another for the "nones" and New Agers of all stripes—and hopefully, a version for Trump Christians. (Once as a teenager I fancied myself getting saved at a Billy Graham rally in the San Francisco Cow Palace. My brother-in-law, a Lutheran minister as I would be, said we had to get to the parking lot and avoid the traffic. I already had four years of Lutheran high school under my belt, and Lutherans never go forward anyway.)

As I thought about my readers, I imagined different terms of engagement appealing to different traditions, each in its native language, each in its familiar biases, each hearing its own vernacular, as at Pentecost. The heavy stuff from other groups' rhetoric would safely be fenced in terms that only they would take seriously. But shouldn't all these readers have to meet some day? Shouldn't they share different approaches on behalf of effective coalitions? (I've grown weary over my lifetime hearing the snotty comments of Lutheran clergy about the Salvation Army or the Gideons. And there's no one as haughty as a Lutheran campus minister disparaging evangelical student groups.) Shouldn't we all have a Pentecost experience in which we try out each other's voices and hear other languages in the same commons? Such a scene, in the early chapters of Acts, became the birth of Christianity.

As we look around, it gradually dawns on us: *We are the ones we have been waiting for.* There is recent enthusiasm in the social sciences for the idea of a "tipping point." When about 10 percent of the public grasp and begin to act on a new idea, they can tip the entire society in their direction. If we all lean in, will a new social gospel reach its tipping point? Even politicians, almost always latecomers with fingers to the wind, will join the parade if there are enough of us to make a breeze. Already in the 1960s, the "Hunger Project," cheerfully championed by John Denver and pitched by Werner Erhard, was claiming that when a certain number of people believe there is no reason why so many people in the world have to be hungry, we will have decided to end it.

> How do we make churches indispensable communities today? In *The Great Spiritual Migration,* Brian McLaren suggests people who want to move institutions forward should begin with questions like (p 134):
>
> What problems are not being solved by current institutions?

What negative effects are current institutions creating? What opportunities are they missing?

What elites have a vested interest in resisting needed change?

What conflicts fragment existing elites to keep them apart?

What values can rally people against elites?

Which allies and advocates can be rallied across various sectors of public life?

What communication tools are available to help movements spread their message?

How do we frame dilemmas and how to conceive the architecture of change?

How will planning and decisions be communicated?

What kind of structures and authority will develop? How will conflicts be avoided? What kind of people are coming forward? What liabilities and talents do they bring?

FAITH-BASED INITIATIVES

To the extent that faith-based initiatives are a cut-and-run to the private sector to throw off the demand for social justice in the public sector, they should partly be resisted. To the extent that they are the band-aids of charity that distract attention from systemic injustice, they do not accomplish as much good as they think. When they serve as the sole evidence of "compassionate conservatism," they are a charade. They cannot be a religiously clothed alternative to or distraction from just economic policies or a free pass for the devastation of unregulated capitalism or a cover for the wholesale abandonment of government's responsibilities to an entire society. They must not be a holy form that privatization movements take in order to lessen government responsibility.

But much good can be said for them. They are religious organizations, doing good in the public sector with the partial use of government funds. They are often more effective and efficient than some governmental programs with a similar mission; at least, they provide rival or alternative approaches so that best practices can emerge. Some kinds of faith-based initiatives receiving federal support have been around for a very long time. President Clinton's "charitable choice" initiatives continued and accentuated them. But President Bush especially championed them, though not without controversy and politicization, and President Obama proceeded cautiously and without notable enthusiasm. It is generally agreed that faith-based initiatives applying for and using federal funds must, while engaging in their work in "sacred places," be devoted to "civic purposes," and that they cannot discriminate in the clientele they serve. But recent court decisions have favored the right of religious institutions, even under federal funding, to hire people who are at one with their religious philosophy and not hire those who are not.

Faith-based initiatives get Christians used to moving in the public square and get the public used to seeing them there. To ban faith-based initiatives outright, in the name of the separation of church and state, defeats the more nuanced view of the public square, in which competing approaches and motivations and ideologies jostle with each other in a society that prizes diversity, difference, multiculturalism—and that do not exclude religious voices or impinge on freedom of religion. Very many people do not get that multiculturalism includes not only ethnicity and varying cultures but religion and spirituality. Decreeing, in effect, that the public square can only be secular is now too self-satisfied a solution that has not kept up with changing times and beliefs and establishes an ideological hegemony in a time of postmodern celebration of multiplicity. Progressive Christians need to stop being obtuse about this.

This book argues for an increasingly vigorous role for a progressive or radical or resisting or dissenting or insurgent religion that mimics the liberating God of the Bible. Nowhere does it argue for a Christian political party, as has sometimes been the case in Europe, and certainly not for anything remotely resembling a Christian theocracy, nor for a Christian sharia law, for which fundamentalists and Catholic bishops are accused of having a special fondness. If not a theocracy and not a political party, including taking over the Democratic party as evangelicals have attempted to take over the Republican party, then the imitation of God argued throughout this book must occur as highly energized religious, moral, and political *movements*—often in alliances and collaborations with government, and as extensions of government—and of course also independent of government. Governments and religious movements can occasionally, and perhaps routinely, extend the common good through mutual collaboration.

One can look around for analogues, such as the Sierra Club or Move On or Common Cause or the ACLU or the Southern Poverty Law Center, or on the international scene, Amnesty International and Human Rights Watch and Oxfam. These nongovernmental organizations are examples of organizing around specific moral causes in ways that arouse the populace, push towards tipping points in public opinion, and lobby governments on behalf especially of the voiceless. They work alongside and often in dialectic relationships with governments, avoiding the latter's bureaucratic inertia and captivity to the interests of the wealthy and the powerful. Sometimes they are prophetic, speaking truth to power, and sometimes they are good allies for governments seeking to do the right thing. They seek *to imagine and enlarge the space for moral action* on a world stage. At best, they have a freedom of movement lacking in political parties and governments. They are a promising model for progressive religion—and an opportunity for collaboration.

But they would never surrender the ambition to influence the government, especially votes in Congress that speak directly to the structure of society and economic regulation and policies for the poor or the imprisoned. In a specifically religious context, <u>Bread for the World</u> works not primarily on behalf of charity for those who are hungry but justice for an entire underclass, here and abroad, who go without sufficient food—often as a result of late capitalism's policies. It is a vigorous lobbying organization, founded by Christians, and it may be one example to be followed. Much larger is World Vision, an imaginative and well-organized evangelical relief organization. The Heifer Project attracts families and others who contribute in the name of others. It pleases me to give cows and goats and flocks of chickens in my children's and grandchildren's name, though they are not always amused. Progressive religion has millions of adherents, and these are typically already "organized" into thousands of "peace and justice" or "reconciling in Christ" parishes. It is a waste of organizing strength and of moral leverage and of the biblical requirement to work for social justice that much more does not come from these people and groups. It is not enough for progressive religion to claim they do not wish to play the game of the Christian Right. The refutation of that un-liberal movement, which does its best to ignore the liberating God of the Bible, is not less religion and less movement, but better religious movements—intellectually convincing, morally imaginative, and theologically driven. We return to the possibility of a vast and effective progressive religious movement in the conclusion of this book.

PERFORMING RELIGION AS SOCIAL MOVEMENT, WITH ALLIES

Will everyone applaud if Christianity, if Christians, start to move? One advantage to the movement of Neo-Anabaptists, the heirs of "free church" movements, is that they live out a counter-story to the current Trump evangelicals, but do not agitate secularists who are always worried about theocracy on the horizon. The free church traditions do not do theocracy. They do the church as a colony of heaven. They think the task of the church is to *be* the church. Being the church *is* their social strategy and their epistemology and their way of seeing. Their language and style and history and ultimate commitments constitute Christian intrusions into the world's settled arrangements. For Christians of every stripe, the task is to recover the God of the Bible, then the true nature of the church as the body of Christ, and then to determine how to reappear in the public square.

Performative faith is a social movement, and a liturgical movement, and a sacramentalizing movement, and a *proleptic anticipation that wants to run forward and meet on the road ahead the God who is coming from the future in our direction.* Early Christianity was an astonishingly successful social movement. Periodically Christianity has reawakened to that memory. Today that much energy is more likely to be happening in the Southern hemisphere, especially sub-Saharan Africa.

Movement types are heady for change, determined to be among that first 10 percent who produce a sea change in society. "Movement people" believe that as ideas and behaviors move from the edges of the social imagination to broader acceptance and practice they transform minority perception to majority practice. This was true in the civil rights and women's and gay rights movements, and very recently in the Black Lives Matter and #MeToo movements and the Occupy movements that sprang up all over the world. Social movements with a spiritual foundation can move mountains. Religious movements, allied with other people of good will, provide social momentum. Jim Wallis of Sojourners calls people of religious vision "wind changers." They do not hold up their finger to see what the times might allow, they see visions of God and bring the times along with them.

For Christian churches or Jewish synagogues, movement might first bring to mind religious liturgies. To call for liturgical movement is to remind that all rituals may be said to have a *performative* dimension. In the 1960s, anti-war and farm worker protests often took the character of ritual movement, with banners carried in procession, through the fields and through urban streets. People who engage in ritual movement *negotiate a passage through the world, as the world passes through their movement.* Ritual processions, always now eventually on YouTube, are energized when heads catch sight of tails. In the Women's March following President Trump's inauguration, I joined two of my daughters in marching through the streets of our college town. A tremendous wave of excitement and exclamation arose when we, on one block heading south, caught sight of the tail of the parade on the next block over heading north. Once it was thought that ritual embodiment and movement was always grounded in archetypal myth and story; now it is seen that the latter often emerges from the former. Out of performative movements we can create and embody our own myths. Get liturgy right; a new social gospel will follow. Ritual movement precedes theological argument, liturgy and worship give rise to theology. Movement is the crucial determinant whether religion and ritual are alive; movement turns inert belief into dynamic action. Religious bodies that never enter the public square change little. The square stays the same and so do they.

Political-religious movement, which is to foretell a new social gospel, is iconic, ritualizing the turn of belief to social action. In the Christian tradition, as symbolized in the three-day rituals from Good Friday to Easter, believers are called to join God in the paschal mystery, the passage from death to life, bondage to freedom, old world to new. Jesus, and those who follow him, constitute hope (and the active intentions of a liberating God) as a performative ritual. Evangelicals need to stop stumbling over the idea of performance, imagining that "performance" means it is not sincere or heartfelt, just acting. Some Protestants, including Lutherans, must also get over worrying that performative ritual is meant to be a "good work" that somehow displaces grace and fails to give God the glory. They should experience performative liturgy as the joyful "call and response" of a new age.

The black church has always known this, and this sensibility is caught in evocative and moving spirituals: "I looked over Jordan and what did I see?"—movement to a new home, and if you know the code you know it's not just a home in the sweet by and by, but a home on a newly claimed earth. It might include an Underground Railroad. As we noticed in chapter 1, the black church has led the way in keeping alive the exodus narrative of a liberating God. Many working- and middle-class white Americans, meanwhile, fail to conceive that America itself could be the Egypt that oppresses and that the journey towards a new and just community is going to have to take us through the troubling and transforming wilderness where we encounter again the liberal God of the Bible.

To call something a movement is to make the obvious point that forward progress has replaced stasis, or even regression, as the new default position. The Greek word for resurrection to describe the emergent Christ at Easter suggests a collective movement up and away from stasis, with Christ leading an earthly community to an awakened eschatological life. Movement also refers to the power of collective action, the whole point of community organizing, in which people get high off each other, calling and responding. Good rituals always happen in community, or generate community. A motto at the liberal Protestant Chicago Theological Seminary is "We're not radical. We're just early." As an expression of religious movement, the United Church of Christ ran a media campaign that proclaimed "God is still speaking" with a voice-over from Gracie Allen, "Never put a period where God has placed a comma."

SOJOURNERS

Sometimes seen as an unexpected fruit of the 1960s Jesus Movement and usually placed under a progressive (even leftist) neo-evangelical or neo-Anabaptist umbrella, Sojourners has evolved into a well-organized movement on behalf of social justice, with extensive print and blog ministries, on "faith, politics, and culture," daily devotions, and a great deal of all-Christian organizing centered in Washington DC. Its founder and editor-in-chief is Jim Wallis, whose well-regarded and influential books include: *God's Politics: Why the Right Gets It Wrong and the Left Doesn't Get It (2006); The (Un) Common Good: How the Gospel Brings Hope to a World Divided (2014);* and *America's Original Sin: Racism, White Privilege, and the Bridge to a New America (2017).*

The Sojourners Community was founded in 1971 and located itself at Trinity Evangelical Divinity School in Deerfield, Illinois. In 1975 it moved to Washington DC, where it has been active in the causes of anti-war, radical critique of free market capitalism, welfare reform, climate change and care of the earth, human trafficking, immigration reform, and in general any social justice issues. In that connection it has popularized the phrase used several times in this book, "Matthew 25 Christians." It has given Christian social activism a high profile. Besides its monthly magazine, it also produces a website and daily digital posts. Although it doesn't choose to call itself the Christian Left, it is the most influential example of such movements. This was Sojourners' original charter:

"Chicago Declaration of Evangelical Social Concern" (1973)

As evangelical Christians committed to the Lord Jesus Christ and the full authority of the Word of God, we affirm that God lays total claim upon the lives of his people. We cannot, therefore, separate our lives from the situation in which God has placed us in the United States and the world.

We confess that we have not acknowledged the complete claim of God on our lives.

We acknowledge that God requires love. But we have not demonstrated the love of God to those suffering social abuses.

We acknowledge that God requires justice. But we have not proclaimed or demonstrated his justice to an unjust American society. Although the Lord calls us to defend the social and economic rights of the poor and oppressed, we have mostly remained silent. We deplore the historic involvement of the church in America with racism and the conspicuous responsibility of the evangelical community for perpetuating the personal attitudes and institutional structures that have divided the body of Christ along color lines. Further, we have failed to condemn the exploitation of racism at home and abroad by our economic system.

We affirm that God abounds in mercy and that he forgives all who repent and turn from their sins. So we call our fellow evangelical Christians to demonstrate repentance in a Christian discipleship that confronts the social and political injustice of our nation. We must attack the materialism of our culture and the maldistribution of the nation's wealth and services. We recognize that as a nation we play a crucial role in the imbalance and injustice of international trade and development. Before God and a billion hungry neighbors, we must rethink our values regarding our present standard of living and promote a more just acquisition and distribution of the world's resources.

We acknowledge our Christian responsibilities of citizenship. Therefore, we must challenge the misplaced trust of the nation in economic and military might—a proud trust that promotes a national pathology of war and violence which victimizes our neighbors at home and abroad. We must resist the temptation to make the nation and its institutions objects of near-religious loyalty.

We acknowledge that we have encouraged men to prideful domination and women to irresponsible passivity. So we call both men and women to mutual submission and active discipleship.

We proclaim no new gospel, but the Gospel of our Lord Jesus Christ who, through the power of the Holy Spirit, frees people from sin so that they might praise God through works of righteousness.

By this declaration, we endorse no political ideology or party, but call our nation's leaders and people to that righteousness which exalts a nation.

We make this declaration in the biblical hope that Christ is coming to consummate the Kingdom and we accept his claim on our total discipleship until he comes.

But consider also the Jewish movement, Tikkun, and its approach of inviting all kinds of people attracted to a movement on behalf of social justice. In Judaism, tikkun means *mend*, heal, transform creation. From its beginning in American Judaism, Tikkun wanted to include a "Network of Spiritual Progressives," including Christians and other spiritually defined people as well as agnostics and atheists. Together they seek to mend

America—and all creation. This is their "Spiritual Covenant with America," to which they invite all comers, including agnostics and atheists:

> We will create a society that promotes rather than undermines loving and caring relationships and families.

> We will take personal responsibility for ethical behavior.

> We will build Social Responsibility into the normal operations of our economic and political Life.

> We will reshape our education system to teach the values of love, caring, generosity, intellectual curiosity, tolerance, gratitude, awe and wonder at the universe.

> We will seek a single-payer national health care plan and also broaden the public's understanding of health care.

> We will be stewards of the environment.

> We will build a safer world and promote a rational approach to immigration through a strategy of nonviolence and generosity that eliminates poverty both in the U.S. and in every other country.

> We will seek the separation of Church, State and Science.

Tikkun imagines a New Bottom Line that measures all public policies not by how well they maximize money and power (the old bottom line), but how they produce, sustain, or enhance our abilities to be loving and kind, generous and caring for others, ethically and ecologically sensitive in our behavior, able to see others as embodiments of the sacred, and living lives not of utilitarian calculus but filled with awe, wonder, and radical amazement. (Note that they actually talk and act as if they believe the Hebrew Bible, including the God of the exodus and the prophets of social justice, could come true!)

So what are we all going to do about this—a weakened Christianity and a corrupted commons? Couldn't we try to proclaim and become a new social gospel, and not just write change off as unrealistic? Shall all people of good will, religious and not, join hands in making the next big play in the evolution of the consciousness of the universe? Of course secular movements have their own contributions to social justice, which can come off as a really *promising maybe,* as documented by Michael Kazin in *American Dreamers: How the Left Changed a Nation.* The Left's cultural victories have come in spite of the fact that the United States, unlike Europe, has no true, viable, left-wing political movement. No socialist parties have ever won a lasting foothold. It is not even permitted to pronounce the word *socialism,* as every electoral cycle demonstrates. In the early nineteenth century, social movements emerged dedicated to the moral transformation of the country. They wrote charters, acted in street protests, and managed media attention. Above all, they sought the abolition of slavery and championed the rights of women. After the Civil War their efforts were often compromised by the racism entrenched in the labor movement and the working class generally, but they nevertheless helped create the reforms of the Progressive Era. Socialist movements that ranged from Wisconsin and Minnesota workers and farmers to secular Jewish immigrants to urban bohemians never succeeded, however, in creating a lasting political movement, and they collapsed with the Red Scare that always accompanied Soviet Communism. The New Left of the 1960s did not follow the Communist Party model and certainly never produced a revolution of the proletariat, but helped change American attitudes towards war and the state.

Several conclusions are possible. The progressive Left, together with others, by the beginning of the twenty-first century, had brought about astonishing changes in cultural attitudes, from the civil rights movement, to feminism, and most recently to gay liberation. #MeToo is well on the way. But some might conclude that Wall Street, much of it culturally liberal, could welcome these changes while remaining steadfastly opposed to fundamental challenges to American capitalism. In this view, radical cultural change, as long as it doesn't include organized labor or wide-ranging social programs, costs Wall Street nothing. Further, Americans, who worship at the altar of individualism, will not tolerate radical economic change and will go to great lengths to crush such movements.

Progressive movement today must occur in the face of great concentrations of wealth amassed against social and economic change. The Republican Party has consented to its self-transformation into an extremist force that is dismissive of the legitimacy of its political opposition and stands decisively with the wealthy. When Democrats somehow win elections, their victories are declared illegitimate and an affront to real Americans. The dark money of the wealthy and the powerful buys political influence, determines the final form of legislation, and generates ideologies that stand in the way of all progressive movement. Cynical billionaires use charlatans and cranks to persuade the masses. The Christian Right, with its tight embrace of an American religion that grows more and more distant from historic

Christianity, joins the alliance. For very many American evangelicals, there is no unforgivable sin Trump could commit—because he is anointed by God to bring about the end of the age, or at least guarantee religious victory in the culture wars. Meanwhile, Democrats mostly run from the social democracy prized in Europe, and they have not succeeded, probably for cultural and religious reasons, in making themselves a populist movement today. Hillary Clinton never gave any speeches to the Salvation Army.

Can the Democrats learn to make a religious argument for a humane and effective state, and could progressive religion nudge them in the right direction, while maintaining its own independence? Could one guess from comfortably centrist Democrats that the God of the Bible denounces the sins of landlords and bankers (lately called banksters), the expropriation of labor, the trashing of community covenants? Isn't it the case that living wages, universal health care, enhanced funding for public and college education, and secure benefits for the elderly and unemployed are appropriate amplifications of God's righteousness? In mid-2018 Seattle was widely attacked as a socialist (and therefore disintegrating) city for pioneering housing for the poor, a $15 minimum wage, and other social programs. Amazon, its largest employer and famous for paying no taxes, had to step in and shut the dreams down. Or threaten to decamp.

Or must Jewish and Christian aspirations rooted in the Bible's liberalism need to look elsewhere than political parties for models and allies? In 1998, when Newt Gingrich and the Republicans in Congress were focusing all of their efforts on impeaching President Clinton over a sex scandal, a very small group of people started a simple online petition: "Censure President Clinton and Move On to Pressing Issues Facing the Nation." The signers of this petition drive had no past political experience, but they proceeded to share it with as many of their friends as they could think of. Within days, the petition went viral and attracted hundreds of thousands of signatures. From that list grew MoveOn.org—an organization of 7 million current members and a powerful progressive force in American politics. Recently MoveOn launched a website called SignOn.org, where anyone can start online petitions to dream and build support for new worlds. Would prophets sign on to online petitions?

I do not call for a new political party specifically infused with religious values (as the Christian democratic parties of Europe originally were), nor for remaking the Democratic Party the way the Christian Right has tried to remake the Republican Party, though it would be good if the Democrats could achieve the courage of their convictions and also discover how crucial to some of their best ambitions would be alliances with progressive religion. The fears and failures of theocracy, especially in the Islamic world but also mimicked in the Christian Right, guarantee there would be secular horror at any Christian political party, and much doubt from Christians and Jews as well.

Because the exodus is best symbolized as *movement* out of oppression and because a "Jesus Movement" underlies the emergence of the New Testament, Christians and Jews can best understand themselves, so far as justice and peace are concerned, as *religious and moral movements, resistance movements, dissenting movements, countercultural communities* within the body politic, making no unqualified alliances or identifications with any political party or platform. A good argument can be made that a Christian or biblical worldview must always be "in opposition," against the grain. What society most needs from the church is not, first of all, political activism, but *the prophetic imagination of alternative realities and their projection onto the screen of the social imaginary,* as new kinds of people become new kinds of communities and institutions. The uncertain steps at the beginning of the third millennium reflect above all a failure of imagination, just as the times were requiring new public space for moral action. Such religious movements, unlike political parties, are bought and paid for by no one—except the God who acts in Jesus Christ.

Movement is the opposite of stasis, not to say regression, and the future is its default mode. In American history we have seen the abolitionist movement, the student movement, the farm workers' movement, the anti-war movement, the civil rights movement, the women's movement, the environmental movement, the gay liberation movement. Movement privileges action and flexibility over fixed order and institution, even if some of the latter may strengthen the former. Of course, the failures of the Occupy movements, such as they are, suggest the necessity of analysis and organization and political action. The Tea Party movement almost immediately entered the political process and won major electoral victories; the Occupy movement chose not to. Which accomplished more? The contemporary paths of movements are the streets and the social media, as like-minded people discover each other and collaborate in becoming a tipping point that leverages structural change.

Progressive religion can draw on an entire history of Jewish and Christian ritual action, in which worship becomes performative, as people move beyond the constraints of pews and ecclesiastical sites and head for the fields and the streets and the airwaves. Rituals almost always arise out of communal experiences, then rituals produce mythologies, and then these stories we tell ourselves about ourselves (myths) become enacted. On the ground liberation happens in community and generates community—as at Seneca Falls, Selma, Stonewall, the Washington Monument.

Think of great reforming movements in Jewish and Christian history. The exodus was the prototypical movement, empowered by a liberating God. The Jesus Movement swept early Christianity across the Mediterranean world. Monastic movements arose every few centuries to recall medieval Catholicism from its stasis and its assimilation to the powers that be. The Protestant Reformation, through the printing press and the universities, moved reforming Christianity across northern Europe. The Jesuit movement arose to reform Catholic spirituality. John Wesley developed a spiritual "method" to extend and reroute the Protestant Reformation.

So never mind longing for a new political party, as tempting as that might be. For Christians, it's enough that we parade through the streets, make our presence an indisputable characteristics of the commons, work for the good of all, and relentlessly suggest this is in fact God's plan for the world. We are on the side of the angels. That's enough, to begin with. All the while reminding ourselves every Sunday that the church's first task is to be the church, to speak the church's language, to witness to the salvation God offers in Christ. Out of this can come a new gospel after Trump.

Epilogue

Collaborative Eschatology

Jesus' announcement of the reign of God was meant to provoke a crisis of decision and an epic response to God's new age. Salvation would come to every disciple and to a new community, the church, called out as God's witness. Paul understood himself to be working towards an eschatological harvest that would reap the abundance of Christ's legacy going public. Every country could become a promised land, every human soul a friend of God, every land a new Eden. Christians constituted as a colony of heaven would be faced with God on the road ahead reaching back from the future into their present. The high Christian calling is to collaborate with God in the ultimate destination of earth and the universe. Contemporary theologians like John Dominic Crossan and Marcus Borg have taken to refer to this destiny as *collaborative eschatology.*

Used to "unbecoming lives," people might *say no* to roles in God's future. Or, because the prospect seems too hard, too unrealistic, too utopian, they might choose a temporizing *maybe,* or *get-back-to-me.* But in sync with the church's mission and in response to the call of the times, and grasping that *Jesus does not imagine an earthly kingdom without God, or God without an earthly reign,* we may rise up to the occasion, to the call of the times, and say *Yes* to a role in God's Becoming and the transformation of the world. At this particular moment in American Christianity after Trump, this may evoke a new social gospel as the church's apt witness to the times.

NOT MY GOSPEL

The Lord has a controversy with his people (Micah 6:2).

> "You are not also one of his disciples, are you?" Peter denied it and said, "I am not." (John 18:25)
>
> "Crucify him!" (Mark 15:14).

The prophet Isaiah said the dawning of the Messianic age would be good news for the poor. Jesus opened his public ministry preaching on the Isaiah text. The New Testament uses the word *gospel* to mean good news from God—not just good news for the poor but good news for all peoples and shalom for the entire earth. *Why don't people, and Americans in particular, welcome a generous God as good news for all and a breakthrough to a new future? Why is a gospel with implications for social justice and the interdependence of the human community with earth so readily ignored or even suppressed?*

A less dramatic way of responding is simply to fall among the nones—none of the above responses to life—from "spiritual not religious" to not spiritual, not religious. So one possible response to God's grace, God's call, as many of us know from our children and grandchildren, is *no*. A bizarre delusion is that by losing one's faith one discovers the meaning of life. The being of God is *becoming* in the evolution of the universe, but we are deciding on *unbecoming*. We fail to notice any teleology built in to us. Saying no may also be a no to the covenanted social justice that Old Testament prophets proclaimed. A gentle no may decline to recognize the societal implications of the reign of God and insist it can only refer to individual freedom to invite Christ into our hearts but not clothe this transaction with a new social gospel. Wall Street is safe as we go forward to our altar call.

The problem with *sin* being mixed into the transaction is that it has become fashionable not to admit to it. Some theologians lately define sin as *unbecoming*. Sin sediments itself in social, economic, and political structures, poisons accumulating in the watersheds—not only in individual hearts. People who are doing well by the status quo may not welcome the radical changes implied by the reign of God. Good news for the poor, or the middle class, (or the environment), will not seem good to those who profit from or exploit those groups, or who think the underclass lacks ambition or worthiness. (Wall Street lacks no certainty about its worthiness.) Slaves do better decoding the exodus narrative than the 1 percent.

A much more certain no, with no remorse and no hesitation, goes like this: Religion is a public embarrassment, God is made up, and no thoughtful person, certainly no scientist or rationalist, entertains the thought that God and humanity and the universe may be on a joint mission. We are what we are.

MAYBE, BUT SEEMS UNREALISTIC, TOO HARD

> I have heard their cry, I know their suffering,
>
> I have come down to deliver them; Let my people go.
>
> Exodus 3:7; 5:1

> Let justice roll down like waters, and righteousness like an ever-flow-
> ing stream.
>
> Amos 5:24

> What does the Lord require of you but to do justice, and to love
> kindness,
>
> and to walk humbly with your God?
>
> Micah 6:8

The doubtful and the unencumbered may decide that the call of God sounds too unrealistic, too hard. God's DNA is a more binding inheritance than we asked for. The unbelieving children of believing parents always fail to see that they are living on borrowed capital. They (or we) are not looking for great commissions. We choose a quieter, less disturbing destiny. The '60s are long over; we are not signed up for revolution. When monastic communities, originating as determined islands of God's presence, lost their will to radical regrouping and reforming, it was called *sloth,* one of the "seven deadly sins" harder to spot. The incarnational message that *earth is capable of heaven* is intriguing but not something we ourselves are ready to undertake.

The softer take on sin than rejecting God's call to our own transforma-tion, or the neighbor's need is the unacknowledged default: the gospel just expects too much, in time, attention, commitment, self-giving. A liberating God means a *high maintenance relationship and a changed life, not just Jesus in an upstairs compartment in our preoccupied life.* Today this comes out as giving up on all that can be dressed up as ironic detachment or disguised as metaphysical abstention from grand wagers.

I hasten to add that secularism in itself does not necessarily reject the biblical vision for a good earth, and many of the nonreligious are acolytes for social justice. Decades ago the lapsed Catholic Michael Harrington, in *The Politics at God's Funeral,* called for fresh and imaginative alliances between secular and religious progressives. Contemporary environmental movements are another example, in which nonreligious and religious activ-ists in the Sierra Club join together in seeing nature as sacred. While the student movements of the 1960s proudly rejected religion, the civil rights movement, especially of course the black social gospel, did not make that mistake. Democrats are slow learners, however, with a history of paying little attention to religion unless it is black. No need to offend their secular, even antireligious wing. In May 2012, the Obama campaign announced that its chief liaison to the white religious community would be a twenty-three-year-old political science major with no Rolodex.

The real conundrum is the number of Christians who cannot accept as good news that the biblical God is liberating and portends the restructuring of society beginning with the poor or outcasts. Some respectable people are determined to reject the sheer grace of such a God as a moral hazard, too likely to attract free riders, and replace it with a system of salvation dispensed by hierarchically controlled religious franchises that specialize in individual religious freedom. Jesus' disciples, too, often did not get him. The call to "repent and accept the good news" must be perennial, and backsliders are always with us. Indeed, backsliders are always us.

But the problems for very many American Christians run deeper. Let it be admitted first that they reject God's liberalism because they do not believe that the Bible proclaims it. Liberation theology is fake news, not good news. Really, though? Are these the same ones who know certainly in their heart that social justice is not God's call because it includes gays and elevates women? (God seems determined to go too far.) And that "a preferential option for the poor" would be a threat to the American way of life? There's the rub. (We wouldn't vote for Denmark's social democracy with its extravagant healthcare, social safety net, and free education even if it were on our ballots. The Democrats are worried about the crazy left in the 2020 elections.) The strange good news of the Bible must be rejected by the many American Christians who, as the Apostle Paul said, follow *another gospel*.

That other gospel is the American mythology of free market capitalism as God's plan for humanity and individualist striving and its attendant success as the reliable sign of God's election. In the heart, true Christianity is believed to be a personal relationship with Jesus through which one achieves an ever more sanctified life of virtue. And gets to heaven. But on the streets, true Christianity is fully pledged to a conservative ideology that lacks the moral imagination of the neighbor, of a worldwide interconnected community, and of the commons whose health is tended by good institutions, including good government. Not to put too fine a point on it, conservative Christians are social Darwinists, and, fully larded with American exceptionalism, that is their other gospel.

But let's admit how wide the circle of "maybe but sounds too hard" is. For nones and dones and detached agnostics and for a lot of church members, joining the parade and staying in it and following where it goes is just too much work, when there are so many other things to do with our lives.

I leave it at this: I've mounted the evidence in this book. Let those who find some other God in the Bible present their evidence. (But it's not fair to first shoot the Bible full of holes, as Thomas Jefferson did.) It is surprising how rarely Christian conservatives construct their worldview from a conspicuous biblical theology. It is easier to find the foundations of their other gospel in libertarianism, even that of Ayn Rand, or in the apotheosis of individual freedom sometimes called libertarianism, or in a culture war that sees everything it hates an adjunct of liberalism, or in the reactionary populism of the Tea Party, or in an Americanism that keeps social ethics close to the national self-interest, or an allergy to anything that sounds socialist, or in a not well-disguised white nationalism. The loudest evangelical preachers do not come to us fresh from hard work in biblical theology; they are fresh troops from the culture wars, which is to say battles over abortion and homosexuality; or they are Republican stand-ins. But conservative evangelicals aren't alone in letting the parade pass them by. As a recent speaker at a military academy noted, there are too many people who simply decline to make their bed when they get up in the morning. Then there's distracting work. And drinks at four. And streaming distracting diversions all evening, which fill our meaning(less) space.

Just as the Hebrew prophets were always contesting rival national narratives to that of the exodus, so progressive religion must proclaim the liberating God of the Bible in the face of a powerful and pervasive American story that drowns out all alternative accounts of the human project. Horatio Alger rings truer than Jesus to the American experience. This is the American tale, for which an unexamined and unheard Jesus has become a national icon. A Darwinian Puritanism conflates loving God and the discipline it takes to succeed in life. Succeeding financially is the measure of a man; the fittest will acquire the most; God clearly loves them and wants the 99 percent to be more like the 1 percent, who seem extraordinarily blessed. Assembling the evidence of God's blessing and approval requires unrelenting competition. It is important to recognize that this comes from individualistic effort. *Assistance from government would actually throw God's plan off and render opaque the mechanism through which God demonstrates approval.* The liberal program attributed to God must be rejected because it shifts our personal piety to government (i.e. taxpayer) programs. Unregulated free enterprise is guided by God's invisible hand. In the conservative view, progressives disturb this clear plan and imply that government can make up for the poor's lack of initiative. Government grants them what only God is supposed to grant—economic success as the sign that God approves of the way they are playing the game.

So here, then, is the last call to the maybes and an urgent invitation to sell all and become a *yes*:

This book opened presenting the evidence that the God of the Bible is an exodus-style liberator—not to be conflated with Left (culture wars) or Right Wing (free market economics) liberalism. The Old Testament makes the exodus the normative portrayal of the nature of God, the wandering in the wilderness the site of Israel's education in the values of neighborhood and community and common land, and the prophetic genome the carrier of God's covenant of social justice as the counter-narrative to the stories told by the powerful and the wealthy. The New Testament proclaims that God left heaven to embody this divine good news on earth, in the person of Jesus, God's liberal paradigm in human form. The Apostle Paul takes God's world-friending public, rendering the Jesus movement a light to the world and declaring the universalizing news that God is intent on making friends with humanity. *What are we going to do with this?* I pause for one last summary before following the arc that reaches from the strange God of the Bible to saying Yes to the God who, in impatient Becoming, calls to us from the future.

The exodus narrative is the prototype of God's liberalism and, some historians say, the *taproot of all revolutions* since. The God of the exodus is intolerant of economic oppression, preoccupied with the enslaved, and comes to life in the Bible as liberator and bountiful provider. This gracious God is acknowledged and performed weekly in the worship of the religious community, endlessly rehearsed in sacred texts, and embedded in Israel's covenant life and Christianity's sacramental life. Transformed into social capital, the Sabbath elicits an economy of grace, above all when imaginatively magnified as a Jubilee Year that periodically dismantles oppressive economic defaults, releases people from enslaving debts, and returns forfeited land to its original owners. In the prophetic imagination, God's social justice exceeds the most ambitious redistribution scheme. Can you imagine—the Hebrew prophets were called to argue God's case in covenant lawsuits against recalcitrant people who think God is going too far?

In the New Testament Jesus incarnates as the earthly paradigm of God's reconciliation with the world. He makes himself subject to every oppression that cries for exodus, as he threatens political jurisdictions, touches the untouchables, reaches out to ostracized women, embraces despised foreigners, associates with public sinners, and heals the socially stigmatized. When challenged, Jesus implies that he is in fact *God on earth as a walking-talking-enacting social justice emancipator/redeemer/savior.* Of course redeemer and savior can be spiritualized, so those other words don't get too down to earth. I don't follow you there, say many modern Christians who fear neighborhood demonstrations and political and economic upheaval. They are not searching the posters of Human Rights Watch for the face of God, and so they are not prepared for the company Jesus keeps. Indeed, Jesus himself was a parable of a liberal God come to earth. If God wanted to portray what human life on earth would be like if fully open to a God of exodus, it would be like the life of Jesus. We do not have to fantasize *"What would Jesus do?"* when we can see plainly *what Jesus did do.* In his first sermon (Luke 4:18–19), Jesus makes the Jubilee vision of Isaiah his own: "The Spirit of the Lord is upon me, because he has anointed me to bring good news to the poor." Not everyone wanted to run God out of town. Some followed. Some chose to stay close.

The Apostle Paul takes God's liberating mission public by turning early Christianity into an inclusive religious movement meant to draw the circle large enough to include the whole world. God's overflowing diversity, freely offered to the world, becomes normative for the Christian mission. All walls of separation, social or political or economic, fall. Paul saw himself founding across the Roman world colonies of heaven, which is to say God's dreams for a new humanity springing up as facts on the ground across the earth. (God's grace is so emancipating it unlocked Luther's bowels, overcame his spiritual constipation, and evoked the freedom of the Christian. Or was that just a rumor in my Lutheran prep school?) Paul's famous theological formula, "justification by grace through faith," means God's free conferral, no prescribed religious trappings and no private passwords required, of friendship on the entire human race. *Earth becomes capable of heaven.* God's coming is good news for the human condition.

But wait. All this is overwhelming, and too much to give one's heart to without second thoughts. So Christians have rarely been able to resist the temptation to let go of Jesus' paradigmatic liberalism, as amplified by Paul, in favor of a more sensible Christianity: not a radical proclamation of God's liberating movement on earth but a church-centered system of salvation, run by the local religious franchise for dues-paying members. Or perhaps a nationalist experiment with Americans as God's ideal people. And so in this new dispensation, those who want to be included must earn their place at Jesus' overflowing table where food and drink had been offered to all, people must meet the criteria stipulated by a religious establishment whose point of view is far more constricting and exclusive than is the imagination of God. Just as Paul's opponents argued that entry into the new community cannot possibly be as easy as "justification by faith" or "grace" seem to make it, so today, in a profound reversal of valences, that liberal God of the Bible is forgotten and the ruthless god of social Darwinism is set up as America's golden calf—or Trump is the golden calf, recently recognized as God's anointed. How hard it is for every age, especially the American age of can-do individualism and a providential market economy, to accept that every good gift comes down from above, that it takes a covenanted community to nurture the new creation, that we live by grace

The martyred and recently canonized Central American Archbishop Oscar Romero wrote: "A church that doesn't provoke any crisis, a gospel that doesn't unsettle, a word of God that doesn't get under anyone's skin, a word of God that doesn't touch the real sin of the society in which it is being proclaimed—what gospel is that?" The biblical God must move and biblical people must define themselves as a religious and social movement. *Churches and synagogues (and declining university humanities programs) may be the last places left in our culture that can engage the public conversation with non-market values.* But many Christians have shot their Bibles full of holes, so all the verses about social justice and the poor are missing. Christianity as a counterculture peopled by "resident aliens," as 1 Peter envisions, will never be a good fit with the prevailing social and political institutions of the day.

The foundational proclamation of early Christianity was "Jesus Christ is Lord." Almost certainly crouching behind this affirmation is the implica-tion, "What would the earth be like if God were caesar and current rulers were not calling the shots?" But a radical kingdom gets lost in translation when Christianity relocates it in heaven. Or when the reign of God is reduced to a spiritual quickening in the believer's heart that takes up no public space and leaves powerful political or economic forces untouched and unexamined. The kingdom of God is not an earth-evacuation order. Jesus' proclamation of the reign of God authorizes new ways to be human on earth—translating a liberating God into earthly justice.

So demonstrating that the God of the Bible has come to set us free is one thing; making that statement intelligible to people who believe all religious assertions are meaningless is another; and still another is getting many deeply conservative American Christians to invite to dinner a God with good news for the lowly. Can we negotiate the return of the Bible's exodus God from exile? Can a liberal God-story be told so compellingly that God could not resist returning to live in it and modern people could not resist embracing it? (This was the dream of the Essene community that went out into the desert to await God just before the time of Jesus.) Isaiah called Israel to prepare a highway for God, the daunting task that hastens a Messianic age. But this may be an assignment for which we now have lost the oompf. It is not on the imaginal horizon of any party. As we have seen at the beginning of this Epilogue, in the Apostle Paul's view, this requires of the new Christian movement a *collaborative eschatology*, a joint venture between a God opening up the future and humans claiming their place in the revolution, initiated in Christ's resurrection, which can be imagined as a holistic rather than individualistic event.

YES: JOINING CHRISTIANITY IN THE PARADE TOWARD A COLLABORATIVE ESCHATOLOGY WITH GOD

> How beautiful upon the mountains are the feet of the messenger who announces peace, who brings good news, who announces salvation, who says to Zion, "Your God reigns."
> Isaiah 52:7

> Jesus came to Galilee, proclaiming the good news of God, and saying, "The time is fulfilled, and the kingdom of God has come near; repent, and believe in the good news."
> Mark 1:14

> Jesus said to them, "Follow me."
> Mark 1:17

> You are the light of the world. A city built on a hill cannot be hid.
> Matthew 5:14

> Your kingdom come. Your will be done on earth as in heaven.
> Matthew 6:10

> He has scattered the proud in the thoughts of their hearts.
> He has brought down the powerful from their thrones, and lifted up the lowly;
> He has filled the hungry with good things, and sent the rich away empty.
> Song of Mary, Luke 1:51–53

> The spirit of the Lord God has sent me to bring good news to the oppressed, to bind up the brokenhearted, to proclaim liberty to the captives, and release to the prisoners; to proclaim the year of the Lord's favor.

(Isaiah 60:1–2) Luke 4:18–19

If anyone is in Christ, there is a new creation, everything has become new.

In Christ God was reconciling the world to himself.

2 Corinthians 5:17, 18

Jesus does not imagine an earthly kingdom without God, or God without an earthly reign. That God has reclaimed and reconciled with humankind, that the reign of God is our destiny and the direction of the universe is both good news for us and everyone we can imagine and an irresistible inheritance to which we say *Yes.* We are not letting this parade pass us by, not declining to turn our earthly journey into a pilgrimage towards God, not falling short of seeing in the church the plausibility structure in which telling the story, being the story, passing on the story is tested and practiced.

Eschatology has been the long-standing theological word for reflecting on the final destiny of humans in the universe, and the role God plays in it. *Collaborative eschatology* is a term adopted in our times to signal that *God's being and human becoming may unite in a joint grand project.* I have allowed myself the fanciful notion that we are joining with God in a double helix. In an evocative and stunning configuration, two strands of this molecule are locked together in embrace and appear to be ascending diagonally wrapped around each other as if on a interlocking ladder. What if God hovers over the earth pulling us along, onward and upward?

Some Christian thinkers today are letting their imaginations, and their cosmologies, run wild as they try to make connections between historical Christian thought and contemporary theoretical physics or "process philosophy." In Roman Catholic scientist Teilhard's view, "the world is not hurtling itself into aimless expansion but is moved by Christ to Christ that God may be all in all. The future of the material universe is intimately linked to the fulfillment of *human beings in whom the universe has come to consciousness.* What we do matters to the 'matter' of the universe, because by our choices we influence the life of the universe. The total Christ is only attained and consummated at the end of universal evolution. That is, the Christ of the physical universe, the Christ of all humanity, the Christ of all religions. In this respect, Christ is not a static figure, like a goal post with a gravitational lure, toward which the universe is moving. Rather, Christ is in evolution because we, human and nonhuman creation, are in evolution. We must take seriously the impact technology and science are causing on the shape of life in the universe." Consider Teilhard's most famous line: "Someday, after mastering the winds, the waves, the tides and gravity, we shall harness for God the energies of love, and then, for a second time in the history of the world, man will have discovered fire." Do these ideas make your Christian head or your heart hurt?

BAPTISMAL COMMISSIONING OF ALL WHO SAY YES

In these final pages I return to the church itself, to the community called out by God, whose ultimate reason for being is to offer up praise to God and witness to the world—lest social justice as a compelling progressive meme seems to swallow up Christianity itself. After all, the Christian mission still begins with its self-understanding and commission as a colony of heaven, the body of Christ on earth, the Spirit-led extension of the incarnation that proclaims the gospel and celebrates the sacraments and confesses the creeds. And, in doing so, turns the love commandment into good news and social justice across the world. *And perhaps a new social gospel in America after Trump.*

So step into the exodus waters God is stirring up. And start walking. Once your feet are wet, pause for the community cheers, renounce the old life, and accept your joyful baptismal commissioning. Baptism is the beginning of the Christian life in the community of the church and the mission to the world and, as Luther saw, the daily reclaiming of our identity.

After Jesus' command at the end of Matthew (go everywhere baptizing everyone) echoes in 1 Peter and 1 Timothy, the meanings of baptism developed in the church's self-understanding and in its ritual life become clear. The early baptismal rites began by renouncing the devil and all his works and ways. Then came the immersion into Christ's own being and a confession of what it means. And then a commission to a new kind of life on earth.

Adults to be baptized would speak for themselves, while godparents would speak for infants. Pouring water at the beginning would be the audible sign that a sacramental transaction was about to begin, and there were allusions to deliverance from Noah's flood. Then prodigious (at least much more than shaking a rosebud) amounts of water were poured three times over the head of the baptized—or even immersion. The baptismal font stood at the west end of the Church opposite the altar at the east end, and perhaps every Sunday congregants would remember their own baptisms by dipping their fingers into the font and making the sign of the cross on their forehead as they entered the church.

The liturgical revival emerging during the middle of the twentieth century among both Catholics and some Protestants sought to recover liturgical continuities between early Christianity and the needs of contemporary Christianity. Among the modern recoveries were attempts to reinstate *renunciations* at the beginning of the baptismal service. Early Christian baptismal rites had been composed of two parts—renunciation (apotaxis) of Satan and his dominions and adherence (syntaxis) to the reign of God. The new Christian life was meant to move from the old to the new.

Why, at the dawn of the third millennium, bring back renouncing the devil and all his works and all his ways now? Indeed, this book has diagnosed many of them and demythologized them so as to name, unmask, and resist them. Demons in Jesus' time meant cosmic forces so powerful and so arrayed against the reign of God that few people could successfully resist them. But how naïve to imagine that no such powers, any sense of the demonic, could exist in our benign modern age! What about economic systems that systematically enrich the 1 percent and impoverish the great majority, that buy political power in order to ward off movements for social justice in the commons? What about the casual destruction of the earth and the inability to mourn the lost mother, the fate of the garden? What about America's "original sin" of racism? What about idolatrous nationalisms and the myth of the state entitled to wreak havoc on neighbors? I have mentioned Walter Wink's New Testament trilogy in which he analyzes *unmasking and naming* "the powers," *renouncing* them, and most importantly *resisting* them. So renewed baptismal rites now aspire to turn individual Christians and all of Christianity into movements of resistance and renunciation and non-conformity. Free space to acknowledge and claim Christ as Lord must be unbound from cultural and national captivities. Catholics especially have seen the spiritual formation required to turn the church into a counterculture. Some Protestant traditions have a long history of nonconformity and resistance. The biblical witness is a mandate for religious insurgency. A careful catechesis walks all baptismal pilgrims through this expectation.

But wait! In this view of baptism as both a renouncing and commissioning ceremony to empower the Christian community to join God in a collaborative eschatology, the question arises: Is *one* baptism going to be enough? Only the sixteenth century Anabaptist movement, the rebaptizers, practiced a second baptism—of adults. They did it as a sign of resistance and nonconformity—so that it would not come to appear that baptism was nothing more than a birth certificate into European civilization. But the Anabaptists wanted to call initiates into a self-conscious reidentification with the Way of Jesus. It was seen as a crime against the state. Against the unification of church and state. The penalty was capital punishment. For not going with the flow. Many Anabaptists were martyred by Catholics and Lutherans and Calvinists for their nonconformity.

Revisioning baptism to include renunciation and counterculture commissioning, and continuing my own themes of secularism as a religion-like ideology and the necessity of the church to recontest public space, brings me to follow the analysis and bibliography of Michael Knippa, "Converted Citizens: From National Allegiance towards Heavenly Adherence" (*Word and World*, Fall 2017), who calls on the modern church to recover lost territory and influence. Likewise, William Cavanaugh's *Migrations of the Holy: God, State, and the Political Meaning of the Church*, argues that in recent centuries *the state has in fact occupied the sacred* and in many ways *replaced the cultural role of the church*. Cavanaugh believes that the migration of the sacred from the church to the state diminishes the possibilities of a unique Christian culture, the possibilities of resistance and nonconformity and insurgency. And the state increasingly demands first allegiance even from people who are religious. Permission not to participate in the absolutizing of the nation might, as Jehovah's' Witnesses discovered, have to go all the way to the Supreme Court. Football players may not sit out the national anthem. The place of the state and of the secular world has displaced the sacred space of the church (or other causes, like Black Lives Matter). The state controls material life and its spaces, while weakened, desacramentalized, privatized space is conceded to religion.

Similarly, in *The Borders of Baptism: Identities, Allegiances, and the Church*, Michael Budde argues that since the Protestant Reformation, political and economic leaders have fragmented the unity of the church in the interests of nationalism, capitalism, and individualism. And so "the bonds of baptism are spiritualized and sidelined in favor of the blood and iron ties of patriotism and ethno-national solidarity." There lies the contemporary decline of moral and spiritual formation, which half-hearted and somewhat rare Confirmation classes cannot make up for. The state becomes the undefined god. Many Catholic and Orthodox moral theologians and Protestant ethicists have decried the formative and corrosive power of American nationalism upon the church, the absolutizing even by Christians of national, ethnic, political, economic, and cultural values. Indeed, consider the readiness of the secular world to call any movement towards a Christian culture an unacceptable and dangerous theocratic displacement of the state. People who do not think this through, especially liberal Christians, are far too ready to *make the state their default* and to declare unacceptable any assertions from the church in public space. Of course they may take this stand as a distancing from right-wing evangelicals or Islamic sharia law.

In recent decades New Testament scholars have come to see that the designation of Jesus Christ as *Lord (Kyrios)* was *political speech* directed in part as a rejection of the deification and worship of the Roman Caesars.

Jesus' ride into Jerusalem on Palm Sunday might be seen as counter to the ceremonial ride-in of Roman troops. Richard Horsley was one of the early leaders of this scholarship, and he noted that St. Paul, a Roman citizen himself, was careful to root the ultimate citizenship of new Christians in the reign of God, not in the Roman Empire. Few contemporary Christians take any notice of these claims. Many Christian pastors and their congregations (often with national flags in their worship space) are pledged to "keep politics out of the pulpit"—not noticing that *all speech is political speech, all speech is occupied speech, all speech is connected to power and part of a worldview, all speech and stories have a social location.*

I close this book and its appeal for a distinctive Christian humanism and a new social gospel after Trump by calling for Christians to become movements in new directions, in alternative spaces. In *Radical Discipleship: A Liturgical Politics of the Gospel,* Jennifer McBride develops her view of theology and liturgy and its political significance in the world from her own experiences of a discipleship that arose from intentionally placing herself in situations calling for social justice. The church's mission is to reduce the distance that separates humans from each other and from God. In bringing our bodies into the proximity of ultimate community, we habituate our actual bodies in the struggle. As they perform their missions, "base communities" in Christianity especially create new social spaces in which Christ becomes visible. Or contest social spaces where secularism reigns.

In Eastern Orthodox depictions of Easter and the Resurrection, Christ is never pictured rising alone; he has Adam and Eve in tow—and by implication millions of others freed from the bondage of the old world. In some Orthodox iconography Jesus' rising up (the Greek word *anastasis*) may be portrayed as rising from sleep or rising up *against* all the forces that stand in the way of God's eschatological plan for the world. This *activist view of the resurrection* also comes to mean that Christians too (and all humanity?) are commissioned in baptism to rise up. And eventually bring the neighborhood with them. Christians are called to live lives anticipating the final resurrection, drawing down into their own lives, their own neighborhoods, their own societies, the resurrecting power of God who meets us in the world and draws us in God's final direction. God is circling. God is intending to arrive in the present, not merely the by and by. Chasing the Holy Spirit, that whirlwind-maker, provides the power for the triumph of spirit over matter.

A prayer that Christians around the world pray every Sunday of their lives, and perhaps every day, the Lord's Prayer, becomes the energy and direction of the Christian life: "Thy kingdom come, Thy will be done, on earth as it is in heaven." For those empowered by a corporate resurrection, these words become revolutionary and anticipatory. God embraces us from out of the future and together with God we participate in God's ultimate plan. No doubt when Paul says "You have been raised with Christ" he is meaning "You should be living risen lives," pointed toward resurrection in the universe. As the prologue of the Gospel of John implies, Jesus the Logos is God's vision for the world and was with God from all eternity. In this (unbelievably?) bold assertion, the universe was from the beginning always about God-in-Christ, through the energy of the Spirit.

Collaborative eschatology means that God is joining with us, and we with God, in a renewed heaven and earth together in a final act of repair and restoration. We, living in the power of a collaborative resurrection first proclaimed at Easter, are participating with God in a world first implied by the Christian celebration of the incarnation at Christmas.

Champions of this view like to quote Augustine: "God without us will not; we without God cannot." What difference would all this make? William James, the psychologist of religious experience, famously asked: "What experiences will be different from those which would obtain if the belief were false? What, in short, is the truth's cash value in experiential terms?" The answer is that if Christ rose, and if we are in on it, and if it becomes the meaning of a future in which God is arriving, then everything about our baptized lives is different.

For a very long time Christians have wanted to think of themselves as God's image-bearers (since we were made originally "in the image of God"). Christian Baptism across the ages is the liturgical performance of how we, together with God in Christ, die and rise again. And become new iterations of social gospel. This is the Christian commission.

Bibliography

Alterman, Eric. *The Cause: The Fight for American Liberalism from Franklin Roosevelt to Barack Obama*. New York: Viking, 2012.

Armstrong, Karen. *The Battle for God: A History of Fundamentalism*. New York: Random House, 2000.

Bacevich, Andrew J. *The Limits of Power: The End of American Exceptionalism*. New York: Holt, 2009.

———. *The New American Militarism: How Americans Are Seduced by War*. New York: Oxford University Press, 2006.

———. *Washington Rules: America's Path to Permanent War*. New York: Metropolitan, 2011.

Baker, Bruce, and Tom Parks. "The Gleaner's Edge: The Modern-day Power of an Old Testament Practice to Transform How We Do Business." *Christianity Today*, July/August 2019, 28–32.

Banerjee, Abhijit, and Esther Duflo. *Poor Economics: A Radical Re-thinking of the Way to Fight Global Poverty*. New York: Public Affairs, 2012.

Barbour, Ian G. *When Science Meets Religion: Enemies, Strangers, or Partners*. San Francisco: Harper One, 2000.

Bass, Diane Butler. *A People's History of Christianity: The Other Side of the Story*. San Francisco: Harper One, 2010.

———. *Christianity After Religion: The End of Church and the Birth of a New Spiritual Awakening*. San Francisco: Harper One, 2016.

———. *Christianity for the Rest of Us: How the Neighborhood Church Is Transforming the Faith*. San Francisco: Harper One, 2006.

———. *Grounded: Finding God in the World, A Spiritual Revolution*. San Francisco: Harper One, 2015.

Bell, Daniel. *The Cultural Contradictions of Capitalism*. New York: Basic, 1996.

Bellah, Robert. *The Broken Covenant: American Civil Religion in Time of Trial*. Chicago: University of Chicago Press, 1992.

———. *Religion in Human Evolution: From the Paleolithic to the Axial Age*. Cambridge, MA: Harvard University Press, 2017.

———. *The Good Society*. New York: Vintage, 1992.

———. *Habits of the Heart: Individualism and Commitment in American Life*. 3rd ed. Berkeley, CA: University of California Press, 2007.

———. *Individualism and Commitment in American Life: Readings on the Themes of the Habits of the Heart*. Berkeley, CA: University of California Press, 1989.

Bettelheim, Bruno. *The Uses of Enchantment*. New York: Knopf, 1976.

Bloch, Ernst. *Atheism in Christianity: The religion of the Exodus and the Kingdom*. New York: Verso, 2009.

———. *The Principle of Hope*. Vol. 1. Boston: MIT Press, 1995.

Borg, Marcus. *Meeting Jesus Again for the First Time*. San Francisco: Harper One, 1995.

———. *The God We Never Knew: Beyond Dogmatic Religion to a More Authentic Contemporary Faith*. San Francisco: Harper One, 2009.

———. *Reading the Bible Again for the First Time: Taking the Bible Seriously but Not Literally*. San Francisco: Harper One, 1995.

———. *The Heart of Christianity: Rediscovering a Life of Faith*. San Francisco: Harper One, 1989.

———. *Jesus: Uncovering the Life, Teachings, and Relevance of a Religious Revolutionary*. San Francisco: Harper One, 2009.

———. *Putting Away Childish Things: A Tale of Modern Faith*. New York: HarperCollins, 2010.

———. *Speaking Christian: Why Christian Words Have Lost Their Meaning*. San Francisco: Harper One, 2011.

Briggs, Kenneth A. *Double-Crossed: Uncovering the Catholic Church's Betrayal of American Nuns*. New York: Doubleday, 2006.

Brooks, Arthur C. *Love Your Enemies: How Decent People Can Save America from the Culture of Contempt*. Northampton, MA: Broadside, 2019.

Brown, Delwin. *What Does a Progressive Christian Believe?: A Guide for the Searching, the Open, and the Curious*. New York: Seabury, 2008.

Brown, Peter. *Augustine of Hippo: A Biography*. Berkeley, CA: University of California Press, 2000.

Buehrens, John A., and Rebecca Ann Parker. *A House for Hope: The Promise of Progressive Religion for the Twenty-first Century*. Boston: Beacon, 2010.

Brueggemann, Walter. *The Prophetic Imagination*. Philadelphia: Fortress, 1978.

———. *Theology of the Old Testament*. Philadelphia: Fortress, 2012.

———. *Journey to the Common Good*. Louisville, KY: Westminster John Knox, 2010.

———. *Finally Comes the Poet: Daring Speech for Proclamation*. Philadelphia: Fortress, 1989.

———. *Sabbath as Resistance*. Louisville, KY: Westminster John Knox, 2017.

Budde, Michael. *The Borders of Baptism: Identities, Allegiances, and the Church*. Eugene, OR: Cascade, 2011.

Carter, Jimmy. *Our Endangered Values: America's Moral Crisis*. New York: Simon and Schuster, 2006.

Carter, Stephen. *God's Name in Vain: The Wrongs and Rights of Religion in Politics*. New York: Basic, 2009.

Cavanaugh, William. *Migrations of the Holy: God, State, and the Political Meaning of the Church*. Grand Rapids: Eerdmans, 2011.

Cobb, John, ed. *Progressive Christians Speak: A Different Voice on Faith and Politics*. Louisville, KY: Westminster John Knox, 2003.

Cochran, Jarrod. *Finding Jesus Outside the Box*. New York: Progressive Christian Alliance, 2008.

Corbin, Alain. *Village Bells: Sound and Meaning in the 19th Century French Countryside*. New York: Columbia University Press, 1998.

Crossan, John Dominic. *God and Empire: Jesus Against Rome Then and Now*. San Francisco: Harper One, 2007.

———. *The Historical Jesus: The Life of a Jewish Mediterranean Peasant.* San Francisco: Harper One, 2010.

———. *Jesus: A Revolutionary Biography.* New York: Harper Collins, 2009.

———. *How to Read the Bible and Still Be a Christian.* San Francisco: Harper One, 2016.

Crossan, John Dominic, and Jonathan L. Reed. *In Search of Paul: How Jesus' Apostle Opposed the Roman Empire with God's Kingdom.* San Francisco: Harper One, 2005.

De Botton, Alain. *Religion for Atheists: A Non-Believer's Guide to the Uses of Religion.* New York: Pantheon, 2012.

De Waal, Esther. *Seeking God: The Way of St. Benedict.* Collegeville, MN: Liturgical, 2001.

Didion, Joan. "In the Realm of the Fisher King." In *After Henry,* 25–46. New York: Vintage, 1993.

Dionne, E. J., and Ming Hsu Chen, eds. *Sacred Places, Civic Purposes: Should Government Help Faith-Based Charity?* Washington DC: Brookings Institution, 2001.

Donaldson, Dave, and Stanley Carlson-Thies. *A Revolution of Compassion: Faith-Based Groups as Full Partners in Fighting America's Social Problems.* Grand Rapids: Baker, 2003.

Dorrien, Gary. *Social Democracy in the Making: Political and Religious Roots of European Socialism.* New Haven, CT: Yale University Press, 2019.

———. *The Making of American Liberal Theology: Crisis, Irony, and Postmodernity, 1950–2005.* Louisville, KY: Westminster John Knox, 2006.

———. *Breaking White Supremacy: Martin Luther King Jr. and the Black Social Gospel.* New Haven, CT: Yale University Press, 2019.

———. *Social Ethics in the Making: Interpreting an American Tradition.* New York: Wiley-Blackwell, 2008.

———. *The New Abolition: W. E. B. Du Bois and the Black Social Gospel.* New Haven, CT: Yale University Press, 2018.

———. *The Making of American Liberal Theology: Imagining Progressive Religion, 1805–1900.* Louisville, KY: Westminster John Knox, 2001.

———. *Reconstructing the Common Good: Theology and the Social Order.* Eugene, OR: Wipf & Stock, 2008.

———. *Economy, Difference, Empire: Social Ethics for Social Justice.* Columbia Series on Religion and Politics. New York: Columbia University Press, 2010.

———. *The Remaking of Evangelical Theology.* Louisville, KY: Westminster John Knox, 1998.

Dreher, Rod. *The Benedict Option.* New York: Sentinel, 2017.

Dunbar-Ortiz, Roxanne. *Loaded: A Disarming History of the Second Amendment.* San Francisco: City Lights, 2018.

———. *Indigenous Peoples' History of the United States.* San Francisco: City Lights, 2018.

Eagleton, Terry. *Reason, Faith, and Revolution: Reflections on the God Debate.* New Haven, CT: Yale University Press, 2009.

Duffy, Eamon. *The Stripping of the Altars: Traditional Religion in England 1400–1580.* New Haven, CT: Yale University Press, 1992.

Ellingson, Stephen. *To Care for Creation: The Emergence of the Religious Environmental Movement.* Chicago: University of Chicago Press, 2016.

Elnes, Eric. *The Phoenix Affirmations: A New Vision for the Future of Christianity.* New York: Jossey-Bass, 2006.

Erlander, Daniel. *Let the Children Come: A Baptism Manual for Parents and Sponsors.* Philadelphia: Augsburg Fortress, 2019.

Farley, Margaret A. *Just Love: A Framework for Christian Sexual Ethics.* New York: Continuum, 2008.

Fea, John. *Believe Me: The Evangelical Road to Donald Trump.* Grand Rapids: Eerdmans, 2018.

Fiorenza, Elizabeth Schussler. *In Memory of Her: A Feminist Theological Reconstruction Of Christian Origins.* New York: Crossroads, 1994.

Fowler, Robert Booth, et al. *Religion and Politics in America: Faith, Culture, and Strategic Choices.* 3rd ed. Abingdon, UK: Routledge, 2018.

Frank, Thomas. *What's the Matter with Kansas?* New York: Metropolitan, 2004.

Freeman, Curtis. *Undomesticated Dissent: Democracy and the Public Virtue of Religious Noncomformity.* Waco, TX: Baylor University Press, 2017.

Froese, Paul. *The Plot to Kill God: Findings from the Soviet Experiment in Secularization.* Berkeley, CA: University of California Press, 2008.

Geertz, Clifford. "Thick Description: Toward an Interpretive Theory of Culture." In *The Interpretation of Cultures: Selected Essays,* 3–32. New York: Basic, 1973.

Gerson, Michael. "The Last Temptation." *Atlantic,* April 1, 2018, cover story.

Giles, Keith. *Jesus Unveiled: Forsaking Church as We Know It for Ekklesia as God Intended.* Orange, CA: Quoir, 2019.

———. *Jesus Untangled: Crucifying Our Politics to Pledge Allegiance to the Lamb.* Orange, CA: Quoir, 2017.

Glover, Donald E. *C. S. Lewis: The Art of Enchantment.* Athens, OH: Ohio University Press, 1981.

Gonzalez, Karen. *The God Who Sees: Immigrants, the Bible, and the Journey to Belong.* Harrisonburg, VA: Herald, 2019.

Gottlieb, Roger S. *Joining Hands: Politics and Religion Together for Social Change.* Boulder, CO: Westview, 2004.

Gundry, Robert Hurton. *Matthew: A Commentary on his Handbook for a Mixed Church under Persecution.* Grand Rapids: Eerdmans, 1995.

Hall, Douglas John. *The End of Christendom and the Future of Christianity.* Eugene, OR: Wipf & Stock, 2002.

Hallie, Philip. *Lest Innocent Blood be Shed.* New York: Harper, 1994.

Hamilton, Mark. *Jesus, King of Strangers: What the Bible Really Says about Immigration.* Grand Rapids: Eerdmans, 2019.

Hanson, Victor Davis. *The Case for Trump.* New York: Basic, 2019.

Harrington, Michael. *The Politics at God's Funeral.* New York: Henry Holt, 1983.

Hauerwas, Stanley. *A Community of Character: Toward a Constructive Christian Social Ethic.* Notre Dame, IN: University of Notre Dame Press, 1981.

———. *Vision and Virtue: Essays in Christian Ethical Reflection.* Notre Dame, IN: University of Notre Dame Press, 1981.

Haught, John F. *Science and Religion: From Conflict to Conversation.* New York: Paulist, 1995.

Hedges, Chris. *When Atheism Becomes Religion: America's New Fundamentalists.* New York: Free, 2009.

Heinz, Donald. *The Last Passage: Recovering a Death of Our Own*. London: Oxford University Press, 1998.

———.*Christmas: Festival of Incarnation Philadelphia*: Philadelphia: Fortress, 2009.

Henry, Carl F. H. *The Uneasy Conscience of Modern Fundamentalism*. Grand Rapids: Eerdmans 2003.

Heschel, Abraham Joshua. *The Prophets*. New York: Harper Perennial, 2001.

———. *The Sabbath*. New York: Farrar, Straus and Giroux, 2005.

Martinez, Hewlitt, and Ted Peters. *Evolution from Creation to New Creation: Conflict, Conversation, and Convergence*. Nashville: Abingdon, 2003.

Hochshild, Arlie Russell. *Strangers in Their Own Land: Anger and Mourning on the American Right*. New York: New, 2018.

Horsley, Richard. *The Liberation of Christmas: The Infancy Narratives in Social Context*. New York: Crossroad, 1989.

———. *Jesus and the Powers: Conflict, Covenant, and the Hope of the Poor*. Philadelphia: Fortress, 2010.

———. *Covenant Economics: A Biblical Vision of Justice for All*. Louisville, KY: Westminster John Knox, 2009.

———. *In the Shadow of Empire: Reclaiming the Bible as a History of Faithful Resistance*. Louisville, KY: Westminster John Knox, 2008.

———. *Jesus and Empire: The Kingdom of God and the New World Disorder*. Philadelphia: Fortress, 2002.

Hudson, Michael. *And Forgive Them Their Debts: Lending, Foreclosure and Redemption from Bronze Age Finance to the Jubilee*. Dresden: Islet-Verlag, 2018.

Hunter, James Davison. *To Change the World: The Irony, Tragedy, and Possibility of Christianity in the Modern World*. London: Oxford University Press, 2010.

Johnson, Chalmers A. *Blowback: The Costs and Consequences of American Empire*. New York: Holt, 2004.

———. *Dismantling the Empire: America's Last Best Hope*. New York: Metropolitan, 2011.

Johnson, Elizabeth. *Quest for the Living God: Mapping Frontiers in the Theology of God*. New York: Continuum, 2011.

Jones, Alan. *Reimagining Christianity: Reconnect Your Spirit without Disconnecting Your Mind*. New York: John Wiley, 2005.

Jones, Robert P. *Progressive and Religious*. New York: Rowan and Littlefield, 2008.

Judt, Tony. *Ill Fares the Land*. New York: Penguin, 2011.

Juergensmeyer, Mark. *Terror in the Mind of God: The Global Rise of Religious Violence*. 3rd ed. Berkeley, CA: University of California Press, 2003.

Kaufman, L. A. *How to Read a Protest: The Art of Organizing and Resistance*. Berkeley, CA: University of California Press, 2018.

Kazin, Michael. *American Dreamers: How the Left Changed a Nation*. New York: Knopf, 2011.

Kempis, Thomas à. *Imitation of Christ*. Ashland, OH: Paraclete, 2008.

Kotsko, Adam. *Politics of Redemption: The Social Logic of Salvation*. New York: T & T Clark, 2010.

Kimball, Charles. *When Religion Becomes Evil: Five Warning Signs*. San Francisco: Harper San Francisco, 2002.

———. *When Religion Becomes Lethal: The Explosive Mix of Politics and Religion in Judaism, Christianity, and Islam*. New York: Jossey-Bass, 2011.

King, David. *God's Internationalists: World Vision and the Age of Evangelical Humanitarianism.* Philadelphia: University of Pennsylvania Press, 2019.

Kinsler, Ross, and Gloria Kinsler. *The Biblical Jubilee and the Struggle for Life: An Invitation to Personal, Ecclesial, and Social Transformation.* Maryknoll, NY: Orbis, 1999.

Knippa, Michael. "Converted Citizens: From National Allegiance towards Heavenly Adherence." *Word and World* 37 (2017) 395–403.

Kruse, Kevin. *One Nation under God: How Corporate America Invented Christian America.* New York: Basic, 2016.

Krugman, Paul. *End This Depression Now.* New York: W. W. Norton, 2012.

———. *A Country Is Not a Company.* Cambridge, MA: Harvard Business School Press, 2009.

———. *The Conscience of a Liberal.* New York: W. W. Norton, 2007.

———. *The Great Unraveling: Losing Our Way in the New Century.* New York: W. W. Norton, 2004.

Lakoff, George. *Don't Think of an Elephant: Know Your Values and Frame the Debate.* Hartford, VT: Chelsea Green, 2014.

Lowery, Richard. *Sabbath and Jubilee.* Atlanta: Chalice, 2012.

Landes, Richard. *Heaven on Earth: The Varieties of the Millennial Experience.* London: Oxford University Press, 2011.

Lathrop, Gordon. *The Pastor: A Spirituality.* Philadelphia: Fortress, 2011.

Lawrence, Bruce B. *Defenders of God: The Fundamentalist Revolt Against the Modern Age.* New York: Harper and Row, 1989.

Lerner, Michael. *Spirit Matters.* New York: Hampton Roads, 2002.

———. *The Left Hand of God: Healing America's Political and Spiritual Crisis.* San Francisco: Harper One, 2007.

———. *The Politics of Meaning: Restoring Hope and Possibility in an Age of Cynicism.* New York: Basic, 1997.

Lovelock, James. *Gaia: A New Look at Life on Earth.* New York: Oxford University Press, 2000.

Luhrmann, T. M. *When God Talks Back: Understanding the American Evangelical Relationship with God.* New York: Knopf, 2012.

MacLean, Nancy. *Democracy in Chains: The Deep History of the Radical Right's Stealth Plan for America.* New York: Penguin, 2018.

Mann, Thomas, and Norman Ornstein. *It's Even Worse than It Looks: How the American Constitutional System Collided with the new Politics of Extremism.* New York: Basic, 2012.

MacIntryre, Alisdair. *After Virtue.* Notre Dame, IN: University of Notre Dame Press, 2007.

McClaren, Brian. *A Generous Orthodoxy.* Grand Rapids: Zondervan, 2006.

———. *The Great Spiritual Migration: How the World's Largest Religion Is Seeking a Better Way to Be Christian.* New York: Convergent, 2017.

———. *A New Kind of Christian.* New York: Jossey-Bass, 2001.

———. *Everything Must Change: Jesus, Global Crises, and a Revolution of Hope.* New York: Thomas Nelson, 2007.

Marsden, George. *Fundamentalism and American Culture: the Shaping of Twentieth-century Evangelicalism.* London: Oxford University Press, 2006.

McBride, Jennifer. *Radical Discipleship: A Liturgical Politics of the Gospel*. Philadelphia: Fortress, 2017.

McFague, Sallie. *The Body of God: An Ecological Theology*. Philadelphia: Fortress, 1993.

———. *Life Abundant: Rethinking Theology and Economy for a Planet in Peril*. Philadelphia: Fortress, 2000.

———. *Metaphorical Theology: Models of God in Religious Language*. Philadelphia: Fortress, 1982.

———. *Super, Natural Christians: How We Should Love Nature*. Philadelphia: Fortress, 2000.

McGrath, Alister. *The Re-enchantment of Nature: The Denial of Religion and the Ecological Crisis*. London: Galilee Trade, 2003.

———. *The Twilight of Atheism: The Rise and Fall of Disbelief in the Modern World*. New York: Doubleday, 2004.

Meyers, Robin. *Saving Jesus From The Church: How To Stop Worshiping Christ and Start Following Jesus*. San Francisco: Harper One, 2010.

———. *Spiritual Defiance: Building a Beloved Community of Resistance*. New Haven, CT: Yale University Press, 2016.

———. *The Underground Church: Reclaiming the Subversive Way of Jesus*. San Francisco: Jossey-Bass, 2012.

Miles, Jack. *Christ: A Crisis in the Life of God*. New York: Knopf, 2001.

Moe-Lobeda, Cynthia D. *Resisting Structural Evil: Love as Ecological-Economic Vocation*. Philadelphia: Fortress, 2013.

Moltmann, Jürgen. *The Crucified God: The Cross of Christ as the Foundation and Criticism of Christian Theology*. Minneapolis: Fortress, 1993.

———. *Theology of Hope*. Minneapolis: Fortress, 1993.

———. *The Church in the Power of the Spirit: A Contribution to Messianic Ecclesiology*. Minneapolis: Fortress, 1993.

———. *The Coming of God: Christian Eschatology*. Minneapolis: Fortress, 1996.

———. *Sun of Righteousness, Arise!: God's Future for Humanity and the Earth*. Minneapolis: Fortress, 1993.

Morse, Christopher. *The Difference Heaven Makes*. London: T & T Clark, 2010.

Myers, Ched. *Our God Is Undocumented: Biblical Faith and Immigrant Justice*. New York: Orbis, 2012.

———. *Binding the Strong Man: A Political Reading of Mark's Story of Jesus*. Maryknoll, NY: Orbis, 2008.

Murray, Charles. *Coming Apart*. New York: Crown Forum, 2013.

Neuhaus, Richard John. *American Babylon*. New York: Basic, 2009.

———. *The Naked Public Square: Religion and Democracy in America*. Grand Rapids: Eerdmans, 1988.

Noll, Mark. *Religion and American Politics: From the colonial period to the 1980s*. London: Oxford University Press, 1989.

———. *The Scandal of the Evangelical Mind: The Rise of Evangelicalism*. Grand Rapids: Eerdmans, 1995.

Noll, Mark, George Marsden, and David Bebbington. *Evangelicals: Who They Have Been, Are Now, and Could Be*. Grand Rapids: Eerdmans, 2019.

Nagel, Thomas. *Mind and Cosmos: Why the Materialist Neo-Darwinian Conception of Nature is Almost Certainly False*. London: Oxford University Press, 2012.

Niebuhr, Reinhold. "The Relevance of an Impossible Ideal." In *An Interpretation of Christian Ethics*, 101–36. New York: Meridian, 1956.

Niebuhr, H. Richard. *The Kingdom of God in America.* Middletown, CT: Wesleyan University Press, 1988.

Pelikan, Jaroslav. *The Christian Tradition: A History of the Development of Doctrine, Volume 1: The Emergence of the Catholic Tradition.* Chicago: University of Chicago Press, 1971.

Piketty, Thomas. *Capitalism in the Twenty-first Century.* Cambridge, MA: The Belknap Press of Harvard University Press, 2017.

Plaskow, Judith. *Sex, Sin, and Grace: Women's Experience and the Theologies of Reinhold Niebuhr and Paul Tillich.* New York: University Press of America, 1979.

———.*Standing Again at Sinai: Judaism from a Feminist Perspective.* San Francisco: Harper One, 1991.

Polkinghorne, John. *The God of Hope and the End of the World.* New Haven, CT: Yale University Press, 2003.

———.*One World: The Interaction of Science and Theology.* West Conshohocken, PA: Templeton, 2007.

———.*The Polkinghorne Reader: Science, Faith, and the Search for Meaning.* West Conshohocken, PA: Templeton, 2010.

———. *Quantum Physics and Theology: An Unexpected Kinship.* New Haven, CT: Yale University Press, 2008.

———. *Questions of Truth: Fifty-One Responses to Questions about God, Science, and Belief.* Louisville, KY: Westminster John Knox, 2009.

Primavesi, Anne. *Sacred Gaia.* New York: Routledge, 2000.

Prothero, Stephen. *American Jesus: How the Son of God Became a National Icon.* New York: Farrar, Strauss and Giroux, 2004.

Putnam, Robert. *Bowling Alone: The Collapse and Revival of American Community.* New York: Simon and Schuster, 2001.

Rauschenbusch, Walter. *The Social Principles of Jesus.* Seattle: CreateSpace, 2015.

Richard, Matthew. *Will the Real Jesus Please Stand Up?: A Debate.* St. Louis: Concordia, 2013.

Rieger, Joerg. *Christ and Empire: From Paul to Postcolonial Times.* Minneapolis: Fortress, 2007.

Robinson, Marilynne. *When I Was a Child I Read Books.* New York: Farrar, Strauss and Giroux, 2012.

Rodgers, Daniel. *As a City on a Hill: The Story of America's Most Famous Lay Sermon.* Princeton, NJ: Princeton University Press, 2018.

Rolsky, L. Benjamin. *The Rise and Fall of the Religious Left: Politics, Television, and Popular Culture in the 1970s and Beyond.* New York: Columbia University Press, 2019.

Root, Andrew. *The Pastor in a Secular Age: Ministry to People Who No Longer Need a God.* Grand Rapids: Baker Academic, 2019.

Ruether, Rosemary Radford. *America, Amerikka: Elect Nation and Imperial Violence.* Sheffield, UK: Equinox, 2007.

———. *Gaia and God: An Ecofeminist Theology of Earth Healing.* San Francisco: Harper One, 1994.

———. *Sexism and God Talk: Toward a Feminist Theology.* New York: Beacon, 1993.

Sandel, Michael. *What Money Can't Buy: The Moral Limits of Markets*. New York: Farrar, Straus and Giroux, 2012.

Schultz, Daniel. *Changing the Script: An Authentically Faithful and Authentically Progressive Political Theology for the 21st Century*. New York: Ig, 2010.

Seidel, Andrew. *The Founding Myth: Why Christian Nationalism Is Un-American*. New York: Starling, 2019.

Sexton, John. *Standing for Reason: The University in a Dogmatic Age*. New Haven, CT: Yale University Press, 2019.

Smith, Christian. *Atheist Overreach*. London: Oxford University Press, 2018.

Sharper, Philip and Sally Sharper. *The Gospel in Art by the Peasants of Solentiname*. Maryknoll, NY: Orbis, 1984.

Sider, Ronald J. *Churches that Make a Difference: Reaching Your Community with Good News and Good Works*. Grand Rapids: Baker, 2002.

———. *Fixing the Moral Deficit: A Balanced Way to Balance the Budget*. Downers Grove, IL: InterVarsity, 2012.

———. *I Am Not A Social Activist: Making Jesus the Agenda*. Scottdale, PA: Herald, 2008.

———. *Just Generosity: A New Vision For Overcoming Poverty in America*. Grand Rapids: Baker, 2007.

———. *Living Like Jesus: Eleven Essentials For Growing A Genuine Faith*. Grand Rapids: Baker, 1998.

———. *Rich Christians in an Age of Hunger: Moving from Affluence to Generosity*. New York: Thomas Nelson, 2005.

———. *The Scandal of the Evangelical Conscience: Why Are Christians Living Just like the Rest of the World?* Grand Rapids: Baker, 2005.

Smith, Huston. *Why Religion Matters: The Fate Of The Human Spirit in an Age Of Disbelief*. San Francisco: Harper One, 2001.

Snyder, Howard, and Joel Scandrett. *Salvation Means Creation Healed: The Ecology of Sin and Grace*. Eugene, OR: Cascade, 2011.

Spong, John Shelby. *A New Christianity for a New World*. San Francisco: Harper San Francisco, 2002.

Stanton, Glenn. *The Myth of the Dying Church: How Christianity Is Actually Thriving in America and the World*.

Stark, Rodney. *The Rise of Christianity: How The Obscure, Marginal Jesus Movement Became The Dominant Religious Force in the Western World in a Few Centuries*. San Francisco: Harper San Francisco, 1996.

Stewart, Jon. *The Daily Show with Jon Stewart Presents America (The Book) Teacher's Edition: A Citizen's Guide to Democracy Inaction*. New York: Grand Central, 2006.

Stiglitz, Joseph. *People, Power, and Profits: Progressive Capitalism For An Age Of Discontent*. New York: Norton, 2019.

Sullivan, Amy. *The Party Faithful: How and Why Democrats are Closing the God Gap*. New York: Scribner, 2014.

Swimme, Brian, and Thomas Berry. *The Universe Story: From the Primordial Flaring Forth to the Ecozoic Era: A Celebration of the Unfolding of the Cosmos*. San Francisco: Harper, 1992.

Tanner, Kathryn. *Christianity and the New Spirit of Capitalism*. New Haven, CT: Yale University Press, 2019.

Taussig, Hal. *A New Spiritual Home: Progressive Christianity at the Grass Roots*. Salem, OR: Polebridge, 2006.

Taylor, Bron. *Dark Green Religion: Nature Spirituality and the Planetary Future*. Berkeley, CA: University of California Press, 2009.

Taylor, Charles. "Disenchantment-Reenchantment." In *The Joy of Secularism*, edited by George Levine, 57–73. Princeton, NJ: Princeton University Press, 2011.

Taylor, Mark Lewis. *Religion, Politics, and the Christian Right: Post 9/11 Powers in American Empire*. Philadelphia: Fortress, 2005.

Tinder, Glenn. *The Political Meaning of Christianity: The Prophetic Stance*. San Francisco: Harper, 1991.

Traister, Rebecca. *Good and Mad: The Revolutionary Power of Women's Anger*. New York: Simon and Schuster, 2018.

Vanden Heuvel, Katrina. *Dictionary of Republicanisms*. New York: Nation, 2005.

Volf, Miroslav. *Flourishing: Why We Need Religion in a Globalized World*. New Haven, CT: Yale University Press, 2017.

Wald, Kenneth. *Religion and Politics In The US, 4th Edition: A Guide To Political Mobilization Of Religious Organizations*. New York: Rowman and Littlefield, 2018.

Wallis, Jim. *America's Original Sin: Racism, White Privilege, and the Bridge to a New America*. Grand Rapids: Brazos, 2017.

———. *Christ in Crisis: Why We Need to Reclaim Jesus*. San Francisco: HarperOne, 2019.

———. *God's Politics: Why The Right Gets It Wrong And The Left Doesn't Get It*. San Francisco: HarperOne, 2005.

———. *The Great Awakening: Seven Ways to Change the World*. San Francisco: HarperOne, 2009.

———. *On God's Side: What Religion Forgets and Politics Hasn't Learned about Serving the Common Good*. Grand Rapids: Brazos, 2014.

———. *(Un)Common Good: How The Gospel Brings Hope To A World Divided*. Grand Rapids: Brazos, 2014.

Wehner, Peter. *The Death of Politics: How To Heal Our Frayed Republic After Trump*. San Francisco: HarperOne, 2019.

Wilken, Robert Louis. *Liberty in the Things of God*. New Haven, CT: Yale University Press, 2019.

Wink, Walter. *Engaging the Powers: Discernment and Resistance in a World of Domination*. Minneapolis: Fortress, 1992.

———. *Naming the Powers: The Language of Power in the New Testament*. Minneapolis: Fortress, 1984.

———. *Unmasking the Powers: The Invisible Forces that Determine Human Existence*. Minneapolis: Fortress, 1986.

Wolterstorff, Nicholas. *Religion in the University*. New Haven, CT: Yale University Press, 2019.

Wright, Lawrence. *The Looming Tower: Al Quaeda and the Road to 9/11*. New York: Vintage, 2007.

Wright, N. T. *Jesus and the Victory of God*. Philadelphia: Fortress, 1994.

———. *The New Testament and the People of God*. Philadelphia: Fortress, 1992.

———. *Paul: A Biography*. San Francisco: HarperOne, 2018.

———. *Paul and the Faithfulness of God*. Philadelphia: Fortress, 2013.

———. *The Resurrection of the Son of God*. Philadelphia: Fortress, 2003.

————. *Simply Good News: Why the Gospel Is News and What Makes It Good.* San Francisco: HarperOne, 2017.

————. *Simply Jesus: A New Vision Of Who He Was What He Did, And Why He Matters.* San Francisco: HarperOne, 2018.

————. *Surprised by Scripture: Engaging Contemporary Issues.* San Francisco: HarperOne, 2015.

————. *Simply Christian: Why Christianity Makes Sense.* San Francisco: HarperOne, 2010.

————.*Surprised by Hope: Rethinking Heaven, The Resurrection, and the Mission of the Church.* San Francisco: HarperOne, 2008.

Wuthnow, Robert. *Left Behind: Decline and Rage in Rural America.* Princeton, NJ: Princeton University Press, 2018.

Zamora, Lois Parkinson, and Wendy B. Faris, eds. *Magical Realism: Theory, History, Community.* Durham, NC: Duke University Press, 1995.